This Luscious Life

Kelley Black

HOLYOKE PUBLIC LIBRARY
250 CHESTNUT STREET
HOLYOKE, MA 01040

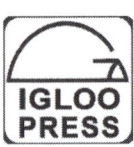

Copyright © 2015 Igloo Press
Tucson, Arizona
San Francisco, California

Editor: W. Scott Stanley
Book Design: Scott Jackson
Cover Images: Alan Cresto
Cover Art: Tracy Brennan Conte

All rights reserved.

ISBN-10: 0978760840
ISBN-13: 978-0978760847

This book is dedicated to my niece Ameena Grace Black

Souls are funny things. They stay constant even when the outside changes, or when the heart makes mistakes. Souls don't really care about good or bad, right or wrong -- They're just true. Everlasting.

~ Miranda July

Hard times arouse an instinctive desire for authenticity.

~Coco Chanel

Be who you are and say what you feel, because those who mind don't matter, and those who matter don't mind.

~ Dr. Seuss

Contents

Introduction

Chapter 1
Paris in New York
1

Chapter 2
Serena, Courage, and the Power of Forgiveness
9

Chapter 3
Shakti, Self-Care, & The Divine Feminine
15

Chapter 4
Across Time & Space: Homage to Unconditional Love
37

Chapter 5
The Support Deficit
49

Chapter 6
Wear Good Underwear. Take Care of Your Skin.
57

Chapter 7
Rituals, Self-Care, and Why I Meditate
61

Chapter 8
Scar Tissue
69

Chapter 9
Storms and the Siren Signifying Support
79

Chapter 10
Maine, Picasso, and the Mogul
85

Chapter 11
The Social Codes of Being Naked
93

Chapter 12
NWA, Race in America, & Being a Mixed Chic
97

Chapter 13
Letting It Breathe on The Way to Finalizing My Divorce
103

Chapter 14
Love
121

Chapter 15
Cinderella Makes It to The Ball
125

Chapter 16
Ode to My Fashion Angel
137

Chapter 17

Ambition Money & Success

149

Chapter 18

The Lost Girls

157

Chapter 19

No Sleepwalking

163

Chapter 20

The Tooth Fairy is Real. She Cleans my Teeth

169

Chapter 21

Reflections on Spirituality

177

Chapter 22
The Silver Chord, True Self and Being a Mermaid

193

Chapter 23
I Love NYC
(And Here's Why)

207

Chapter 24
Everything is Energy

215

Chapter 25
The Power of Dreaming

221

Chapter 26
Ameena and Michael's Relationship Lesson

227

Chapter 27
Hogwarts & A Night in NYC

233

Chapter 1

Paris in New York

You know what the issue is with this world? Everyone wants a magical solution to their problem, and everyone refuses to believe in magic.

~ Lewis Carroll, Alice in Wonderland

It's Friday the 13th of November. Earlier in the day I had a colonoscopy and an endoscopy. Cameras down one orifice and up another. I am laughing to myself remembering a friend of mine telling me, "Think of it as an expedited fast." He'd made me laugh about it. Who needs green juice and bone broth when you can take some Suprep and be cleared completely out in just 24 hours?

I'm drained. Drained from not sleeping the night leading up to the procedure. Drained from being in the bathroom all night. Drained from the Suprep, which I've had to hold my nose to get down and keep down; drained having not eaten for 24 hours. Tired and spacey. I can feel the anesthesia and whatever else wearing off. Fentanyl, Lidocaine, Propofol all need to clear my system. I've always been sensitive to drugs, even caffeine, feeling like they can linger in my system. I've been cleaned out.

As I walk into my apartment lobby, I'm dreaming of watching Velvet, the Netflix series out of Spain about the family dynasty of a luxury department store in the 60's. It's got just the stuff that makes lying on the couch and spacing out fun - love triangles, temperamental designers, class friction, orphans . . . a melodramatic microcosm of the human experience. And I'm looking forward to getting lost in it.

Then through my haze I hear Julio, my doorman, with his voice raised calling me, "Kelley, Kelley, do you know what's happening in France, in Paris? Get upstairs now. Check on your friends, your people there. It's very, very bad. State of emergency." I feel a wave start to hit me. My hands are shaking and I quietly say, "Okay" and step in the elevator.

I don't have a television, so I hop on my computer. And then I have a meltdown . . . bomb goes off outside the Stade de France, there is a shooting in the Bataclan, the reports go on and on. This is happening half way around the world and it feels to me like 9/11 all over again. My hands are shaking and I start to cry. I cannot get hold of anyone I know in Paris, I feel like my heart is breaking and I am starting to feel as though I'm in shock. I can't take in the images I'm seeing on the news, the reports I'm reading, what I'm hearing in real time. Time slows.

I reach to the powerful men who I know. By initials, *K*, *R*, and *A* . . . all of them people who have a deep well of sensitivity, understanding and empathy. High vibration men with Mars and Sun and Mercury in their charts. They all have a particular masculine energy that balances out my Venus and Moon. My connection with each of them is profound and soul connected. I believe it is these qualities that make me feel the safest. Each in their own way have the ability to steady me when I speak to them, hear their voices, or read their written responses to my notes or emails. As I hear back from them, I feel myself go back into my body. I start to ground.

In response to me saying it feels like 9/11 *R* tells me "I wouldn't go that far, but it's frightening and horrible." Although *R*'s friend in Paris tells him that it's worse than what is being reported.

I send an SOS to *A* in Eastern Europe. I'm in such a state that I don't realize its one or two in the morning there. I write to him,

Please say a prayer for Paris
My heart is breaking at the moment for France and the world. It's all

upside down. Please pray. You are powerful. Everyone on the side of Light must ask God to help.

I immediately get a note back saying, "I will!" and the little girl inside me stops panicking. I notice my breath rate slows down. I'm grounding myself. He understands me. And it's the understanding, the empathy, that makes me feel safe. I stop being unhinged. I ground.

The following day I feel emotionally drained, but even then inspired by the things I've seen posted on the social networks. One especially makes me laugh . . .

Friends from the whole world, thank you for your #prayforparis. But we don't need any more religion! Our faith goes to music! Kisses! Life! Champagne and joy! #Parisisaboutlife!

I realize it's time to stop being shell-shocked; stop being sad that maybe the best way to pray for Paris is to set my intention to have a great day. I head out with no expectation other than to experience life on Saturday the 14th. On my way to my first stop, I get a call from the Salon berating me about being five minutes late. The caller is so wound tight, so NYC, so intense about a hair appointment -- at that moment, from where I am, I just can't relate to the urgency of it. But I honestly try to understand, and assure them I'm two blocks away.

You couldn't have told me there was magic coming . . . And so, after the salon, I'm on the other side of town at *Symphony Space for the Women, Fashion and Film Festival*. I'm excited to see the panel on *Women Coming of Age: Sharing Life Experiences*. One of the inspirations of my life, Pat Cleveland, is on that panel.

I have come to see my life experience has blessed me in equal measure with joy and pain. And in so doing, the balance has tilted toward joy. So here I am on a late Saturday afternoon in a dark theater enjoying my solitude when I feel a tap on my shoulder and look up. A gentleman says, "I love that sweater and you have a great body." I laugh and say, "Thank you" and shake his hand.

Then he says, "You have to move up to the front. Sit in front of Pat. Don't worry, she isn't going to call on you, it's not school." I laugh again and say ok.

There I am two rows back and struck by the energy of being so close to someone I've dreamt of meeting since I was a child. She is natural, fun, witty and when they ask the panel members *what are you afraid of?* she says, "I'm not afraid. I have always just kept moving forward and I don't waste time on what isn't working." Then I'm close enough to hear her repeat under her breath, "I'm not afraid."

When the panel is done she is exiting the stage and is surrounded by men gushing over her. Telling her she is the ultimate and this makes me feel inspired. They are enthralled and mesmerized by a woman in her early 60's. And again I am inspired. As I stand there in my own vortex, one of the men grabs my arm and says, "I want her in the picture too."

So there I am, me, a man from the UN, and Pat Cleveland standing in front of a hedge of amateurs and professionals lifting iPhone cameras and fat photographic lenses. I can feel the clickety-click-click-click sounding from the tight crescent of cameras flashing around us.

As she is walking toward her husband after the photos, I say to her, "Excuse me Pat, can I talk to you for a moment? She graciously turns and says yes. And then my heart opens. I tell her that seeing her image made me think that someone like me, someone who looks like me, could have a big life, a *luscious* life. She helped me dream beyond my immediate reality and past slights. She was proof for me that my dream was real. And for a girl of mixed race who didn't fit in, who felt adrift, I saw in Pat Cleveland a much bigger world, one that would accept me, because . . . it accepted her.

She asks me, "what's your background, your heritage, where are you from? You look like me." And I tell her French, Cherokee Indian, and African-American. And so she shares her heritage too.

Then she puts her arm next to mine and says we're the same color. And I smile and say, "Precisely." I tell her about this book and my passion for a luscious life, and she asks where she can buy it. And then the talk turns back to Paris.

I tell her I'm headed to Paris soon for my book-launch. Then she shares with me that Anna, her daughter, was in Paris in the 10th Arrondisment when all hell broke loose there. She tells me, "Please be careful." I tell her, "Thank God your daughter is okay." With that we're both silent for a moment and then she says, "You must meet Alva . . . and no matter what, Paris, well it's *Paris*! . . . and we both grin from ear to ear.

When I look at that photo of the two of us, I see magic all over it. The huge smile on my face looks like an exclamation point to the words, *life is magic*! I see the ease and magic of life, if we allow it to flow, if we can move from control and certainty to possibility and magic -- to faith and love. An exclamation point on the joy of human connection, the joy and power of never knowing who is going to show up, and what opportunity may present itself to you. The joy of embracing life, all of it, big and small -- bitter and sad and ecstatically happy. And I know that in the space of less than 24 hours, I've been gifted with the emotions of all of that. I see it as a kind of a metaphor for the journey of my life. I feel beautiful and grateful.

Over the next couple of days, I find myself having and bearing witness to conversations about Paris, — on social media, in passing, after ballet class, on the street. I am struck by the tendency to judge — to judge where people are placing their empathy. Judgments about too much empathy for Paris and not enough for Beirut, Kenya, Mexico City, and for black-lives-mattering. I think to myself *really*? Since when is pain a competition? . . . I notice I weep so easily now. When pressed to explain why I've wept for Paris I say, "Well, lay it on me. I'm so raw at the moment. I'm ready. Name a city. Who do you want me to weep for?"

I write to friends:

> *Pray for Paris and pray for peace throughout the world. Send Love, Peace and Light to the planet. Pray for all of humanity. Pray that all divisions cease, that all hearts open and that the bloodshed everywhere stops.*

In my writing, I realize how much we have a tendency to process through the lens of our own experience. When asked why I'm so saddened by Paris and not weeping for Beirut, I struggle not to get defensive. The truth is that I'm saddened by violence everywhere. But the truth also is that I am especially saddened by Paris. I feel so personally connected to it. Paris holds a special place in my heart perhaps because of a deep association I have with what I hold most dear — a sweet or even misguided belief that no country does life like France, in the enjoyment of life in its bright ignition of the heart and the senses. And, perhaps, a deep enjoyment of life is the *big* prayer – the prayer to embrace all life, the bitter, the sweet, all of it. To truly enjoy life is the richness of a spiritual life, of a *life* – a tribute to the sacred gift of our humanity.

And then my phone rings, it's the third musketeer. It's *K*. I had written to him via text when I couldn't get him on the phone . . .

> *OMG my heart is breaking for Paris. It's under siege. They have closed the borders of France. You are powerful. Please pray for France. Please. It's horrible and I cannot reach my friends.*

He says, "I wanted to respond to you. My plane is about to take off." Then he tells me there has been a death in his family, and he's had to dash off to Europe. He gives me his itinerary and when he'll be back. We ask each other if we're okay. There is an implicit understanding, a connection, an empathy between us.

I say *big hugs* and he says *same to you*. My eyes fill up and I say *travel safely* and he says *I will* and then we hang up. There's the *"I will"* again and I think to myself, there is something so powerfully comforting when a man says *I will* with a certain tone.

I smile. Because when you least expect it, life gives you exactly what you need. It synchronizes, and if you pay attention you notice the connections, the empathy and understanding that make life luscious. And I keep smiling. Because, ultimately, if I'm asking myself, *what makes me feel most safe?* — it's not money or power. It's something much more internal — it's the shared moments of love and showing up that connects me to the lusciousness of life no matter what is going on.

Chapter 2

Serena, Courage, and the Power of Forgiveness

No matter what gets damaged, life rearranges itself to compensate for your loss

~ Hanya Yanagihara

It's March 2015, and the Indian Wells Tennis Masters is happening. There is talk of a Serena Slam. She is on the cover of New York Magazine and the New York Times Magazine. Serena seems to be everywhere. There is a lot being written about how she is a symbol of the racial schizophrenia in the US and simultaneously a symbol of a particular black excellence. And *I am* reading. I'm also watching. I see something in her as a woman that captivates my attention. But even as a bi-racial woman, I find myself most inspired by her humanity. And, of course, as an athlete she is beyond awe-inspiring. The New York Times has called her The Greatest, a label formerly reserved for Muhammad Ali.

It's her greatness as a human being refusing to be anything other than who she is that inspires me to believe in personal excellence. And maybe that is the most courageous stand any of us can take. She refuses to diminish herself to make other people more comfortable. She plays her game and makes no apologies for it.

I'm gushing here for a reason. Serena deeply touched me when she decided to go back to Indian Wells. And if you don't know what happened at Indian Wells, we'll be there in a moment. But I'll say first that I tend to not place myself in locations that remind me of my own diminishing experiences -- places I feel will contract my energy, or pull me back to a past I want to forget. I consciously choose to not go there. For instance, it's been years since I've been back to North Carolina — not since my grandmother's 80th birthday party. As a young girl there, I recall my alcoholic aunt screaming at me, "You think you are white, but you're black just like all of us." And the truth is then I didn't know how to think of myself as either. I was a bi-racial child in the 1970s who didn't identify with conventional black culture or fit with the Caucasian ideal. My aunt was half into a bottle of vodka at the time, but the thought of stepping foot anywhere near there still sends shivers down my spine. I can't imagine being 19 on TV and in front of a massive stadium audience yelling racial epithets. I simply can't imagine it. I can't.

But after 14 years, Serena returned to Indian Wells. This time, instead of boos and racial epithets, she was greeted with an ovation. And before the match began, she wept. Many of us watching or reading about it did a bit of that as well.

I wept for all the times I had summoned courage even when I was shaking in my boots. I wept for the moments of cruelty I had endured and also hoped to be forgiven for any cruelty, conscious or unconscious, that I had levied on others.
I wept out of awe for the power of the human spirit.

Anyone who plays tennis, follows sports or reads the papers probably remembers what happened at Indian Wells 14 years ago. It was so much bigger than tennis. Courage, forgiveness, and heart — a liberation trifecta.

Courage

I asked myself, how often do I have the courage to face what scares me the most? So Serena was a mere 19 when she was booed for hours and pelted with racial slurs while playing at Indian Wells in 2001. This occurred in her home state of California just miles from where she grew up. The scale of ugliness directed at a girl this age is still unfathomable to me. Equally unfathomable was an American crowd cheering for her Belgian opponent Kim Clijsters to crush her. But rather than withdraw from the match she held her center, played, and won. Then she vowed to never play there again. And so for 14 years she didn't. But then something in her heart moved her to face her fears and when she walked on that court in the spring of 2015 it resonated beyond tennis. Because facing fear is something we all have to do, if we want to live at our highest state — healed of injury.

My biggest act of courage has been to love myself and to admit to myself that my biggest fear over the fifty years of my life has been that I wouldn't be loved because of being bi-racial — that I wasn't lovable. This terrorized me for most of my life and was at the root of so many of my dysfunctional choices. This was my deepest wound. And to heal it I had to first admit it to myself and then face everything, every trauma I faced growing up and also in my adult life.

Things I had long buried like the memory of a father, who to avoid the wrath of my mother after coming home from seeing his mistress would climb into my bed. I am not saying that I was sexually abused in the traditional sense, but I will say that he had, and until I stopped allowing him to take from me, always had an unnatural attachment to me. The courage to remember really painful things that happened before I could understand them meant I also had to have the courage to stop trying to cope by over-identifying with my father's pain. That was my foot on the path to loving myself and allowing real love into my life.

Courage to get real about my personal agendas. Courage to get clear on my choices and my intentions. The courage to own all of me — the shadows and the light without apology. The courage to get and be real, vulnerable, and authentic. Following Serena over the years inspired me to do all of this.

Forgiveness

It has been said that forgiveness is one of the most powerful things we can do. It is also one of the hardest, I feel, because forgiveness is also as much about forgiving ourselves as forgiving another person, *especially* when we've been deeply hurt.

Forgiveness liberates the one who does the forgiving, and those forgiven. When I forgave my mother for not understanding me, my lifestyle, and my choices, I stopped putting energy into trying to forge a connection where there wasn't one. I dropped that agenda. I cleared my intentions with her when I stopped berating her for all the times she didn't show up for me. I let go of the pressures I'd internalized from all the times she'd leaned on me emotionally, even as she rendered me invisible through the lens of her own emotional needs. She used to proudly tell the story of how, as a child, I would comfort her during her divorce and tell her how it would all be alright. She never asked me how I felt even when I became anorexic and bulimic. It was all about leaning on me and me trying to hold things up, me trying to make it better. I was 12 years old.

Her level of emotional unavailability taught me to shut down and distance myself from my own emotional landscape. I resented it for years, even as I functioned under its ongoing presence. For years I was angry with her. When I finally forgave her for never really being a mother to me, I forgave myself for expecting her to give me something she was incapable of giving. When I finally accepted that, I was liberated to become emotionally available to myself. Forgiving her meant stopping my agenda, my exhausting agenda, of trying to win people's love. Forgiving my mother re-clocked my field to connecting with the highest, most responsive people. To allow myself to open to people who are responsive. Forgiving and letting go liberated me from wasting my time on people who are just into themselves. I no longer spend time on people who don't appreciate my time.

This led me to forgive myself for any choice I've made that didn't have healthy boundaries or went against loving myself. I forgave myself for any time I was self-abusive.

Serena's return to Indian Wells demonstrates to me what happens beyond ourselves when we move beyond bitterness. The effect can be vast, beyond our immediate field of view — something we may only witness once we step back onto the court. I find it so curious how often forgiveness, as a state of being, is rooted to a physical place and to physical action. Forgiving the past, letting go of it, is an act of cleansing. While I can't delete the past I can heal the patterns of the past and in doing so no longer be controlled by it.

Serena's presence in tennis is an ongoing act of forgiveness that allows a community, well beyond her life or the sport, to move beyond defensiveness, intolerance, and bigotry, to transition to repentance and finally love. It illustrates to me that when we genuinely forgive, we provide the platform for something equally important and often overlooked — that, in forgiveness, the forgiven is given the room to be honestly repentant. And I think her daring to be herself on the court with no apologies makes people reflect on their own biases and perhaps grow in some way, big or small beyond them.

Heart

Serena's return showed me the power of aligning with our hearts, despite what people think. People have strong opinions about her playing at Indian Wells. Some wanted her to continue to boycott the tournament. It's nothing to judge.

To this day, Venus refuses to play there.

But Serena's playing demonstrates her willingness to listen to her own heart — to follow her own internal compass and wisdom. There is nothing more powerful than that. When I listen to my heart and follow it there is a powerful ripple effect. I discover there an authenticity that compels me to take my frequency higher. I've also discovered that it's contagious. One of my students wrote me recently:

"Thank you so much for giving of yourself for an incredible Wednesday class, where I gained more wisdom and confidence in a little over an hour than I have in years of my life. This journey that I am on is surely interesting and exciting and I am grateful that I have been blessed with a master teacher like you to guide us."

So I vow to have the courage to forgive and live from my heart. To listen to my heart and allow myself to be vulnerable. To have the courage to keep it real and authentic and to use every bit of every experience in my luscious life to keep my heart open to my truth. My deepest prayer is that keeping this vow expands my capacity to love – unconditionally.

And although I've come to an answer for now, I know from time to time I'll reflect on this again and ask, W*here is my own Indian Wells?*

Chapter 3
Shakti, Self-Care, & The Divine Feminine

Femininity requires energy. Without energy, we can't be feminine. We can't bring all those priceless qualities to the people we love. When we do too much and don't take care of ourselves, we have no energy to be what women can be.

~Anonymous

Every Wednesday evening at 6:30 I teach a Naam Yoga class for women on the upper west side of Manhattan. We gather weekly for an hour and fifteen minutes to open our hearts to the cosmic energy of the Divine Mother, Divine Intelligence and Divine Love. That's the intention of the class - to reconnect women with the Divine Feminine, the feeling of it, the experience of it; their deep primal connection to Her.

When I was asked to teach the class at what was then the new Naam Yoga Center, I hesitated. Truth be told, after serving on the Naam Yoga board following their transitional phase and headquarters move from New York to Los Angeles, I was burnt out. I had also just come through major surgery and my focus was on self-care and getting really strong and healthy again. By necessity, I was committed to my own well-being first and foremost. I was interested in getting stronger. I wouldn't commit to anything that exhausted me.

So I spoke with Dr. Levry, founder of Naam Yoga, who pushed me to teach. "You have so much to offer, you have integrated the teachings in the most practical way. You live in your heart, and you hold a frequency, a frequency that can really touch and transform women's lives. I told you a long time ago that you will help a lot of women. Teach the class. And you never know who might show up in your class that will give you opportunities as well." After he told me that I decided to go for it. The truth was teaching energized me when it was taken out of the context of running the studio or serving on the board. My agreement with him was that if I could teach a niche class for women and no longer be on the board or involved in the running of the studio, I would do it.

There were women I wanted to reach as part of my own healing. I don't believe we heal ourselves in isolation. Simone de Beauvoir famously wrote in 1949 in her book The Second Sex, "One is not born a woman, but becomes one." I believe it. My desire for the class was born out of my own journey to birth myself into a full-fledged woman, following my partial hysterectomy and divorce. I knew I had fundamentally changed. I also knew that this would not happen alone, in the same way that we do not become women alone.

Shakti

While I believe with my whole heart that all females possess the capacity to become women, sometimes this mysterious force, this Shakti, lies dormant. Like all aspects of the human experience, I've seen how Shakti respects free will. Expressing her is a choice. It's a challenge as there is not much in the dark flower of our contemporary Western culture that honors and exalts womanhood. When you look around you see a culture that deifies the external: doing valued over being, productivity valued over playfulness, action valued over receptivity — which all serves to undervalue and then suppress the innate qualities of being a woman.

Hard skills like intellect and empiricism are valued above states of being, states evocative of intuition and the simple knowing of the great mysteries of life. I've found that to be a woman means integrating the whole in the center of our being where our Shakti lives. You can't integrate the *whole* by focusing on integrating the half — the half outside of yourself — as if organizing a list, any list, is some kind of recipe for having it all. If you go that way, you will fail. And when you fail, if you haven't already, there will be some wisdom in that. I'm not suggesting a plan for keeping positive. This isn't a plan at all.

It's about acceptance of your direct experience, witnessing your states of mood and mind. There's honesty and self-awareness in that. Conformity of mood is a lie. You might have noticed but conformity to externals is just the tip of a very large and very cold iceberg.

I believe the Divine Feminine Goddess energy is something that lives in every woman. In yogic teachings this force is labeled Shakti, the female principle of divine energy, especially when personified as the supreme deity. In Hinduism, *Shakti Power,* or *empowerment*, is the primordial cosmic energy and represents the dynamic forces that are thought to move through the entire Universe. Shakti is the concept, or personification, of divine feminine creative power, sometimes referred to as "The Great Divine Mother." Shakti is responsible for creation. Also, consider Shakti the agent of all change. It also exists in men in its potential unmanifested form. Shakti is cosmic existence as well as liberation, its most significant form being the Kundalini Shakti, a mysterious psycho-spiritual force.

What I am proposing is that you connect with this force to become a force of nature. This is an internal, not an external, "job." Being a force of nature means being the force that underlies action. Here again the emphasis is on your state of being, which is to say where there is action there is also an awareness of one's internal state — your being, your beingness. What is the ineffable spark that opens your hand at your command? Follow that question along your hand's synapsis to your brain and further still. Follow it right down to your own intent. What is that? What is your intent?

Ironically, my partial hysterectomy was the ultimate catalyst for moving fully into my state of being as a woman, into *being* a woman. When they removed the tumors in my uterus there was a vacuum that was created. I lost 10 pounds shortly after the surgery. The resulting vacuum left room for me to hold more light, to vibrate at a different, higher energetic frequency. It was after my surgery that I came to a different relationship with my Shakti. After the surgery I was fully able to embrace and express her. I wanted to help others do the same.

My mother used to say to me, "Decide what type of woman you want to be. If you are really connected to you, to who you are, then you don't have to make a big fuss about it. People will feel it when you walk into a room. The way you make them feel will move everything, and you won't need to try to do it. You will be *it*."

At the time I didn't have a clue what she meant but I did know that things seemed to stop when she walked into a room. She is tiny and she wasn't glamorous. It was an essence and an energy that commanded respect without saying or doing anything in particular. She was also afraid of her own power. She suppressed her fear only to have that fear spin on her. When we were kids she had the most amazing fits of rage, slamming cabinets, throwing china -- all expressions reserved for inside our home. In the external world, she conveyed a sort of restrained power – she was simultaneously warm and sweet and could also slay with a glance. Her students and often those around her were drawn to her. There were exceptions, of course, including my father. But as a child and teenager, I witnessed this powerful force in her as something she never really named for me. Over time, however, I came to recognize it in myself.

After my surgery, I vibrated on a different level. Odd and amazing things happened. For instance, I was at a party and a friend, a successful man, was telling me that the only woman he ever wanted to sleep with but hadn't was me. I suppose he thought he was complementing me. He wanted me to stay in Berlin, to put me up in an apartment, to sidestep his mistress with me, to consider getting serious with me. He was wealthy. Connected. But he needed time, he said. So strange. My answer to him was, *seriously*? You need time? You're incongruent with even yourself. You don't know yourself, and you certainly have no idea about me. And when I looked at his martini glass he was holding, it simply shattered. Weird.

I made a conscious decision to spend more time in Europe. As soon as I did, teaching engagements popped up in Berlin, Brussels and Paris. I was at a party in NYC and found a bride-to-be, who I didn't know well, pleading with me to come to her wedding. Her ex-boyfriend, friend of my ex-husband, was saying, "Stop that. Don't pressure her to fly to Africa. It's far and expensive and you don't even know each other that well." It was a moment that I knew was bigger than the wedding. I wasn't close to her. He was right. But I did revere Nelson Mandela, and had always longed to go to South Africa and also to see Robbins Island. Something in me knew that she was a portal to getting me there. Little did I know that the timing of her wedding would coincide with one of the messiest times of my life. But that trip was Divinely guided. I cried every day there, discovered I had a heart condition I needed to address, and got my head/heart around my pending divorce. The energy in South Africa is so powerful. It's one of the most beautiful places on earth; it was the perfect respite from the drama at home in NYC.

And so began an interesting period of being invited to weddings of people I wasn't close to, or who I hadn't seen in a long time. Just a few months after I went to South Africa, I found myself invited to a wedding in Saint Maarten. This invitation came from a former client who I hadn't spoken to or seen in seven years. Energetically, seven is a complete cycle and somehow this felt like a sign of my own completed cycle and possibilities for the future which included a lot of traveling. Social and professional invitations took me to South Africa, Saint Maarten, Brussels, Berlin, Paris, and London -- all in the space of a few months. I road through Bosnia on a bus and witnessed a sea of white crosses on unmarked graves. Simultaneously, my teachers, Dr. Levry and Mary Grace O'Hearn, helped me make peace with the collapse of my life and aspirations as I had known them. They helped me unravel the coincidence, prophesy dreams, intuitive connections with the unseen, and other mysterious experiences. I had regularly since having surgery and leaving my husband.

"You are one of the living embodiments of the Divine Feminine walking the earth. You are an agent of change and you not only contain but are fully connected to the psycho-spiritual force. What you are experiencing and embodying is a deeper level of independence. Shakti is self-born, and is unable to be created or destroyed by any other existence. Now use this ability to help women and the world." This was the message I kept getting in dreams and in my waking life. The process of my surgery had been a birthing of sorts. It was this experience that was my portal to being a woman.

More and more people, both men and women, approached me with the longing to understand this force. For example, men showed up on Wednesdays asking to take the women's class, asking me to teach more workshops that weren't gender specific. Male clients laughed and said, "Get out of my head. It's like you read my mind and you're ahead of time and space. It's like you just know. Teach me how to access that."

Self-Care

Before I agreed to teach the class, I had gone through my own odyssey as a woman, including painful miscarriages and a partial hysterectomy. The breadth of my life experiences had led me to a desire to understand myself not exclusively as a human being but as a woman. I wanted to not only understand the meaning of my life but also to feel fully alive.

For instance, I had spent most of my life achieving, striving, driving myself to be "successful." It was only after my surgery that I started to accept that success meant a lot more than how I had been defining it. It also meant accepting that I was no longer willing to maintain any sort of façade. I was ready to be, to really be, who I am -- to be my true self, which as it turns out, was pretty different from the self people had been experiencing up to that point. A veil had lifted and I was clear, unbound, free to create. I felt fully alive. Anything else suddenly had zero appeal. And on December 21, 2012 this desire intensified in parallel to the sudden increase in popular culture on the topic. I decided that Dr. Levry was correct and that I did have something to offer.

Ironically, many men had urged me over the years to work with women. Men feel comfortable around me. As my friend Richard says, "You are a woman but you're not a girly girl. You're like Sonia Rykiel. All women can't do it so well, but you can hang with the men's club and still be a woman." My Spiritual Mother Mary Grace O'Hearn once told me, "You have a perfect balance of yin and yang. This is why men and women in equal measure really like you. Some fall in love with you, and the ones that don't really like you."

Shakti & Self-Care

I count it as a gift that the traumas of my life forced me to learn about who I am. I became conscious that I could participate in my transformation or not. But change was *certain*, which is a weird notion when you think about it -- especially when you want certainty, when you NEED certainty. I now believe that the Universe gifted me with a variety of experiences that would give me what I needed to birth myself and my Shakti. I just had to pay attention and learn to accept rather than fight against certain experiences that felt brutally unfair. I had to connect to my "*I AM*" to the essence of who I am and my truth to heal and thrive.

I also know what it is like to live the life of an urban career woman - I am one. At my core I have the driving qualities needed for a career in equal measure to my softness, nurturing and compassionate nature. Part of my journey as a woman is mastering the integration of the totality of myself. This happens in the small day-to-day experiences of life and how mindfully I respond to them. Only from this place can I feel comfortable under my own skin regardless of external circumstances.

As I transformed, what I noticed in my female friends, business associates, and clients is that they were all struggling with this balance. They wanted to be more receptive. They wanted to have more fun, but worked so much and were driving themselves so hard that they had forgotten how. They were only alive from the neck up most of the time.

I've noticed that many of the women I work with are longing to connect with the Divine Feminine Goddess energy. They want to bring that spirit into their professional and personal lives. I also saw that the more I healed and connected with this Shakti, this essence within myself, this *I AM* -- the more successful I became in all areas of my life -- successful in this way that I was both happy and proud of what I was doing.

Shakti at Work

The Athena Doctrine by John Gerzema draws data from 65,000 people across 13 nations that supports that "feminine," aka "soft" skills, are essential for success in a global economy. This is the age of the Divine Feminine and the hard numbers essentially prove it. But the more important proof here is direct experience. Direct experience is the soft-skill of being present to your life. Let me say, there's no running from your story. If you do, what you have is a story of someone running from themselves – running from their direct experience, avoiding the *experience* of living. So you might look good on paper, you might not. But there is no avoiding that all the demanding substitutes for direct experience will unsettle you. You are not a transportation unit for your skull. You are a being. Feel it. Live it. Why not? Because you're too busy or bored or hurt to participate in the *experience* of your own life? Maybe you haven't considered it lately, you know, but you're breathing. Make the next breath just so slightly deeper. And in that breath is something bigger than yourself. There are others beginning to breath deeper too. It's a bit of a massive wave of human evolution, you know. As Gerzema describes it, this global wave is building now. So ride it. That's no abstract. Blink. You're holding it in your hands.

I've been hired to sit in on high-level negotiations in Manhattan, hired essentially to be present as an empath. I remember a CEO turning to me after one particularly intense session to ask me, "So what did you see?" And at this point I could then translate my soft-skills into the language of negotiation strategy. I could identify the top three initiatives and look at how they were supported at the tactical level. My focus for organizations is often to translate meetings in the c-suite to the level of *why-am-doing-this* for the rest of the organization. I love being hired specifically to be present in the room — to pay attention in ways that also allow you to focus on the bottom-line business realities of building things out, making deals, winning contracts, and getting the organization on board. Feeling the direct experience of the room has a tangible bottom-line result, as long as your personal energies are integrated. That is, as long as you know yourself as a being that perceives outwardly and inwardly. Place your attention on your physical form, on your breath, on your moods, on the light of your eyes, on silence and sound. Live there, as a perceiving being — and just see what happens. Be there, someone needs to be. But my duh moment after years of experience is simply this: you avoid awareness of your sensations in the present moment at your own peril.

For most females there is a tangible longing in our souls to express the potential of the Divine Feminine Goddess energy. We feel the pull even if we can't always name it or don't always have the courage to express this powerful potential. But it is essential to being authentic and aligned with our true selves. It is the source of our truth, power and creativity.

So this is my 'why' for teaching the Naam Yoga for Women, and why my class is packed to capacity every Wednesday. Men ask me why I don't let them in the class. I laugh and say, "Because women need their own space to cultivate themselves as women. Then they can go back into the world and interact at a higher level with all of you." I often add, "Just like you need your 'man pad,' fraternities, etc." I feel the Wednesday class is a female version of that. I know this, and this is why I'm not offended by the need men have to have a man pad, or be part of a men's club. We all need a space and support for our *I AM,* and gender plays a part. Men and women are different and *viva la difference!*

We all need our safe space where we can be what and who we are, and then we can be more authentic with each other regardless of gender. I'd like to think the Wednesday class I teach supports women in being better partners, run more successful businesses but most of all heal the collective imprint of anger, jealousy and fear that is rampant in the collective unconscious of women. Perhaps my greatest contribution is healing this in myself and being a catalyst to this healing in others. From my personal experience, we all are challenged by at least one of the above. For me, anger was always my biggest challenge. I remember doing a particular yogic posture and after thirty seconds my arms were shaking and I found myself bursting into tears. It was only later that I learned that this posture worked on stored anger in the heart chakra. That posture helped me to first accept that I was royally pissed off about a lot of things that had occurred in my life and then to be present to what I needed to heal in myself. Namely, it helped me to stop playing the same tapes and telling myself the same stories, in order to unbind myself from the past.

It was a process. But over time, I learned that healing had nothing to do with being positive or denying what I felt. It meant feeling all of it and approaching it from a softer place in myself. The softness of compassion, the softness of letting myself breathe into it, and the softness of being with it, ironically opened the portal for me to no longer be stuck in it.

Connecting to Shakti requires embracing the shadows and the light. And often our shadows show up in our "negative" emotional states. But I believe these states are as valuable to us as our "positive" states because they wake us up. It's not striving to be positive or holy that heals us. It's striving to be more receptive, more present to our personal defenses and judgments, more honest, *more human* – this is what heals and helps us grow, to have an independence that co-exists with acceptance. By staying in my own frequency, staying clear about my I AM, and staying authentic, I continually rediscover a deep trust for abundance of all kinds.

I conclude a client engagement and allow the space that is left to be. Within what seems like a miniscule amount of time more clients come. I pray before I teach. I pray to be an extension of something bigger than myself. I pray that I be a vessel of Light in service to the good of my students and the class is always full without actively promoting it. These are all signs that being more human, more trusting, combined with healthy boundaries and not being afraid to be, results in more opportunities than I sometimes have the time to accept. This is beneficial because when my schedule is overbooked I know it's time to pause and really assess what is in alignment with me, my values, and my intent – what I want to create.

Self-Care, Intuition, & Acceptance

For instance, I've become more aware of my need to have space all by myself. This is how I restore and refuel. I get energy by being still, so I consciously intend not to over book myself. I am also notorious for embracing the value of sleeping. I refuse to exhaust myself to the point that it's almost a joke within my circle of friends. Unlike many New Yorkers who have the motto "I'll sleep when I'm dead," I actually sleep now. Because I know I cannot be fully alive and receptive unless I get enough rest.

I vowed to show up in my own life differently after the surgery. As I contained more light my capacity to pay attention increased. And because I gave it time, my intuition breathed into my experience. I am now acutely aware of what is happening around me both in matter (what is seen) and the subtle energy of what is not seen. My intuition leads me into experience. My experience sharpens my intuition. I feel I live in a place where my intuition and experience meet. I live in congruence with nature on a whole different level. And this includes my own innate nature, my I AM. I don't multi-task as much. I move slower. I notice what is being given and why. I see what I am willing to give and why. I keep an eye out for patterns. I always know where the moon is. I pause. I brake. I do my best to give people my full attention. And this necessitates healthy boundaries. There is a higher quality to my choices. I am less rigid and more adaptable and healthy boundaries are what tend the garden gate of this beautiful life. I know how to adapt and pivot without losing myself. I stand for my own life and take care of myself differently. I check in with my heart and my closest advisors before I commit to things. I follow the God in my heart.

For instance, I am inherently in love with children. But without cultivating acceptance and the desire for deeper understanding, the miscarriages and a partial hysterectomy I experienced would have crushed my spirit. At one level, I see how easy it could have been to have become bitter and armored. After the doctor told me that I needed the partial hysterectomy, I couldn't believe it. It was just so mammoth. I went into shock. I actually had to go back the next day. The doctor must have gotten something wrong. All of it wrong. Somehow she fit me into the day's schedule. But in the doctor's office on the next day, I found she was really able to hold space. And it helped. But it was no cure. I had to step up.

I can see now how easily I might have gone to a bitter place: *I've always wanted kids. I love kids. Look, at all these people who hate kids. They hate them, and they have them anyway.*

I stepped right up to the edge of that and had to step back. It's no place to dwell.

Having kids, It's such a big thing for women now. There's such a panic around the kid thing. All I can do is speak to my experience and what I've discovered about the acceptance of suffering.

Shakti for Ourselves & The Love of Men

I also love men and male energy. At heart I am a romantic and someone who values connection and intimate relationship. Again, without cultivating my spiritual practice as a means of healing old emotional wounds, my divorce would have crushed me. Rather than that happening it liberated me.

On my journey as a woman one of the things that helps me understand me is to own and acknowledge that men are different, and to embrace that difference. I believe in gender parity, but I also hold a conviction that we have fundamentally different operating systems. I try to understand the male operating system rather than expecting it to function as a female operating system does. When the man I love doesn't respond right away, I know it's not personal. I've grown to understand that even when he seems to be not doing anything he is doing something — most likely focusing on how to figure something out. So I give him room. I let it breathe. I focus on my side of the fence, on intentionally expanding my container of light and what I have control over. I accept that everyone has their own timing. By not pushing situations and relationships, my life experience tends to synchronize and turn out exactly how it's meant to. I have realized that there is no need to try to control everything.

Do your internal work and then things will unfold. I don't worry about chasing after somebody – whatever everyone else is doing. For instance, I will do my best to make this the best book I can. I don't worry about pleasing men or anyone else for that matter. I don't worry at all. But I do intend to stop criticizing, nagging and holding other people responsible for how my life is unfolding. I'm responsible for my life. My life is a result of my choices and my willingness to do my own internal work; to set my intention, to be mindful and compassionate and honest, when I'm scared to acknowledge that too, even if it's irrational. When the man I love was shooting off the side of a 60-story building I got anxious and kind of freaked out. I was scared for him even though he was completely nonchalant about the whole thing. So even though it seemed irrational I told him and was so relieved when he sent me photos showing me he was safe up there. I've learned that part of being healthy and whole is to express how I feel and to not be concerned with how rational it is or not.

To unfold with what you feel and think – you must be congruent – you can't separate yourself into compartments with funny locks and keys. But when you are congruent you hold more space and more light. Without congruencies you're full of little boxes. Place your breath on your heart. Breathe from your heart. Is there something you need to speak to? Then try to come from that place, with your breath from your heart. For those who don't, do you think you can control everyone by compartmentalizing everything? then you're not your real self, which is to say, you're not even real at all. You may have all the external trappings but without the internal congruence eventually it all becomes nothing more than a diversion.

So the rich guy says to me, stay in Berlin. Don't go back to New York. After a month, I'll be able to deal with how I feel. I say, what are you talking about? You don't make sense. I could never ever get close to you. He says, You're the kind of woman that would break my heart. I say, What are you talking about? You're not a congruent person. I see how you have all the externals. You've got it all on paper. Believe me, I know this. Everyone is so impressed with you. So many women are so easily bought by you, but that doesn't move me. When I met you in South Africa you showed me your heart, you were real there. And this is why I'm here with you in Berlin having lunch. But I can't connect with you now. You have too many boxes. You go from room to room in those boxy spaces. And you call that a mansion. I can't connect with someone who is trying to buy me. And you're an atheist on top of it all. Where's your inner life?

Let me just say that for women who say otherwise, I think most guys are good guys – don't blame them for your choices. When I got back to NYC from Berlin, more than one person I shared the story with said, "Well, I would have stayed in Berlin." *Really?!* I said. You would cancel all your plans for the holidays? And then you would have blamed him when he didn't leave his girlfriend. This is a heartbreak for me? This is it? Is this the level everyone is going to function at to make a connection? This stinks. It really stinks. Ick! There's a smell in here. You know what he said to me? He said, "You're the only woman I wanted to sleep with that I haven't." You'd be surprised. He really does sleep with anyone he wants to sleep with. Where's the guy I met in Africa, I ask, the one who helps with the post-apartheid election, and works with Desmond Tutu. Where did he go?

My message here is, Do your work and keep being open to the truth. Lift the veil. When someone shows you who they are, believe it. Engage based on being honest with yourself about what kind of relationships you want, and if that person is a match for that. My Grandmother once said to me, "Marry what is, not what might be." At the time I had no clue what she was talking about, but at 50 somehow I get it. Canceling my holiday plans, waiting in some posh hotel for what might have been — well, that's not my style.

Along this journey to being a woman, I learned on different levels that men, gay, straight and everything in between, long for Shakti. It heals their wounds, soothes their spirits and recharges their batteries. And when women are connected to this energy we recognize that they are really sensitive – as sensitive as we are but with different operating systems, so it shows differently.

Shakti respects and honors the different operating systems. In so doing, it awakens the dormant Shakti in men. It honors where people are in their own development. A woman connected to Shakti can hold her own in authenticity and creative expression. I know my yin and yang are balanced and I'm fully living in the embodiment when I am not criticizing, complaining or nagging. I did all three in my marriage out of my own wounds and patterns. My ex-husband was emotionally unavailable most of the time, but I knew this when I married him, and I still married him. That was my bad, not his. He is who he is, and if I had really let myself see all of this 11 years ago I would have made a different choice. Essentially, I married a version of my parents, blinded at the time by my wounds and my willful refusal to see the warning signs. It took me 11 years to reduce my ego to the point that I could accept that it wasn't working. That no matter how much I meditated and prayed I had to accept that it was over. Once I accepted that I had no choice but to move beyond certainty into the unknown of life as a divorcee.

Beware the person, male or female, who feels threatened by your success. If someone can't celebrate you in your glory, it's no good. From my experience, many people are more comfortable around the wound than the success. Steer clear of this energy. Engage in it at your own peril.

Part of my paying attention is to live in accordance with the cycles of nature. For me, being a woman means understanding and flowing with nature, knowing my cycles and how they wax and wane like the moon. Like Mother Moon, they impact my moods. Having the discipline to slow down and understand where I am in any calendar year. Where are the stars? What are they saying to me? This creates more room for flowing and ease. Merging with the energies at play instead of fighting against them makes things easier. It facilitates having more abundance and working less. It exponentially cuts down on stress. I live in NYC and have a thriving business and personal life. Most of the time I'm not stressed. Why? I know how to set healthy boundaries, I don't get attached. I'm not in a rush and I let things breathe. I don't take action until I'm sure. I only reach this clarity when I check with my heart.

To hold the energy for the Wednesday class I need to balance the yin and yang energy within myself. On a practical level this means I hold my center while allowing for the totality of my experience which includes allowing myself to feel -- being in my emotions without getting stuck in them. Sometimes I cry when I meditate and I don't know why. I let myself be with my tears. When I'm patient and compassionate with myself they reveal to me why they are there.

I utilize it in the perfect frequency and it supports me in the joy I carry and in the times I'm sad. I can feel, allowing my feelings to wash over me. I can stay real and authentic. I can fully feel without being taken over by my unconscious emotions.

I've noticed when I'm unbalanced and need to recalibrate. Too much yin and unconscious emotions take over and blind me. Too much yang and it's ambition in overdrive without heart -- tunnel, ego-driven vision. Neither space is useful without the perspective of the other. This is the gift of paying attention and giving myself permission for the totality of my experience. I can make a correction and get back to the centered space.

Something magical happens during my Wednesday yoga class. Magical enough that it pulls people in from all over town and Europe. I am blessed to have students who fly in from Amsterdam and London just to take my class. I'm happy to create a space where women can be real. From my perspective, so much is misunderstood about walking a spiritual path. I say openly in the class that I don't want to be an oracle, and I'm not one. I'm a woman and everything that goes with that. I don't sit on high preaching one way. Rather my intention with the class is to share whatever wisdom I have gathered from my own experience of life, love, and the Divine. I believe the Divine is everywhere.

My wish is that everyone saw with their hearts.

Truth be told, I don't plan my Wednesday class. I always get a kick out of the faces in the room when they hear this for the first time. What, there's no formula? No precise plan?

Nope. There isn't.

I lock into the frequency of the Divine Feminine and the Shakti within and it gets downloaded to me. It unfolds organically. Anyone who comes to the class knows that I go into a sort of trance-like state before I teach. I pray and set my intention that the class unfolds for the glory of God on earth. That I teach from my heart motivated not by spiritual ego (pride), but out of a sincere desire to help everyone there become a woman and raise the frequency of being a woman. I have the sincere hope that when I teach I help everyone get more connected to their hearts, that I can be a proper vehicle for the transmission of energy that is heart-centered and healing -- that I can be an extension of the Divine.

Prayer of Love Peace & Light

Love before me
Love Behind me
Love at my left

Love at my right
Love above me
Love below me

Love unto me
Love in my surroundings Love to all

Love to the Universe

Peace before me
Peace Behind me
Peace at my left
Peace at my right
Peace above me
Peace below me
Peace unto me
Peace in my surroundings Peace to all

Peace to the Universe

Light before me
Light Behind me
Light at my left
Light at my right
Light above me
Light below me
Light unto me
Light in my surroundings Light to all

Light to the Universe

    The prayer above is something I say before I teach and also every morning. It's a simple way to ask for blessings while also giving a reciprocal energy to the world. It's a prayer of balanced giving and receiving.

    I have been told by my students that to bear witness to this level of surrender is a powerful example, even if it freaks them out a little bit. I can't explain in a linear way how the class occurs, I just know it's magical for all of us and the energy of the beautiful women who come every week makes it happen. It's not me in a vacuum, it's a magical alchemy that occurs and it's fun.

Something magical happens in the class. Here is what one of my students recently shared with me . . .

"Thank you so much for giving of yourself for an incredible Wednesday class, where I gained more wisdom and confidence in a little over an hour, than I have in years of my life. You have no idea how sacred your classes are and how much I missed coming. YOU ARE AN AMAZING BEING OF LIGHT."

When I received her note I exhaled and thought, wow, it's happening. I am making a difference for people. My experiences do matter beyond me. Note to self: keep giving yourself permission to share your truth, your experiences, your messy bits . . .

Here are some of my essentials for staying in the space called Shakti:

Compassion is paramount. I see how I have the ability to enter into another person's world. But I can be overly empathic in the sense that I can feel what it feels like to be in another's world even while I stay in my own shoes. At its core, it's the energy of the Divine Mother -- the ability to feel what someone needs from me, to see beyond my own needs, to ask questions and not assume. Compassion and empathetic inquiry help me to be nurturing and effective rather than bossy and meddling.

Compassion is integral to femininity. All expressions of the feminine need compassion to inform them. Compassion gives us the ability to sense what someone in front of us needs. It contributes to successful teamwork and collaboration. It is essential for nurturing our most intimate relationships. Without compassion it's very easy to *assume* what another person needs and to become pushy, over-giving, or meddling, instead of nurturing and effective.

Generosity is key. Often we are able to be generous materially. We buy things for people, and that's lovely. But the foundation of generosity rests on compassion. Generosity grounded in the heart allows people to have their own process --

and allows that process to proceed in a gentle, mindful way. There's power in this. There's also a counter tendency to want to control another person's experience of something. But doing this doesn't honor your shared humanity. Influencing is different than controlling (more on this later in the book). Generosity that allows people their process, without trying to shape their perception, does something extraordinary. It manifests compassion. Consider what happens when you give others the highest qualities of your attention. That's a kind of generosity indistinguishable from compassion. And in being generous in this unplanned way, you're rewarded in ways you hadn't *planned* on.

Receptivity is a requirement for expressing the Divine Feminine Goddess energy. Being receptive takes courage, because it requires a level of openness and vulnerability that is often way out of our comfort zones. It can feel like leaping off a ledge without seeing the bottom.

To fully receive the gifts that life has to offer us, we need to choose to let the spirit and gifts of the giver in. It requires an opening of the heart. Ironically, receiving is a gift to the giver. Receptivity completes every cycle of giving. It is not possible to give freely and to love unconditionally, unless you give yourself permission to be receptive. Receptivity balances your cycle of giving and receiving and is a gift to the giver.

Breathing with intention is a way to practice receiving. Breathe with your attention placed on your heart. For a minute or so practice long, slow, deep breaths with your attention placed on your heart. It creates a softening around the heart-center that will help you get comfortable with the art of being receptive.

Breath is a sure way to master the mind and open the heart. When I feel myself spinning, spiraling, or feeling rejected, I put my hands on my heart with my left hand on top, and inhale deeply. When I cannot inhale anymore I say "*I AM*" silently. Then I exhale and before I breathe in again I say silently to myself "*I AM.*" This powerful breathing technique immediately connects me to my heart, to my soul's truth, to my center. In doing it, I am able to be present to the lesson of the moment. I AM able to live my life in the truth of my own vibration and frequency. The breath is one of my greatest teachers.

Playfulness. Many people tell me that I'm chic, sophisticated, smart etc. I'm also told that I have the energy of a five year old. I think that's because I laugh . . . a lot. I like to have a good time. I like good food, good conversation, good sex, and good wine. I like challenging my intellect and to engage in different points of view. And I make a point to have all of them. And to not be too serious, I place a premium on joy, pleasure and happiness: seeing the spontaneity of a child experiencing something in the moment, buying fresh flowers from the farmers' market, sleeping naked in really soft sheets, shopping for glasses with my beloved. I realize as I get older, it's often the small intimacies of daily life that give me the most pleasure.

I am 50, and the older I get the less serious I am. I laugh more and know that everything I've been through has cracked me open. And it's in that open space where I want to stay, laughing.

Chapter 4

Across Time & Space: Homage to Unconditional Love

When love beckons to you, follow him. He is for your growth.

~Rumi

Sitting with my teacher Dr. Levry, I show him a picture. He asks me, "Who is he? That guy loves you." Tears spontaneously come to my eyes. "I love him too, but I lost him a long time ago," I say. The memories come flooding back. I don't know what to do or if there is anything to do. What I do know is that in this present moment, I'm married to someone I don't love. Actually, probably never did. Not the kind of love that shows in that picture anyway.

That picture is from 2000, taken by my sister in London somewhere between Holland Park, Kensington and Notting Hill. That time is past but the relationship has taken a different form and shape over the years. Somehow through time, space, and being married to different people, we both accept this. It's been 15 years since the last time we shared a bed. I noticed when I looked at that picture, that while I'm radiantly happy in it, somehow I seem smaller. I stand slightly behind him. Maybe that's one of the reasons why we didn't end up together. I don't think I am meant to stand behind anyone. Beside someone, yes, but never behind him or anyone else.

At the height of the pain of my failing marriage, I longed for him. The memory of his courage and steadiness seemed to ground me and I conveniently erased the volatility and the pain that we caused each other. No matter what, I wanted him to know that I was sorry. Sorry for letting him down. Sorry I couldn't leave NYC to go to London so many years ago. Sorry from the depths of my heart for having hurt him. I reached out to him and told him all of it, while at the same time asking that he come and see me in NYC. Intuitively, I knew that he still felt for me as well and that if I could only show him that my woundedness had healed that perhaps we could try again. I admit, I was suspending reality a bit. A man of his caliber doesn't walk out on his family. His courage is such that he keeps his commitments. His biggest commitment is to his family, especially his daughters.

He told me his daughters wanted to go to Paris and perhaps we could meet there. At the time, he was in the Middle East. I wouldn't go and then posted on FB how much I loved Paris. He exploded publicly, on my FB page, about how London far surpasses Paris! Fifty plus people came to my defense defending Paris as a perfectly lovely destination. I sensed the same frustration that he had with me over the course of our intimate friendship over the years. I always had a way of driving him crazy in both negative and positive ways. For many years he did the same to me. We never labeled any of it, and there was much hidden. I know on my side it is only recently that I've been able to put words to something that is ineffable and sometimes indefinable.

The truth is that he has been in my heart but, as time has passed, he hasn't been there physically. In some shape or form for nearly 30 years, since my early 20's, he has lived in my heart. The pull between us was once so strong that I almost felt that it made me crazy. It is only now, many years later, when we're both in the middle of our lives, that I realize the heavens have graced me at least once in my life with an experience of real and transcendent love, love that makes both people want to be better people. While not united in the day to day, this love has been a constant presence in both our lives.

I also know now that it was no accident that Sacred Heart, the Catholic School I went to growing up, was Polish. As a child, even

I wondered why I was there. After all, I'm not Polish – not one drop of Eastern European blood flows in my veins. I'm French and African American. My Grandmothers on both sides of the family gave my mom a lot of shit about this, what is also etched in my mind. I recall my black Grandmother saying, "Why isn't she learning French? Polish, what is that going to do for her?" But my mother has always been willful and stubborn. When she decides something, that's it. It's very difficult to oppose her or turn the boat around. So Saint Mary's it was, beginning in kindergarten.

Only when I arrived in NYC did this piece of the puzzle start to sort of make sense to me. Being in that Polish Catholic School meant I was also exposed to the culture and the food. Pierogi and potato pancakes were favorites through my childhood. I also liked the earthiness of the culture, the realness of the people who crossed my path at that school. Another result is that I always felt at home in a church.

Early on in NYC, I was running a gallery in a design firm called ISD. I was also an administrative assistant. The truth was I had no clear vision of what I wanted when I failed the Foreign Service Exam. I just knew I wanted to go to NYC and I had a friend from college who could rent me a room in his railroad flat in Hoboken, New Jersey for $200 a month. Hoboken was just on the other side of the river. A quick PATH train got me into town.

One day I was puttering around the design firm. I was laughing with the guy who ran marketing. He was older, 28. His age seemed ancient to me at the time. He said that a friend of his was coming to the gallery opening later that night. He said that we should meet. That night the place was filled with people. This was 1989 and NYC was a different place — not as expensive and a bit more creative as a result. There was a pulse in the city that felt like anything was possible, that all worlds could collide, regardless of income.

That night they did collide. I looked up and saw a purposeful banker striding through the crowd. That stride over the years would always make me feel safe. When I saw him walk like that whether it was across the bedroom after making love, at the Barbican going into the Philharmonic in London, or across a tennis court after kicking someone's ass, the purposefulness and self-containment of that walk was irresistible.

I guess something in me knew that first day that something was about to happen. Like all magic in life, the inner knowing is ahead of time and space. But even though the evidence had yet to come, my heart knew something explosive was going to happen.

Life has taught me that when mighty unseen forces want to make something of our lives, they conspire for change. Maybe this is the knowing, this feeling that something beyond rational thinking is taking hold.

He spotted me also and we were introduced. So handsome he was, self-contained, and entirely himself. He was in possession of a spark. He was and still is unlike anyone I had ever met. I guess when you have the courage to get political asylum and to walk out of a fencing tournament and never look back, as he did, you don't get shaken up at an art opening by a beautiful girl who is entranced by you.

To this day, both my sister and I marvel that we have been so close to someone who had such courage. It's not an easy life as a woman when the bar is set that high at such a young age. It would seem that no one can come close, and the legend gets bigger and bigger over time.

A few weeks later his friend the marketing guy told me some of the Polish expat's story. He worked for a Japanese bank and lived with his girlfriend who was American and taught him English when he first arrived in NYC. So I was told that he was driven, powerful and intense. His friend was candid, telling me that at times he was intensely difficult and exacting in his standards. He said that he would like it if I joined them for a dinner party.

The part that was conveniently left out was that his girlfriend was away the night of the dinner party. That night we made a small dinner party of four. There was a couple, the Polish expat, and myself at his apartment. Eating dinner with these three people, I was shaking in my boots and acutely aware that I had never met anyone like him. He just seemed so in control and on top of everything, despite everything that he had been through, and despite not knowing if he could ever go home. It was 1989 and the wall hadn't fallen yet. Political asylum could easily have meant never returning home. He seemed to so confidently look forward.

After a lot of food and wine no one felt like going home. By 3:00 in the morning, the couple decided they'd stay over. I remember saying, "Well, I think I will go call someone to walk me or help me get a cab. That's when I knew I was cooked. They all laughed and said, *Oh just stay over.* I declined – where would I sleep? They said *sleep on his bed with him.* I said, "He lives with his girlfriend, I can't sleep in the bed with him." Then they all said, *She is so American, isn't she?* I remember thinking they are all so self-assured and older than me. I felt naïve, and I was naïve. But it was clear that I would stay.

He gave me a pair of his sweat pants, a t-shirt and a sweatshirt. My heart was racing out of my chest. The truth was I wanted him, wanted to be with him. But at 23 I was not in my center enough to own this desire I felt for him. Curled up on the side of the bed in my layers, I breathed and turned to face him and he kissed me. I kissed him back. When I woke up the layers were gone.

He made me coffee in the morning and breakfast. We laughed. He walked me home. I knew at that moment I was in way over my head. I felt something so primal, raw and powerful that night. It was beyond anything I could or can name to this day. It is still a powerful force in my life. We both live on separate continents but there is an energy that binds us still.

When I came down to earth, I thought, *What am I doing? He lives with his girlfriend.* But no matter what, I had decided that he would be mine. So I left a message on his answering machine saying that, by the way, I slept with your boyfriend last night. Juvenile, hurtful, something I'm not proud of. He hit the roof, and she did too. I told him to move out. He thought I was crazy. But he did move out.

We continued to sleep together but we also got to know each other outside of the bedroom. He took me to the Polish restaurants on 2nd Avenue and I took him to Danal, one of my favorite French restaurants. Sometimes we would just walk together and talk, sometimes we would walk together and fight. Our relationship was volatile. He couldn't understand my temper, and I couldn't understand why he was so hard on me. Now I realize that he was so hard on me because he saw me. He saw who I really was beyond the wounds and the insecurities, and he expected me to live into that — into my true self.

He moved back to London and the continent. I moved in with the all-American guy who would be my first fiancé. But my Polish expat would come back to New York sometimes. He had business here as well as in London. He always let me know when he was in NYC, and I always arranged to meet him. He never approved of said fiancé, and because he saw me, he knew that I needed someone as powerful as him or that it wouldn't work. He was right.

One day after one of his visits to NYC, and the inevitable coupling with him when he was in town, I handed my engagement ring back to my fiancé, who I think always knew that I was in love with someone else. But he accepted it. He accepted it, because he thought the steadiness of his commitment would override the passion I felt for someone else. When I handed him the ring he looked at me with ice-blue eyes and said, "You've got to be fucking kidding me."

I left my fiancé, and while I later had boyfriends in New York, nothing could take the place of my Polish expat. I may have slept with someone else but he was always in my heart. I safely held him close to the deepest part of me, and I prayed for his greatest happiness. He had set a standard that no one could touch and through this standard had revealed to me what was possible in a man. I idolized him. The intimacy was raw, passionate and primal. We could laugh and talk and fight with each other. Despite all of it, we never let go of each other, until we let go of each other.

The last time I saw him was just before 9/11, when I flew from New York to London to see him. My sister and two friends were in London with us from Paris, when he made his declaration. He walked his walk out of the WC in a pub in Notting Hill and over to the table. He said to the table at large without addressing me directly, "I don't know what's wrong with me. I can't commit to her. I can't marry her." The energy was sucked out of the room. My sister, not knowing just how to respond, got up and asked a couple of Brits if she could borrow their fluffy white dog. The friends from Paris ordered more drinks. The supremely-awkward-moment-rent-a-dog sat at the table with us and yipped. No one knew what to do other than to distract and anesthetize.

We left them and went back to his place. I was incensed and became even more so when he made it clear that we would not be making love that night. How dare he deal me two double rejections. I huddled with my sister in the kitchen, enraged and crying while she told me, "I think he won't sleep with you out of respect for you. He doesn't want to hurt you any more than he has. He is afraid he is damaging you." I thought, *Complete nonsense*.

Ego kicks in, overriding heart. Not good. The next day he is off to the office, and I tell my sister to pack her things. We're leaving early. Back to NYC. At his flat, I see a postcard I had once sent him from Provence. It's in his study pinned to the bulletin board where he sees it every day. For a moment my heart softens. But then I attach to the slight and I think, No. *I'm leaving*. I write a note and truth be told I have no remembrance of what it said. It was a goodbye note with the subtext of testing: *Goodbye but come to NYC and get me. Bring me back to London even though I've made it clear that I won't move without some guarantee of a life together, something clearly defined.*

Many years later I reflect how emotionally immature and distrusting I was. I reflect how I would make things impossible through my inability to convey the depth of what I felt. So I upped the ante for proof of the love. I placed conditions. There was a spy in the house of love, sabotaging the love of my life. The spy was so covert I had no idea it was myself.

That visit to London was the last time I saw him. I wept for the whole flight back. He didn't come to get me. In his devastation, he met someone else, and he married her.

Seven years following, I too was married. In my devastation, I thought *good enough* would be good enough. Out of fear of not finding that primal passion again, I settled for that which was less than. I focused on building my business. The next phase of doing that meant going to Sarasota Florida for my executive coaching certification. A woman there turned out to be a Polish expat and very successful executive in the pharmaceutical industry. It wasn't lost on me that she worked for Sanofi and lived in Southern France and somehow had ended up in Sarasota, Florida in my executive coaching program. Sure, it's a draw run by an ex-McKinsey exec and Harvard Graduate. But it's off the beaten path in western Florida.

She and I quickly bonded. We had an easy camaraderie through the program. Out of the blue she mentioned she was writing a book about successful Polish expats. The book was about people who had the immigrant experience, and had then gone back to Europe successfully as she had. She had interviewed her full list of subjects with the exception of one man, the one she wanted to get to most.

I had chills up and down my spine when I asked his name. Even before I asked, I knew. I also knew it was God, working through her to put us back in touch. What is the rational likelihood that a Polish expat who lives in Southern France turns up at a coaching program in the states in Sarasota Florida at the precise time I am doing the program? Synchronicity and the higher world are always working through mortals. Read the writing on the wall. It's there.

She was frustrated. No one could get to him. I smiled and told her that I could. She was a bit stunned. Of course, she wanted to know how. I have always been very protective of him, and vice versa. So I told her, "Please trust me, if I tell him to connect with you he will. The rest isn't important."

So I reached out to him. We spoke of how we were both married now, and clearly not to each other. The longing was still there but it was somehow beginning to correspond with the reality of our chosen adult lives. He was in the Middle East and I was still in NYC. While I still felt that primal raw pull toward him, and I believe vice versa, space, time, and history separated us. We both had commitments and he now had two children and a wife. But as I knew he would, he agreed to speak to my colleague.

This opened the portal for us to be in touch. I asked his advice about some things that happened with my niece. He asked me to do the energetic charts for him and his two daughters. I wrote the charts, bound them, and sent them to the Middle East. FedEx is a beautiful thing. He moved back to Poland. I stayed in NYC.

Over time something has evolved between us. I am acutely aware of the absence of agenda between us. We are old dear friends, and there is a special understanding between us. I believe there is a special love we hold for each other that is untouchable, unbreakable and that will be through space and time. I have no expectation that we will be together. I accept that time has past. I have my own commitments on my side of the great pond to someone I love very much.

There remains an energy between us. We are Facebook friends and we have a habit of liking each other's posts. I wish him happy birthday and now that I am clear within myself that I have no agenda with him other than to be supportive and honoring of our connection, I say whatever I feel to him and vice versa. I have no fear of saying or doing the wrong thing. I just am, and sense that he just is as well.

We still love each other and in our own ways do our best to be supportive of each other. Our energy is still with each other. We remind each other of this every now and then. There is a deep and mutual knowing and deep trust between us. We are each other's cheerleaders and I am comforted by the knowledge that there is someone on this earth who truly wants what is best for me without agenda. I wish the same for him.

I feel like there is a radiant circle of Light around both of us that only we know about. I say that because it defies explanation and I wouldn't want it tainted by trying to explain it to people. I feel like something bigger than both of us brought us together and keeps us together against all odds.

Over time, lust turned to love turned to unconditional love. They say great love requires great courage, and I believe we both have been blessed by having this courage. Our mutual reward is the energy exchange irrespective of time and space. Bound by it, intentionally or not, we are always on each other's horizons.

We cannot be together as man and woman now. Truth be told, I don't know what I will do when I see him. As much as things have changed, in some ways I bet they haven't. I wonder sometimes if I would have the discipline to not jump into bed with him just one last time.

But perhaps that is the romantic in me. The practical side of me acknowledges that time has passed. He told me his great love at the moment is his dog – his French bulldog. I thought, *Well, at least there is something French that you love*, and I slightly chuckled to myself.

We have other sacred contracts to fulfill. We both know this. I have finally accepted this – fully accepted it. I know it's what's correct and at the highest alignment of light.

Now I am grateful for the connection and to know what it means to really love someone – intimate love, raw, primal love, volatile passionate love, and ultimately unconditional love. All of this is his gift to me.

My sister recently said to me, "I'm glad you guys keep in touch."

"Me too but why do you say that," I said.

"I always really liked him," she said. "He is good-looking, really smart, has a great sense of humor, and is honorable with so much integrity."

I laughed and said, "It's all true."

"But most of all," she said, pausing, "I always really liked him because I always knew how much he loved you. Even though you're not together in the day-to-day sense, you never left each other. His love for you, ultimately, helped you love yourself."

Spurred on by this comment I reached out to him by email. "Writing this book has been such a profound emotional excavation," I wrote him. "I have such deep love and respect for you always that is not about us being together. It's interesting to read about my own life and who has influenced it. Writing and then reading what I write about you makes me realize how primal and powerful our connection was. I am grateful for our paths crossing and in some ways big or small, I hope you've received as much from our connection as I have. Living on different continents I have to say this through technology rather than in person. Not optimal but better than not saying it at all."

The next day I woke up to a note from him, saying, "Our connection is important. And in some ways intentionally or not, your voice is there reminding me of very important things, 'Don't forget spirituality, don't forget higher purpose in the Universe, don't forget to dream.'"

I read it and cried. Happy tears. Grateful tears. My heart was overflowing with gratitude that I have given him as much as he has given me. How could I have any idea that 25 years ago that a feeling, an electric energy between a girl standing in a design firm with a glass of wine in her hand and a man striding across a room toward her would land here. I couldn't have told you that those layers of sweat clothes we peeled off would have ever helped us both understand anything so profound as our layered selves.

We'd been incarnated in each other's lives as lovers, combatants and ultimately friends. Those transient incarnations actually outlasted many other people who passed through our lives. What's at the core of a life when everything must pass? I don't know what happens next or if I'll ever see him again. But what I do know is that I'm not attached to knowing. What I do know is that I'll always love him.

Chapter 5

The Support Deficit

Think not that you can direct the course of love. For love, if it finds you worthy, directs your course.
~ Kahlil Gibran

The US culture has spun the myth of self-sufficiency into countless books and movies. It fosters it; celebrates it; and exports it. But while I am very independent, the "self-sufficiency" stuff has increasingly felt like nonsense to me. Great love isn't built alone, and guess what else? Neither are great careers, friendships, organizations, cities, or artistic achievements. Nothing is achieved "on our own." Nothing.

Trying to prove we can do everything ourselves costs much more than it gains. Trying to be self-sufficient is like tacitly agreeing to be disconnected, armored, and exhausted. Ease and flow drains out of life when you go it alone. It becomes all about driving and pushing. But it all also becomes ingratitude for all the support you do receive but don't recognize. Big *ICK* on both counts!

Being of a certain age, and growing up in a college town in the land of the Seven Sisters (Smith, Mount Holyoke, Wellesley), I also came of age with the advent of feminism. It's only now that I've come to realize that the message I got in my home growing up was different than its intended definition. Gloria Steinem's definition of feminism simply described social and economic equality between men and women, across-the-board.

Steinem did not intend feminism to mean *going it alone*. Even the early bra burning rallies show crowds of women. While the bra burning photos don't resonate with me, (too homogenous and I love my beautiful French lingerie), the camaraderie and shared purpose of women coming together always felt powerful to me.

Now even though I was a reserved child, I liked the idea of community. I just hadn't found one that I felt I fit in. Rather, I found myself floating though different tribes, white on one side and black on the other. The jocks and the AP kids. The Catholics and the atheists. I was, and am still, like water, flowing and adapting, but not solidly fitting into one group. Somehow, even though this has been isolating at times, ultimately it taught me to move easily between social codes, countries, and business sectors without being locked into any one of them. I adopted my own ideas about where I want to be.

Growing up, I witnessed my mom trying to do it all herself. She prided herself on being the single mom who had a career, raised 2 children My sister and I received a consistent, pressurizing message that to be safe was to be self-sufficient.

I remember, after one of many blizzards, watching my mother all of 5"2" and maybe 105 pounds put on a parka and snow boots to shovel out a very long driveway in the driving snow. I thought to myself, *Why is she doing this by herself? Why doesn't she ask for and accept help?* I heard neighbors asking her if she wanted help. Even the guy who drove the snowplow would ask if she wanted help when he saw us shoveling. This was Western Massachusetts in the 1970s. We routinely got a foot or more of snow. We had a long driveway, and shoveling out was no small task.

Mom was the master at saying, "I got it." It was probably because my dad and others had let her down so often. Asking for and accepting help was really tough for her. Interconnectedness didn't resonate with Mom. Independence and self-sufficiency did. She felt that she could keep us all safe by proving that she was an island unto herself. All that *proving* that she could do it herself, made her emotionally inaccessible to everyone, including my sister and me. I can articulate it now At the time it was something I felt without words to clearly express it. But emotional unavailability definitely didn't feel safe, as it doesn't feel safe today.

She would also sometimes say, "You can't have it all, and you can't do it all on your own." She was also shoveling mixed messages. They were probably mixed because she wasn't completely sure herself. It was the 1970s, and there was change all over the place, including feminism, Title 9, even my neighbor – a girl-playing baseball with the boys instead of softball with the girls. All around me were girls and women doing things on their own . . . starting with mom. But her overreliance on self-reliance put its own spin on the broader message. If I could have articulated it at the time, I would have told her something like, *independence doesn't mean isolation. Balancing a life doesn't mean imbalance. Real community doesn't express itself through lack of heartfelt connection.*

She held a master's degree and a very successful career in education. She was also a single mom, so I want to acknowledge her and how much she had on her plate. After surrounding herself with emotionally unavailable people, I think she bought into being a super self-sufficient woman as a survival strategy. But the people she surrounded herself with mirrored her own emotional unavailability. That's a hell of a way to build a support group.

Truth be told, she wasn't doing it all on her own either. I need to acknowledge my Grandmother, who helped out in essential ways, even if it was difficult for my mother to ask for and accept her help. At home, self-reliance was the law of the land. Do it on your own or risk getting devastated by life. The message was clear enough, even if left unspoken: *don't ask for help, reach out, or show vulnerability until you're at the absolute breaking point.* As a young woman, I tried to follow her example as a way of protecting myself from getting hurt, but ultimately and ironically this way of being hurt myself. Over time, I lost a great love because I wouldn't allow myself to tell him how I really felt. I couldn't tell him that I wanted him in every way a woman can want a man, that I wanted to have his children. I had wanted us to build a life together. Until recently, we both paid a heavy price for my inability to be vulnerable and real. This was one of the heavy costs of being a cool girl who wasn't sharing how she really felt. In the end, the effort to keep up my cool façade and control all the facets of my life became too much of an effort. I burnt out.

It was only when I was much older that I gradually let my barriers down and accepted that trying to do everything myself didn't get me the goodies; certainly not the really juicy stuff that keeps you warm at night. The drive and the pushing got me titles and a good salary but it didn't help me relax or accept myself. Rather, it made me push harder to prove that I was lovable based on my achievements, not based on who I was.

Now that I'm older I realize that my greatest fear has always been that I wouldn't be loved. Maybe it's because I never felt accepted and loved as a child beyond the praise I got for my achievements. Unconsciously, I perpetuated the support deficit in my own life.

As I've slowed down and aligned with my values and ideas, I realize how motivated by connection I am. That at my heart, what I desire most is a family and great love. Upon reflection, it becomes clearer and clearer how far I had to walk away from myself in order to live in this space of self-sufficiency. What's also clear is how the long walk back to living in my heart has rendered something entirely different than what I struggled for before.

Today I realize how much I internalized this imprint of hyper-independence as a defensive posture. I had lived in a kind of crouch mode, one I masked with a detached exterior because I was mirroring the examples I had known. I had actually exalted my living with a cool-girl posture. But with it I had exalted my defenses as the face of my identity. As I result, I rarely let my guard down. In the process, I created my own support deficit. I internalized my mother's unconscious beliefs, some subtle form of *I'm not good enough*. By doing so, I earned my mother's approval. She relished how successful and independent I was as well as what an overachiever I was. I know now that while I received my mother's approval in many ways, I betrayed my own highest self and true potential by behaving this way.

As I developed my spiritual practice, I learned of the seven karmic influences. These influences are the imprinting you receive when your soul incarnates into lifetimes and passes through the developmental stages on into adulthood, the inheritance of not only genetic predisposition to various disease states but also to the dis-ease of various beliefs and automatic behaviors. All this has its consequences in outcomes that don't serve our highest good, feeding back into a cycle of living from our body of pain.

For a long time I had a deep fear of disappointing my mother, and then one day I didn't care anymore. Maybe this is the gift of being in your 40s. For me, I became more afraid of living someone else's life, and repeating someone else's life mistakes in my own.

For a long time, I operated on a strictly unconscious level with my mother. I now realize I felt that if I affirmed my own power and potential, my mother would experience this as a personal rejection.

I didn't want to risk losing my mother's love and approval, so internalizing these limiting, unconscious beliefs was a form of loyalty and emotional survival for much of my adult life in NYC. I came to NYC thinking that if I don't let anyone in I won't get hurt. Okay, that lasted until I became bat shit mad crazy in love with a man who had the same primal draw to me. Although we both hurt each other, he remains a constant source of support even though we live on separate continents. My unwillingness to accept his help and support is one of the things that ultimately sabotaged our relationship. I could only let him in up to a point and then I would pick a fight, test him, keep raising the bar higher and higher until it was humanly impossible for him to do what I was asking. I now know how I created this and later used it to justify creating my own support deficit -- my own belief that he wasn't showing up. He really tried to, and he did. I just wouldn't let him in when he showed up.

This went on for many years. I was once told something like,

"Everyone thinks you're so great because you listen well. But anyone paying attention can tell that you aren't revealing anything about yourself. None of us know anything beyond the surface stuff – biracial, Boston College Jesuit education, ambitious, successful – also prone to drinking too much sometimes and to having a bad temper and alcohol fueled crying jags."

All my armoring wasn't getting me what I needed or wanted in my life. But I was mirroring what I knew from the example I grew up with – my body of pain and karmic influences were steering the ship. Feeling something was quickly addressed by a glass of wine, I wasn't running deep with myself. My Grandmother as loving as she was, always had a "high ball" in one hand and a cigarette in the other. I needed to look for other models and understand my motivations.

INTERDEPENDENCE VS. PROVING WE CAN DO IT OURSELVES

Fast forward and I'm all grown up at the age of fifty. But it's not the numerical age that makes me feel like a grown up. Maturity for me means finally allowing myself to fully experience myself and others. I can connect, be vulnerable, and live along a middle path. My absolutes are gone. I'm open and I don't walk around with a contingency plan. I am open to life, to people, to knowing that everyone who crosses my path is sent from a force higher than myself. I live in the knowing that nothing is an accident. All of this has made me a lot less controlling and a lot happier.

As I observe my students and my clients, many, but certainly not all, are women. Those who really thrive are living connected, interdependent personal and professional lives. The ones who are trying to prove that they can do it all themselves are often frustrated, exhausted and brittle.

Living in NYC it can be easy to buy into the illusion of self-sufficiency. We become experts at "driving" everything and, if we're not alert to the signs, pull too far to the masculine sides of ourselves. Then, if we are lucky, through the twists and turns of our lives we wake up. But that luck, at the time, can feel anything but lucky. It can feel like grief and loss.

I have finally grown up enough to admit that I need people and deep connection in my life. Once I fully accepted this, the most amazing things began to flow continually through my life. They'd show up in the form of clients, my beloved, and a whole host of incredible souls. Perhaps they were circling me all along.

I accept that I am far from perfect, and have stopped trying to be any semblance of that. What I prefer over battering at perfection is an honest view of myself. It is that gentle honest awareness that I hope to hone. And because of that I extend my love to being fully human with all the inherent messy bits. Awareness, honesty, and acceptance in this way are luscious. I am no longer afraid to fully feel. Raw, vulnerable, graceful, wise and sometimes moody, I allow myself the totality of my experience. When people ask me how I am, I honestly tell them. I no longer do the knee jerk "*I'm good*" response. As I've let myself be more fully myself, my connections deepen. The more I soften and receive, the more often life shows up to support me, often from the places I least expect it.

Chapter 6

Wear Good Underwear.
Take Care of Your Skin.

Clothes, like good architecture, have to correspond to the rhythm of life.
       ~ Jacqueline de Ribes

I am not close to my mother. I think it's safe to say we never really bonded. She had me when she was 22, after defying the social codes of the day and marrying my father. She is French American and he is African American. Like most of us, the *us* being African Americans, my father is a mix of a few things. In addition to his African heritage, he carries a bit of European and a bit of Cherokee Indian. My mother is as fair as a piece of white linen and as crisp. My Father is black.

I was left with my Grandmother for the first two years of my life. My Mimi raised me. I'm told she would show me a picture of my parents and tell me that that is who and where I came from. That was as close as I got to my parents for the first two years of life. I don't recall being shown a photo of my absentee parents, but I do recall how my Mimi loved me with her whole heart and how they were all laughing at our first reunion, when I ran back for my Mimi. It was to always be that way. Living with my parents or not, I reflect that the relationship with my parents could often feel like an awkward reunion with people I hardly knew.

But a few things from my mom stuck with me.

Wear good underwear

We never had droopy drawers. Mom made sure of that. And she was right. Good underwear is a sort of reinforcement. Now that I'm older it's not because I may get into an accident and have to go to the hospital. God forbid the emergency room doctor saw me in a pair of droopy drawers when I was being admitted for surgery.

No, now that I'm older, what I wear underneath is like a beautiful sensual secret that is with me every day. Beautiful lingerie makes me more confident and more connected to me. It's a way of honoring myself. It's a ritual that makes me happy and more secure. And every time I'm in Paris, I laugh on my way to the lingerie shop as I tell myself that I'm so worth it.

From the beginning, with my beloved, lingerie made me more confident. There is something quite amazing about disrobing and seeing the look on a man wanting to devour you. When you have beautiful lingerie you become more comfortable in your own skin, and this bestows confidence and sensuality.

Choose your poison. Fifi Chachnil is my favorite. Maybe yours is La Perla, or Wacoal. From the most basic to the most frilly, and everything in between, wear good underwear. Ditch the bloomers.

Take Care of Your Skin

Mom and Mimi always had the most beautiful skin. No nipping and tucking for them. No Botox, no facelifts. Just radiant skin that glowed. Even as they grew older, the wrinkles seemed to glow. They both have miniscule pores.

Even mentioning nipping and tucking would elicit a snort of disgust with them. Why would you ever cut your beautiful face? It was unfathomable to them. And believe me they are both vain women who passed that on to me as well. The women in my family like being beautiful, and walk around like it's a woman's God-given right.

But they never subscribed to a cookie-cutter idea of being beautiful. Just the opposite. One of the greatest insults ever lobbed at my mother was when one of her students told her she had a "big nose." For the record, with the exception of my niece Ameena Grace, we all have "big noses." But mom never thought of her nose as big, or any of ours as big. Rather, she said we had royal, aquiline noses. Hah! That seemed like the biggest load of crap of all when I was a kid. I was surrounded in school by kids with little button noses. My nose felt like it took up my whole face.

Mom would say, "*Don't be ridiculous! You are beautiful.* Someday you'll get it, and other people will too." That seemed like such an abstraction back then -- even though years later, like most things she said, she was proven right.

Just take care of your skin. From a young age forward, even after my parents got divorced, there were always potions in the bathroom. My mom wasn't taking care of her skin for a man. She was doing it for herself. She reminded herself day and night that she was worth it. It was about her feeling nurtured, cared for, and liking what she saw first and foremost for herself. What I also took from her was that she took care of herself this way as a sign of respect for others and the Creator. Why go out without putting your best foot forward?

My mother's creams, nail files, lotions… they were all behind the cabinets. She didn't wear much make up – some mascara and lip gloss and well-groomed eyebrows. These were her secret weapons. There to herald the cry, "*Don't be ridiculous. Take care of your skin!*"

Fast forward, and I'm 50. I am grateful to my mother's advice. It's funny what stays with you into adulthood. My bathroom cabinets are also filled with potions and I wouldn't think of cutting my beautiful face. I've even developed a different relationship with my nose. I like it. Rather than feeling like it takes up my whole face, I feel like it fits my face. I'm glad that when some girls in my class were getting nose jobs as a sweet 16, my mom was not having any of it.

Monthly facials are like taking a bath. It's just what you do to take care of yourself. Necessity, not luxury. This goes for my body creams as well.

Even though mom never articulated it this way, perhaps this is what she meant all along. Taking care of your skin can be one of the most sensual rituals of all. It's the biggest membrane, and absorbs everything you put on it. When you take care of it, you get comfortable feeling with your whole form, making not only touch but smell, sight, sound, even taste, a whole-body affair. Skin runs deep, if you let it.

As mom always said, "Take care of your skin."

Chapter 7

Rituals, Self-Care, and Why I Meditate

The most precious gift we can offer others is our presence.

~ Thich Nhat Hanh

I am, and have always been, a ritual-oriented person. Ritual is my favorite part about church: communion, incense, candles, holy water. The ritual of the service can be counted on in the US and in any church I've been to in Europe or Mexico. They can be counted on when I walk into a Catholic church. The Homily may or may not resonate with me, but I will take communion, I will do the Stations of the Cross blessing myself with holy water, I will light a candle, kneel and pray.

I carry rituals into my daily life. When I walk into my home I take my shoes off and light at least one candle. There is always at least one candle burning in my home. And since I've been a small child I give thanks when I wake up and pray before I go to bed. *Now I lay me down to sleep I pray the Lord my soul to keep. If I die before I wake I pray the Lord my soul to take.* I said this as my little ritual with a Hail Mary and an Our Father before bed, since I was 3 years old. Even then it settled me, gave me peace even when all around me was filled with instability and rapidly changing.

Rituals sustain me still. There are many in my life. There are the rituals of being a woman and these include monthly facials, ballet barre class in the morning, and lots of creams, perfumes and potions. I also sit in the tub a lot with candles burning with my favorite books and magazines. Rituals are a way I order and center myself in my life.

Most of them I realize connect me to source in some way. My facialist is a Slovakian intuitive who has a powerful capacity to heal with her hands. Technically, she is an aesthetician but I have never felt that does her justice. She is so much more than the technical prowess of cleaning my pores. She can lay her hands on my skin and tap into my field, into what is going on with me and during my sessions we speak a lot about why we were drawn to each other and how the Universe makes no mistakes.

The *Physique 57* ballet studio on Spring Street is one of my womanly rituals. It's the estrogen club and on the odd chance that a man shows up it's jolting. Why? Because there is a sacredness to our tribe -- to our grown up sorority without the mean girls. A crew of us, about 8 women, see each other regularly at 9:30 AM. The shared experience of getting stretched and, quite literally, rotated to our limits is a bonding experience. The experience of going there and seeing the same people is comforting in a city that moves so fast. The class may move fast on most days, but the sharing of this experience creates a bonding in the moment. We laugh a lot together and connect about simple aspects of being a woman – our vanity, the children in our lives, the men in our lives, the challenges we go through. They all bubble up before, during and after class. We pay attention to our highs and lows, celebrating our triumphs and giving a hug or lending an ear when someone's going through something. Meanwhile, we notice when someone's away. In the most natural, organic way, this ballet studio creates community.

The *Physique 57* founder and her team have created an energy and experience that has been a sustaining ritual for me for so many years. When I had surgery, these wonderful people were so nurturing and supportive as I struggled to work my way back to the advanced class. When I hurt my back, they all checked in with an attention to detail in my movements that ensured a speedy recovery. Going to class there is a moving meditation of sorts. It's so darn hard that I have no choice but to be completely present to the moment, which is a great lesson when I head out of the studio into my day.

It's also a great energy of women supporting each other, which can be challenging to find due to the collective imprint of jealousy, anger and fear in the collective unconscious of women. Intentionally or not, this class contributes to healing that imprint. In all the seven years I have been taking this class, I never heard anyone make a snarky comment or do anything that is less than supportive in the studio. When I came back after major surgery, I was missed by both my fellow students and the teachers. Everyone I knew asked how they could be supportive. It was so welcoming my first day back after eight months away that it made me teary.

It is also the space to make new friends, which is not always so easy as a "grown up" with a busy life. I have made multiple new friends, some who have helped propel my business forward, others who have brought me into their networks, and others still who just love having a glass of wine and a laugh as much as I do. This studio is one of my happy places.

Rituals are part of the way I make the space for self-care. Self-care is not a luxury for me, or something that I need to think about. Self-care is as necessary and natural to me as going to the bathroom. This includes sleep – lots of it. Downtime where I'm not doing anything but perhaps rolling around in my Egyptian cotton sheets (with or without my beloved). Eating well -- I invest in eating well and also to getting bodywork done. I give so much to my relationships and to my work that to excel at it I vowed to take good care of myself. I keep this vow and it's a powerful force in my life. To be a woman and live in the space of the Divine Feminine is impossible without self-care. I offer that lack of self-care is a form of self-abuse.

Meditating is one of my essentials in the ritual of self-care. Chanting and working with my mala and cards in the tarot deck all help keep me centered in the space of conscious choice. It balances my yin and yang so that I can support myself through times of intense joy and happiness. It helps me stay connected to my heart and to have the courage to move beyond my own self-limiting ego -- to be able to move to a higher frequency of acceptance and clarity.

The meditation practice that I have done for more than 15 years is chanting the word or mantra. I learned this practice during my multiple hours spent with Dr. Levry, founder of Naam Yoga, in his workshops, teacher trainings, Harmonyum Healing trainings, and literally sitting at the feet of a Spiritual Master. Working with mantra put me in the space of seeing the interconnectedness of life as well as the Divine purpose of my own life.

I feel like my life exists in the space before meditating and after meditating. Meditating raised my frequency so that I could move beyond being the victim of my circumstances. It opened and healed my heart as well as helped me rewire my internal dialogue. It helped me to tap into Divine Intelligence, and deepen my faith as well as my ability to read the signs.

Meditating with mantra and breath work helps me support my nervous system. It gives me the capacity to navigate my life force. It clocks my mind in the present so that my mind works for me even as I'm connected and guided by Spirit. Meditation gives me freedom, the freedom that comes from connecting with wisdom, intuition, and Divine Guidance.

Meditating elevates my consciousness to the level of intuitive intelligence, which creates efficiencies in my life. This is the space that prevents me from sabotaging myself. It also activates my pituitary gland so that I can attract amazing relationships and people to my life.

For me, meditating has and is a way of activating my superpowers. Meditating, including chanting mantra, supports my frontal lobe and activates my pituitary gland. It enables me to receive Light from the unseen world as well as to communicate with the Higher world. I am able to receive more light, wisdom and guidance from Divine Intelligence. This connection creates more magic, ease and flow. By meditating I also wake up to lessons more quickly. I am able to avoid wasting time. It also gives me perspective on embodying patience, patience beyond any I'd ever imagined.

The relationship between my heart and my brain has also changed. Working with the Divine Word has given me the power to overcome my genetic lineage, what has given me many gifts. My great grandmother on my Father's side was a shaman and my father has a lot of spiritual gifts. They are insanely good looking. In equal measure to everything mentioned above, that side of my lineage is also filled with addiction and depression issues.

On my mother's side there is the Iron will -- steely French people with the will to survive cold winters and make a life out of very little financial resources. Education was limited. My Grandmother was only educated till the 8th grade but went back to school in her 50s, completing her GRE and going on to get an undergraduate degree. Both my parents were the first generation to finish high school, university, and graduate school. There is this steely will that runs deep in the veins of my ancestors on both sides. I'm grateful for this. There is also an irreverent streak that is present on my mother's side.

My great grandmother lived to 105 and had 3 husbands. She died in her own home simply of old age. I remember as a 10 year-old kid asking her how it felt to be so old. I wanted to know how she got there. She lit a cigarette and laughed. Then she said, "Darling, I made choices that made me happy even when they really pissed everyone else off." And she laughed. That always stuck with me -- the correlation between happiness and the courage to stand for her own life. These are all characteristics that flow in my gene pool. The women in my family are strong-willed.

But, like those on my father's side, they also suffer from mental illness. Nervous breakdowns happened in every generation. My Grandmother, my mother, and myself each had nervous breakdowns. My sister had one in college. Nervous breakdowns and clinical depression are part of my lineage and both always scared me. Nothing was scarier than going through it myself in my early 30s when I was so depressed that I couldn't get out of bed.

So when I was gifted with meeting Dr. Levry and given specific mantra to help my brain disconnect from the karmic lineage it was a game changer. This practice is a gift beyond my own life, because it is high spiritual wisdom. It's been said that if even one person in the family breaks the lineage of negativity it is healing for the entire family. I see it already in my niece. Meditating as a way of disconnecting from my past and my lineage enables me to rise above my childhood conditioning. It enabled me to destroy and eradicate the imprint of self-abuse, so that I could love myself. From the beginning, both my sister and I have reinforced my nieces connection to self-love and her *I AM*.

Loving myself deactivates the negative aspects of my lineage, and hopefully has helped deactivate it in my niece. It is not an accident that despite suffering miscarriages, a nervous breakdown, major surgery and a contentious divorce that I have never experienced depression again. I attribute this to my Naam Yoga and meditation practice.

Another gift of meditation is that the science of working with the word is broad and vast. Essentially I learned how to "prescribe" a meditation practice based on the gaps that people wanted to close in their lives. There are specific mantras to increase prosperity, abundance, self-confidence, self-love, and to right health imbalances and mental illness, etc. Working with mantra is a powerful tool to bring balance and harmony, and in turn become a positive life force on the planet.

Meditation and studying the great esoteric wisdom in the teachings of Dr. Levry helped me move beyond the *negative* in problems and see the problems as a gift, even when they pissed me off. It is not a white washing of emotions, but rather a way to see the problem as a vehicle for perceiving the solution to the "problems" roots.

This practice and ritual of self-care helps me to embrace the totality of my emotional landscape and transmute negative experiences like divorce, depression, miscarriages into gateways for the positive. It has helped me to stop contributing to my own suffering.

Here is why transmutation of my emotional landscape is so important to me. My emotions are unconscious feelings. And my feelings effect how I think. The way I use my mind determines my health. It's all connected to the quality and frequency of the life I am able to create. How I feel is at the root of how I use my mind, and how I feel is contingent on the awareness I have of my emotional state. If I am on automatic in my emotional state, if I go into denial, or shut down, or get hijacked by moods and overreact in my in dealing with people, then the frequency for which I'm caretaker is diminished.

Meditating helps me to respond, but not react, even to the most ridiculous things. It also helps me to stay in the space of authenticity combined with love. Like the time when a female client who had just turned 40 looked at me in the middle of a meeting and said to me, "It's not fair." I said, "What's not fair." I thought I would get something around strategy and business as we were working on a particularly complicated strategic reorganization. Instead she said, "You are 10 years older than me and have no wrinkles and you haven't had any surgery."

Okay, have I mentioned there is often a collective imprint of anger, fear and jealousy in even the most accomplished women. Instead of being hurt, I laughed and said, "that's not true." She got really worked up and said, *"It is, and it's not fair."* I said, "Sweetie, it's true. Lean over your desk and look at my forehead." Then she was vindicated and said, "Hah you're right, you have three lines on your forehead." I said, "Yup told you so. Do you want to keep talking about my forehead or shall we get back to business?" She laughed and said, "Okay, back to strategy. Because I was able to stay in an accepting space, it didn't turn funky. It just moved from awkward and random to funny. So we both could laugh.

I'm not suggesting that meditating makes me able to transmute every awkward moment, but it does make me better able to stay out of the swirl of other people's emotional states. It makes me able to own my side of the fence and to see clearly most of the time regardless of what gets thrown at me. This serves me well when dealing with corporate boards, clients as well as in my personal life. It helps me to be more mindful, and genuinely present with a positive mental attitude. My teacher calls me the "positive transformer."

My favorite mantra at the moment is Om Namo Bhagavate Vasudevaya. Om Namo Bhagavate Vasudevaya is a powerful yogic mantra of pure consciousness. It calls upon the higher and loving consciousness, the Love principle, to act through you. By working with this formula your thoughts, words and deeds all become extensions of the Divine, eliminating all discord in the body and mind. In turn, you become healthy and radiant. The world, through you, is healed. Om Namo Bhagavate Vasudevaya translates as, *"I bow to the Lord, the Indweller, the Christ Consciousness, the higher and loving consciousness, that is omnipresent, omnipotent, immortal and divine, and lives in the hearts of all."* It means, "Lord, may Thy will be done," which calls for the complete surrender of the individual self to the Divine. This mantra of Lord Vishnu is written about in the Bhagavad Gita, stating that those who recite it will be delivered from all sins. It generates healing energy within you by awakening the higher spiritual centers that may otherwise remain dormant for the entirety of a lifetime, and in so doing activates healing on all levels of your being. It balances both the physical and psychic bodies and brings faith so that your prayers may be answered.

These are rituals of daily self-care that help me to create and open to the whole experience of my life. For me, they are essential and not a luxury. I feel grateful and blessed to know this. I also know my rituals are inherently a personal choice and reflect the bigger picture of how I view life and what's important: spiritual growth, beauty, love, nurturing – they reflect my larger values and keep me out of auto-piloting my life.

Rituals are like invocations to conscious action. Without them, where is the conscious action in a life? So I've had to ask myself over time, *what are your supporting rituals?* So now, I ask you.

Chapter 8

Scar Tissue

As women we have a unique power of creativity in our reproductive system. That power is used not only to create new life, but also to bring personal projects into being. However, that energy can be blocked by physical, emotional, or spiritual trauma to the pelvic floor and the female organs. The pelvic floor, including the vagina and uterus, places that often hold our deepest wounds: sexual abuse, rape, abortions, surgeries, childbirth tearing and scars, self-esteem, and negative images about our femininity. To heal the pelvic floor and related areas opens up the portal to experience new possibilities for renewed feminine energy, greater health, and a deeper sense of pleasure in being a woman. It also often deepens our connection to the earth and by extension to ourselves.

~ Suzanne Scurlock-Durana

September 19, 2012 I had the surgery that would change my life.

When I found out that I had to have major surgery, I was in shock. But in retrospect it all makes sense. As a small child, I had been emotionally abandoned by both my parents. I was a very sensitive child who always wanted to help. That was my imprinting, and intentionally or not, my parents took full advantage of that. They were not ready to give up their darkness, their wounds, and as a result they were not as ready as they thought they were to be parents.

They were inherently non-supportive and pejorative, while at the same time consciously and most often unconsciously putting me in the position of being the validation for their union. One that had been scorned by both black and white. I believe, I was the product of love. But in 1965, the time of my conception, my parents were in defiance of both the social codes of the day and the law. If they had not been on an army base, they would also have been subject to the miscegenation laws that were still on the books in many states, including North Carolina where I was born. It is also notable that the year of my birth North Carolina had the largest Klan membership, 10,000 people – more than all the other southern states combined. This gives you a context for the energy into which I was born. Much to everyone's delight, I came out light, bright and almost white. And even on an army base, the hospital staff thought my mom was European. The conventional thinking was that no American white woman, from a middleclass background would be crazy enough to marry and have a child with a black man.

My mother also endured a lot of emotional abuse from her parents, while she was pregnant with me. Despite their disdain for the choice she had made, they adored me. I believe she internalized these energies during the nine month gestation period. Shortly after I was born, she took a bus to Massachusetts and left me with my Grandmother. I was not breastfed, held, or anything that creates a bond between mother and child. So as a result my mother and I never bonded.

At the age of 2, I was taken back to live with my parents after being raised by my Grandmother for the first two years of my life. My grandmother would recall for me how I ran back to her when they came to pick me. Throughout my childhood, I would turn to her and the Catholicism of my upbringing for support. And while my mother would rail against the dogma and hypocrisy of the Catholic Church, it was our spiritual portal. She had gone to church every morning when she was growing up to pray the rosary. 108 beads, 54 Our Father's and 54 Hail Mary's every day. So regardless of how she railed against the priest that told her it was a sin to marry my father, I was sent to Sacred Heart Catholic School. We went to church. I was baptized, did my first communion and confirmation. But most of all I prayed.

I believe the emotional abandonment by my parents was largely unconscious on their part, including my father's unnatural attachment to me and dependence on me even as a small child to "save" him from his addictions to womanizing, alcoholism, and drugs. It was default automatic behavior rather than a conscious choice. But the message I got was that my accomplishments, my goodness, my innate compassion would be the salvation of the family. That pressure was there as long as I can remember -- to receive any love required that I "make it better" for everyone.

Fast forward to 2012. On the surface I was healthy strong and fit. I was married and had a successful coaching practice. On the surface it all looked stable and correct, but it was not. I was married to someone who, like my parents, offered no emotional support and regularly abandoned me. He also regularly chose darkness, and expected me to save him from himself.

On that day in the office of my OB/GYN office, I realized that this partial hysterectomy operation was the culmination of years of emotional and spiritual trauma. The physical manifestation of it all was as real as three tumors, each one, at 9 x 11 centimeters, as big as a grapefruit.

Stunned at the news, I froze on the examining table. I couldn't cope. I had always wondered in my 20's why I hadn't gotten pregnant. Then I was so in love with a European man who was five years older. We were often sloppy with our birth control method. His preference was a lambskin condom, but even that was not consistently used and at the time I wasn't on the pill. I used to wonder why I didn't get pregnant. We were in our 20's and crazy about each other. We couldn't be in the same room with each other for long without making love. Such was the chemistry between us. Still every month, I would get very, very heavy periods, sometimes with clotting.

Fast forward again, so many years later, I was married. I wanted kids. There was no question. So I was devastated when I couldn't hold to term, and I miscarried our baby. Something in me knew that something wasn't correct in my female parts, but year after year my OB/GYN visits came back with a clean bill of health. I have never had an STD. I was the perfect weight for my height. My thyroid was fine. Even so, I never could carry a baby to full term.

When my spiritual teacher told me I would hold the energy of the Divine Feminine for many, many people, who would in essence be my "children." I remember thinking, "That feels like a lot and I think about, I would rather just have a child." But the Divine Intelligence of the Universe, has a direction and a plan for all of us. So deep in me, I knew that I needed to catch sight of some bigger plan -- some deeper reason beyond me and what I could then see. This is what I told myself, and it gave me a small measure of comfort. I prayed that God reveal to me the bigger purpose. But it would only be revealed to me after the surgery, during the healing process, and the implosion of my life as I knew it.

I am a Cancer, cardinal water sign, nurturer of the Zodiac. I was the girl who *ooooed* and *aaahed* at babies on the street. I loved being around children. And now, here I was, feet in the stirrups being told that my uterus had to come out. My spiritual teacher told me I had a malformed uterus. From an energetic standpoint, when I was growing up through my adolescence and formative years, I had taken such a hit emotionally and psychically that my uterus had absorbed all of that and prevented me from becoming very ill during those years. But in return, it had been malformed. That's why, when I first came to NYC, after so much lovemaking with a man I truly loved I never got pregnant.

I could not grasp what my Doctor was telling me. So strong was my inability to take in the news that I would lose my uterus, that I pushed my way back onto the doctor's schedule the next day to talk it through. In between, I sent the test results to my mentor and teacher who is a Master Kabbalist and also to one of the top Chinese medicine doctors in NYC. Both told me to have the surgery done immediately. When Dr. Levry tells you to do something immediately, believe me, you do it. I remember sobbing and saying, "Can't you give me a kriya or a mantra to prevent this. We are kabbalists, isn't there something else we can do. I am terrified to have that surgery."

In no uncertain terms I was told by three sources to have the surgery. One of the top living spiritual masters and master kabbalist, top OB/GYN women's health expert and a top Chinese medicine specializing in women's health. Bells were going off. *HAVE THE SURGERY NOW!!* Three experts, who rarely get alarmed, now had a sense of urgency. I am very sensitive to energy and I picked up on their alarm. This snapped me into dealing with the whole thing on a practical level. Schedule the surgery, tell my clients what was happening, prepare myself spiritually for what was about to happen, ask for help. The last one was the hardest.

I was very accustomed to extending my heart out to others. I always wanted to help, but I had conditioned myself not to ask for help because during my formative years there had rarely been help. This inability to ask for and receive help would cause me to make my life harder than it needed to be for much of my adulthood. It would also cause me to make zany choices. When the man I loved so much when I first came to NYC tried to take care of me, I resisted. This dysfunction in me was something deep and profound that the surgery would wake me up to healing.

When I realized that my OB/GYN would do the surgery, I felt marginally better. I have to say that it is a misnomer to lump all western doctors into the category of being solely evidence-based. My OB/GYN and surgeon had framed words of Moses Maimonides in her office.

> *There is one disease which is widespread, and from which men rarely escape. This disease varies in degree in different men ... I refer to this: that every person thinks his mind... more clever and more learned than it is.*

When I was having my meltdown, my doctor said I wasn't leaving her office until I had my head and heart wrapped around what was going to happen to me. She also told me the straight scoop. She said conventional wisdom would say that in 6 weeks I could go back to work. With reverence and gratitude in my heart I recall her saying, "This is what they tell people but...it will take you a year and then some to recover from what you're going to go through. The healing process is more that the incisions closing and coming off the morphine painkillers."

She continued… "There will be a deep energetic, emotional, and spiritual healing that will take time. *Can you give yourself this time?*" It was at that moment that I committed to healing myself on another level. The surgery was the catalyst to healing something so much deeper within myself. I reached out to the man I had loved so long ago. We lived on different continents. We were married to different people, but I trusted his power, his strength, and his goodness. I reached out to him and asked him to pray for me. He said he would, and then followed that with. *"You will be fine. Nothing bad will happen to you."* His clarity and complete belief in his words reassured me. They always had.

I meditated and prayed a lot, the morning of my surgery. This was not unusual for me. Since I was a small child, I had prayed to Mary, to Archangel Gabriel, to Jesus, to God. This had only grown stronger after I began my yogic and kabbalah studies with Dr. Joseph Michael Levry 15 years earlier. My faith was unwavering. Through prayer and meditation I had settled into a peace around the surgery.

Accompanied by my then husband, we arrived at NYU at 6:30 am. I checked the box saying I declined an epidural. The head anesthesiologist asked to speak to me. He said, "I respect your choice but I also feel obligated to give you a context to make that choice. Do you understand that you will be cut almost back to your spine. Without an epidural the pain you will experience will be beyond anything you can imagine." Then we talked about why I was scared of epidurals. His compassion was astounding and this compassion would continue with everyone who had a hand in the surgery. I changed my mind and elected to have the epidural. I also asked everyone in the surgical theater to say the Christ Prayer. My doctor held my hand and told me to breathe and to let her know when I was ready. While I was breathing, the attending anesthesiologist slipped the epidural into my spine. I didn't feel a thing.

When I woke up I was very cold. I was also in critical care and feeling completely disembodied. But I felt no pain. I felt like I was in a cotton ball. Everything soft and fuzzy and surreal. I guess that's what buckets of morphine pain killers do. Feel no pain.

The first thing my mother asked my doctor was if I would gain weight. The disgust on my doctor's face was palpable, but this was my mother. She could not connect to anything unpleasant so her default was to connect to things she felt were in her control – weight was always one of her primary focuses so I wasn't surprised.

When I finally got into my room, a young resident came to tell me about her experience witnessing my surgery. She told me what a privilege it was. She told me that she had not seen anything like it even in the medical books. I remember her saying, "You will not believe what we took out of you. It was incredible." She said it looked like something out of the movie *Aliens*. At this, I saw my then husband's face turn crimson and he looked like he wanted to ring her neck. He barked out, "Stop this talk right now. It's totally inappropriate." But from my experience it was like being told a science fiction story. I wanted to hear more. She was so enthusiastic and positive about her experience and I was pushing the button on the morphine drip repeatedly. I was enjoying the tale she was telling, then, well, I realized it was about me. And then, well, I continued to enjoy it, until my-then-husband asked her to get the hell out. He wasn't enjoying it as much as we were, which was understandable. I recognize that I was high – which was probably why it was so amusing to me.

What is not amusing is not being able to go to the bathroom and having three Caribbean nurses telling me to drink another, and then another liter of water. There was a deadline, you see. On the third day in the hospital I was told by the nursing staff that I had to go to the bathroom on my own or they were going to do something to make me go which I was not going to like. I took their word for it. It is a funny thing to pray to pee and pray to perhaps be graced with being able to poop also. Amazing how these times raised my consciousness, in gratitude to my body's basic functions.

Following the surgery, it took six months of allowing my body to heal. Giving it the time to heal. That time allowed me to hold more light, which in turn caused me to be able to expand. My earth body needed to be able to expand, which required deep energy work, care, and love. I got weekly Harmonyum treatments and went to the top Pilates pelvic rehab specialist. I also prayed to Divine Intelligence, to God, to give me the courage to also work on my external world -- to give me the courage to release any lower consciousness within myself and outside of myself. I committed to choosing only love and light and asked the Higher Worlds to support this intention.

I also developed a fundamentally different relationship to my body. I asked her to guide my pacing. I asked her what to do and I listened. I had been an athlete all my life, so I had a driving/achieving relationship to my body. I knew how to push my body to its limits -- to shave a second or two off my swimming records. I knew how to play tennis in the middle of the day, on a hard court, in the blazing summer heat . . . and win the point. I knew how to rotate my legs out of the hip sockets in the most insane ballet barre positions to keep my bum where I wanted it. I could drive my body to do all these things. But this, this was the first time I slowed down. Slowed down, asked for her guidance, and listened.

Two years later I realized there was still a lot of healing to be done in this area. I had physical scar tissue, of course. But the energetic and emotional scar tissue ran deepest. In my meditation one morning I was literally guided to a gifted healer – a technical wizard, body mechanic, and shaman. She fully tapped into the great Source for true healing. With her help I got myself through the last bit of healing the energy left frozen along those scar lines. My pelvic area was put on the road to complete healing – orgasms and all. I feel orgasms as more than the physical pleasure, the small and sacred death. They are in their deepest manifestation, another connection to the Divine. Why settle for a life without them?

So in healing, I listen to my body and the accompanying flow of my energy. It's an incredible experience to develop that kind of relationship to your body. The body is unlike the mind in that it doesn't rationalize. The human body is the most magnificent creation. She doesn't intellectualize. She tells you the straight scoop. My connection to my body post-surgery gave me what I needed to shift my vibratory frequency, to clock myself to the field of who I really am. It was then that the magic really kicked in.

Chapter 9

Storms and the Siren Signifying Support

Life is happening through you, not just to you.

~ Kelley Black

Hurricane Sandy was the deadliest and most destructive hurricane of the 2012 Atlantic hurricane season. It was the second-costliest hurricane in United States history. It disrupted millions of lives. It hit NYC just a month after my partial hysterectomy. I remember that night. We lived all the way downtown on the LES of Manhattan and my then husband was on the phone. I was still loaded up on opiate pain killers. Lying on the couch I heard him say, "Holy Shit." Then everything went black in the apartment. He had witnessed the Con Edison explosion as Sandy's storm surge hit New York City on October 29, flooding streets, tunnels and subway lines and cutting power in and around the city.

He was always at his best during a crisis or holiday. Extreme stress or pleasure seemed to kick in his highest self. Consistency was challenging for him. But he could definitely be counted on in a catastrophe. He is a recreational camper and a professional architect with a sharp intellect and problem solving capacity. So while I was dwelling in the surreal world of opiate intake, combined with a very weak body, he was lighting candles and checking the phone lines. We were on the 15th floor and the elevators were out.

So we snuggled in for the night. The next morning we became acutely aware that our part of the city was under a state of emergency. Governor Cuomo ordered the closure of the MTA and its subway on October 28. The MTA suspended all subway, bus, and commuter rail service beginning at 2300 UTC. After Hurricane Irene nearly submerged subways and tunnels in 2011, entrances and grates were covered just before Sandy. They were still flooded. PATH train service and stations, as well as the Port Authority Bus Terminal, were shut down in the early morning hours of October 29th.

I must emphasize that said ex-husband is really good in this type of situation. He packed our bags and said we are getting out of here. "There is no water, electricity, heat and you aren't well. We can't stay here," he told me holding a candle in the dim light of the apartment. All of that was true. We were actually fortunate to be able to stay in Brooklyn Heights just across the East River. The challenge became how to get there.

So while he got a pile of cash out of the hiding spot I got dressed. He was carrying everything; I was under orders not to lift anything because of the fear that my stitches would tear. This was a primal irrational fear every time I went to the bathroom. Even so, it sure hurt a lot whenever the pain killers wore off.

We walked through desolate water soaked streets and past lines of people queuing for water and provisions at the neighborhood bodegas. I have lived in NYC, and had seen big blackouts. The last one had been years ago. This time no one was price gouging water. The consciousness had shifted.

Taxis hissed as he tried to flag down the odd car. There was no car service or taxis. So my then husband was trying to find anyone who could drive us to Brooklyn Heights.

Finally, a man stopped. NYC is always filled with people who seize opportunity. This storm was no different. Lucky for us the guy was trying to make an extra buck. We were equally lucky that he was asking for a fair price. Truth is we would have paid 10X the fair rate to get to Hicks Street, but this man balanced commerce with compassion.

And so we arrived on the other side of the river, where nothing had changed. Simple things take greater importance during times like these: traffic lights being lit, the glow of light in restaurants, open stores with stocked shelves, the hum of business as usual. Yes, I found comfort in simple and predictable things like street lights working. I felt gratitude for a meal with friends and a warm place to sleep.

We stayed with friendship and gratitude on Hicks Street. Our friend, also a rock star architect, whose office was on Wall Street, preferred to work from home. So, for the duration of the week, we all lived together.

Some funny things occurred while I was on opiate painkillers and holed up in our friends apartment. We were sleeping in the loft bed. My husband had gone out for something, our friend was on the phone to China, and I had to go to the bathroom. This required me to walk down a steep flight of stairs. I was focused on getting safely down the stairs, which had no railing. Usually, one of the guys helped me. I was gingerly making some negotiated steps past his open living space with the broad architect's table. He was pacing and staring out the large windows of his beautiful apartment in the St.George Hotel. Then I saw him spin around with his jaw dropped. Thinking he was in awe of me walking on my own, I laughed, and said, "*Keep going*. I can do it." His jaw was swinging. He was staring, and I was laughing. Then he said to his client, "Can you hold on for a moment."

I said to him, "You didn't have to do that," as I stepped down the last stair and delicately made my way to the bathroom. He looked speechless. I was thinking whether I'd be able to go to the bathroom. When I got to the WC I looked in the mirror. I saw myself standing there with nothing on but my underpants. I started cracking up.

Context matters, doesn't it? The same man has seen me topless on a sailboat and swimming topless in the Aegean. But somehow in the context of a hurricane with my husband absent the whole thing takes on an entirely different context. Later that night, over some red wine, we all laughed. I was done with my last painkiller and now it was back to normal – the normalcy of red wine over dinner. To the Bayonne, to Hoboken, to Port Authority, to the Lower East Side of Manhattan. Still bleak – South Street Sea Port, Manhattan water line. Our storage container – books soaked and pasted shut. Tennis rackets preserved. Camping tent and equipment mildewed.

Then a week passed and we were home from Brooklyn back in Manhattan. It was 9:00 a.m. The lights were on but we had no hot water and the elevator was a bit sketchy. We were settling back in after having been home for one night. Now that I was back at home I was realizing a second hurricane was hitting my life. Now that I was off the opiates and clearer I could see that something fundamentally had been altered. I had the acute sense, a deep feeling that my marriage was fundamentally broken. It was the insidiousness of no connection when the external world was back to "normal." I realized there was nothing to bond us. We were pleasant in the way that people who have a "good polite upbringing" are pleasant, but there was no depth, no internal connection.

My then husband was getting ready for the office when he heard the key turn as well. I was reading, catching up, getting myself organized for what was to come: pelvis healing, re-engaging with business, doing internal work. I felt I needed to prepare for a time when I knew what these feelings meant. Externally and internally – I leaned into those feelings not knowing just then what they meant. Now that I could walk around I walked like I was cut in half. I literally couldn't feel my pelvic area.

It was like there was an abyss in the space between my lower rib cage and my pubic bone.

Little things at the time felt like a breakthrough and I'd start to weep. I would sit for a half hour where I could hopefully engage my pelvic floor. I worked with a Pilates expert to rehab my pelvis. As I'd start to reconnect with that area, I'd begin to sob. I remember beginning to sob in her office saying, "Oh my God, my marriage is over." I was like, oh my God, what next — and not knowing what was next. Seeing things in my dreams – oh fuck, here we go. I could feel a second storm brewing.

And then one morning I heard that inevitable click as Hilda, our housekeeper, made her way in the door. She was smiling, cheerful. "Good morning, Kel," she said sweetly.

I said, "Hilda, how did you get here? The transportation isn't working so well."

She laughed generously, "Oh, well four buses and three hours."

"Oh my God," I said, "we don't even have hot water for you to clean with."

"Kel, I grew up in the *Philippines,*" she said. "I know hurricanes. When you get home – there's no heat. No hot water. On-off electricity. It's ok, I'm going to get you a hot water bottle. Just go under a blanket. It's so cold."

"Hilda, we're without running water, never mind hot water," I said.

Again, she laughed and said, "I promised to help you a month ago when you came home from the hospital. Don't you know, I'm keeping my word? I'm here." She pulled out the biggest pots we had and started boiling water to clean and wash with. I started crying. I was speechless. "Come on now," she said. "It's all alright."

"It really isn't," I said. She looked perplexed.

My then husband came out of the bedroom and irritated said, "Hilda, what are you doing here? We don't have any hot water. You can't do anything."

Calmly, this minute woman looked this 6'2" man in the eye and said, "Yes, I can. And I made a promise." I continued to cry and somehow through her kindness knew that if I kept faith and listened the Universe would keep its promise -- the promise of support as the next part of my life fell apart.

Chapter 10

Maine, Picasso, and the Mogul

You have to trust yourself (and you can't fake that). That's the most important thing. In order to trust yourself, you have to have a relationship with yourself. The relationship you have with yourself is everywhere, every moment of the day ~ to be able to be alone, to be able to think, to be inspired, to give yourself advice. To be your own best friend (and no matter what happens, never be a victim).

~ Diane von Furstenberg

I'm back in New England, a world away from my day-to-day life. Kennebunkport, Maine: sea, lobsters, artists and my childhood friend KGirl. She and I grew up together, first meeting in 9th grade in a small college town in Massachusetts. We bonded many years ago over our shared displacement and passion for swimming. Our differences are many and maybe always were. She's an atheist, and I'm a big believer in the Saints, God, and the greater influence of all things seen and unseen. She takes things at face value, and I look for the layers and nuances. I left our small town and never looked back, landing in NYC and 25 years later I'm still there. She lived most of her adult life in suburbs and small towns. She lives in a small town now with her husband.

Despite not seeing each other for years, as the plane descends into Portland, I feel excited and happy. Going through the airport I hear the hard, nasal-A accent in the speech of people. It's only a 45-minute flight and a whole world away.

The first thing we do after hugging each other is start telling stories. The energy feels familiar in its simplicity. I remember her kinetic, loud, booming voice and her sense of humor. It all brings me back to junior high. We would write notes on our hands to remind ourselves to tell each other funny stories.

My longings in the moment are to be by the sea (easy we're in Kennebunkport) and to eat lobster and crab. All the things that back in the day made me want to leave New England suddenly wash over me and make me happy.

KGirl asks me if I've seen the latest episode of the View or Housewives. I laugh and say I don't have a TV. Then we both laugh. She laughs at the idea of not having a TV and I laugh at spending time watching the View. Again we are worlds apart but what is shared is our ability to laugh at life, and I realize this is what has bonded us since childhood.

KGirl tells me that I really have to meet Picasso. He's an absolute character here in Kennebunkport. I say I love characters. I find them interesting.

Picasso has a gallery in town, and instead of painting the Bush compound or still lifes, he paints nudes -- abstract, provocative nudes that have this preppy, conservative town in a twist. Apparently, he has been told for years that he better switch his subject matter, if he is going to make a living here. 18 years and 6 kids later, he is still painting nudes.

Pulling into his driveway, we park the car. Standing there is a mannequin that has been turned into a pot with flowers coming out of it. This strikes me as reverential. Its flowers reach out of a rainbow-colored women's pelvis atop a long set of legs. Strikes me as symbolic. I feel a magical mystery tour about to begin.

Salt and peppered, he emerges and KGirl introduces us. She is nervous, not knowing how it will go. He is provocative. His customers include Courtney Love, Jenna Bush, and Gwyneth Paltrow – to name a few whose crotches have been abstractly immortalized. I think, *Why is she so nervous?* I'm not offended by immortalized crotches or by being asked to have mine painted. So many others have come before me. She whispers to me, "Don't feed the beast." And I start laughing. She starts laughing too. Then we are all laughing.

His paintings are provocative but they are also extremely sensual and beautiful. This guy clearly has an appreciation for women. And at 63, that he still appreciates women, is fun. What strikes me is how people in the town are so offended by this work. They can't see beyond the breasts and crotches through to the nuance and energy of the work. The paintings are far from safe in pushing boundaries but they make you feel something. What I feel is that this is the work of someone who really loves women.

KGirl and Picasso start talking about The Mogul and his multi-millionaire deals. How he is the richest guy in town, the local mogul. He is going to be at David's in Kennebunkport. I'm told we should go *NOW*. I say to my friend, *My God, you are such a social climber. You're driven to meet this mogul.* Picasso knows the Mogul and she is pushing -- *are they at the restaurant? when are they coming to the restaurant? let's go so we can catch them at the restaurant?* Picasso's brother is the Mogul's banker so there's the opening for her. Even in this small town in August people have an agenda.

So we stroll over to the restaurant. The Mogul hasn't arrived but he has his table inside. I don't care about The Mogul and his money and connections. And I don't want to sit inside on such a beautiful day stalking the guy. I say this. And I tell her to breathe. He may be the town mogul but he's not GOD. Money and power in and of themselves don't move me.

We sit outside. KGirl has her phone out and is staring inside, fixated on the Mogul's grand entrance. She asks Picasso, "Have you heard from your brother, are they coming?"

He says, "Drink your cava and have an oyster." We all start laughing and then he looks at me and says what could be better than this. I say nothing. This moment is pretty perfect.

KGirl refocuses and starts telling Picasso that I have super powers. She tells him that I can see people and tell them who they are just from knowing their birthdate. He laughs and says, "Do it Kell, tell him who he is." Then she gets serious and says to him, "She is deadly accurate. She knows how to read the numbers."

I'm laughing and drinking my Cava and say, "I am an irresistible mystical creature."

Now I'm the provocative person in his eyes as he asks what that means. I say, "Tell me your birthday and then you can decide."

I proceed to tell him what I see and he is mesmerized. Spirituality, Cava, oysters and king crab cakes, everyone is settling in to just being rather than verbally jousting. In the being, the door opens and everyone allows a peak into himself or herself.

KGirl is jubilant and proud. She rests her case. Her old friend from childhood is still a mystical creature. He finishes the oyster and his tequila. He looks up and says, "Now I'm horny."

I say, "What?!!" . . . and then we all start laughing.

More oysters, more Cava – we take some photos of us with the sea and the boats behind us. KGirl says the Fisherman won't let Picasso paint me. I laugh and say, "Why not?" Then we all laugh again.

Next, it's like the Red Sea is parting. He is here. He is here. Three Cavas in, I start laughing. I'm laughing a lot here. I like to laugh as often as possible. Then a New England poster boy for the sailing prepster walks out. Blond, chiseled, 52 and exuding old money and power in his Lacoste shirt, boat shoes and lime green shorts. It's evident that he is used to the sea parting when he arrives. It's also evident how guarded he is. His entourage is there as well. Bankers and financial holy-wick candlestick makers. They all pull chairs up to the table by the sea with the boats behind it and the American flag. He is sitting across from me. I'm not saying anything. I am listening, taking in the social codes and nuances.

The entourage and the King have been wheeling and dealing all day. They are also into their cups. This is a quintessential sailing New England moment. Buffed-out, wealthy guys, making deals after drinking all day. But somehow no one is drunk. Everyone is focused on The Mogul but me. He notices me watching the dynamic. Clearly, he doesn't miss much, including the subtlety, and it is apparent that not focusing on him is a unique identifying factor.

KGirl notices also and says, "Tim, Kelley has super powers. She is a mystical creature. She can tell you who you are."

He says "Really." His skepticism is palpable. I can feel him saying *really*? It's oozing out of his pores and I see his steely blue eyes size me up. Shit, I think. I just want to relax and keep enjoying my oysters and Cava. I don't want to get into a thing with the mogul or have my friend treating wisdom as a parlor game to get his attention. I turn my head to her and say, turning my head to her, "This stuff isn't a parlor game."

"I'm sorry Kel, I know I'm sort of pimping you out," says KGirl with a smile.

"Sort of feels like that," I say, a bit exasperated. I stop talking. A cool breeze flutters the napkins under the drinks.

KGirl gets the message but the game is on. Mogul says to me, "Okay, tell me who I am." I ask him his birthday. Silence falls. He says August 24th but I ask him to give me the whole thing *including the year*. And for a second he flinches. It's evident that he's used to the sea parting and people being deferential to him. One thing I am not is deferential to anyone, especially based on money and social status. A long pregnant pause ensues. I look at the boats in the harbor. The sun is setting. I breathe in and I say a small prayer in my head. May this unfold for the glory of God and the benefit of all. I exhale. Why not? People are looking at me like, What is she doing. Then he speaks up and gives me the year. And I go. I read the numbers. At first he looks defiant. Then mesmerized. Then teary, like a shell around him has broken open.

I say, if anything doesn't resonate, that's okay. I'm just telling you top line what I see.

Then that swirling little vortex breaks and dissolves. We move on. The table starts talking business again. But he keeps looking at me - not the way a man looks at a woman with longing. (I do find out later he is gay.) He looks at me with more the look of someone who has heard the truth. Then I say to him, "It's not an intellectual thing. It's a gift that comes from someplace beyond me that works through me. In the same way you have instincts for how to make money, I know how to do this. It's a gift. We all have them."

Then in the middle of the conversation, he gets up and walks around everyone and says, "Can I give you a hug." I just hug him, and he hugs me back. As he is hugging me, he whispers in my ear, "Thank you." And I say I hope it was helpful. He says, very.

When the embrace ends, he is back wheeling and dealing. He says to the entourage *let's go*. There's more money to be made, more things to wrap up. As they are walking out, he looks back at me and nods. I smile. As he walks through the restaurant, the sea parts and *he-they* are gone.

"*Holy shit, he really likes you*. He actually gave you a hug," says Picasso.

"Maybe it's because he knows I don't want anything from him. I don't have an agenda," I say simply, while we linger at the table with the sky changing color into orange and magenta.

"But that's the Mogul, he is never like that. He doesn't let anyone in," says Picasso, tapping his chest lightly with a finger.

"Okay, maybe he is never like that. But maybe that hug, that's who he really is," I say.

We all pause. Then I start laughing, "Who knows? Certainly not me. I don't even know him."

Picasso steps on my words. "Clearly you do!" he says, leaning in. We laugh some more. I sip my Cava, eat another oyster, and smile.

Chapter 11

The Social Codes of Being Naked

Art can never exist without naked beauty displayed.

~ William Blake

Okay, I will say up front that I like being naked. I sleep naked on Egyptian white cotton sheets. No, they are not ironed but they are soft and they feel great. I also have a tendency on weekend mornings to put on favorite artists like a Kygo remix of Marvin Gaye's *Gotta Give It Up* or *Firestorm* on up to Taylor Swift's *Shake it off*. Maybe even some old-school Bee Gees or Barry White. I like to shake it off and dance around my apartment.

The townhouses in front of me have beautiful gardens on top, and the view stretches to the bottom of Manhattan Island. I can see the water while I dance around. I tell myself that my unobstructed view from this high floor apartment prevents people from seeing me dance around naked, but I will say that if they can see me hopefully some of the associated freedom rubs off.

Maybe it's because of my half-French bloodline, time spent on European beaches and in locker rooms from a young age. One thing I am comfortable with is being naked.

A couple of recent experiences showed me that like many aspects of life, nakedness also has its social codes.

When I was in the middle of my divorce, I was going to Europe a lot and teaching workshops on the Divine Feminine in Berlin. While in Berlin I visited the Liquidrom Berlin. It is a gorgeous spa with the most amazing sauna's both wet and dry. Germans really know about saunas. Excited, I visited with a native

Berliner and an American friend who flew in from London. First, we visited the main pool which is an otherworldly experience in chilling out. Next the sauna. On the approach to the sauna there was a sign saying no bathing suits. My native Berliner and I quickly stripped, hanging our bikinis on the hooks. The third musketeer, an American living in the UK, kept her's on. We filed in to a very hot steamy sauna. We strategically chose the top level, since heat rises and we wanted to sweat. It was still cold out and it was nice to be somewhere super hot.

Eyes closed, I relaxed into the heat and the vibe. A man entered with a very serious expression. The sign was being enforced. He was the sauna policeman. I don't know how to speak any German. So when he began barking I had no idea what he was barking about. But I could tell from the tone that something was wrong. I looked at my native Berliner to see her horrified expression. She is German and clearly speaks the language. Turns out he was flipping out because our friend had on her bathing suit. Super sauna *nein nein*. I see my native Berliner whispering to her and see her slink out. I think to myself, *who cares if she wears a suit or not?* But rules are rules and as I look around I see that there are clearly people who are happy that she got ejected.

I return to NYC and a few months later I'm living in my epic building with the pool and two saunas. Having been in a co-ed sauna a mere few months before, I think certainly there should be no problem being naked in the women's only sauna.

As it turned out, I had hurt my back doing some insane extension and rotation of my leg in my ballet class. So first week in my building, I thought: *right, it's no problem, I'll go for a swim followed by a wet sauna. That will fix me right up.* I know by now when I hurt my back in ballet it's muscular, not structural, and if I can just get everything to relax I'll be fine. Wet sauna is perfect for that. At 120 degrees or more and filled with steam, spotlessly clean, it is a white-tiled nirvana.

After my swim, I entered the women's only sauna naked. I do a yoga posture to release my back. It's also great against a wall in my apartment. But in the wet sauna after about 15 minutes, I am fixed right up. I assume the position at the highest level where it is hottest and scoot my bum up against the wall with my legs straight and flush against the wall. Feeling my femur bone drop into my hip socket and my back relaxing, I'm exhaling. I find exhaling difficult when I'm scared and when my back hurts.

Here I am relieved, happy, relaxed, when suddenly I hear the door to the sauna open, followed by a shrill noise. Because of the steam, it's difficult to see. I am not upsetting my own apple cart by coming out of the posture. My back is finally feeling better. I turn my head and ask what's wrong. Little do I know I am what's wrong. As my eyes adjust I see a small middle aged woman in her bathing suit and swim cap staring at me, mouth agape in horror. Then it dawns on me, it's me. I've broken the social code. I am the problem. But unlike the spa enforcer at liquidrom Berlin, she is a fellow tenant with no authority. She is clearly horrified, and I think, *what sort of fool wears a swimming cap in a sauna?* Or a suit for that matter. The suit I can live with, but a cap? Come on!

For what seems like eternity, there is a standoff. She doesn't move and neither do I. Then she turns and storms through the steam out of the sauna. I check in with a German friend of mine later that day. He laughs indignantly at the prudish nature of Americans. He finds it absurd that someone would wear a bathing suit and cap in a sauna. Renewed in my nude confidence, I continue to sauna. Yesterday, I swam and took a sauna afterwards . . . Commando style.

Chapter 12

NWA, Race in America, & Being a Mixed Chic

It always seems impossible until it's done.

~Nelson Mandela

As the credits rolled on Straight Outa Compton, I sat in the theater deep in reflection – mesmerized really. I am old enough to remember when the census form had boxes that read *Black* and *Caucasian*. Growing up it was so strange to be mixed race, so unaccepted on both sides of the fence, that there was a constant pressure to choose one of the boxes. But I couldn't choose. As I wrote earlier, I always chose "other." It was the non-choice choice. Sometimes I scribbled next to it *mixed black/white* but even as a child I felt that whoever was reading it would probably not really get it and just put me in the black box. There I would be, living in a black box, living in a white box, living in a fishbowl.

As I watched the movie, I understood how deeply different my experience had been from the one on screen. I did not grow up in a ghetto, but rather a college town. I am acutely aware that while I have heard racial slurs uttered in my midst by people thinking I was Italian, Jewish, Israeli or something other than what I am, I have also had certain privileges because of my light skin and green eyes.

So why am I mesmerized? I am mesmerized by the magic that happens when you really know and own who you are. How the courage to speak the truth shines a light so bright that the truth is undeniable. I'm mesmerized at the cost and reward of doing this. The truth was being honest about their experience, and they were both crucified, persecuted and ultimately vindicated for having the courage to do it. They refused to be silenced or to be boxed into someone else's comfort zone – in refusing to do so they made a lot of people uncomfortable but they also woke a lot of people up to the reality for many people of what it is to be black in this country.

Ultimately, it is a great, inspiring story about the courage to dream a dream that is bigger than your reality.

It's the dreamy part that I relate to most about the story. For a long time I had a sort of post-racial fantasy. I recently had lunch with a colleague and was exhausted that the conversation centered on race for 3 hours. But I also have very light skin and after the conversation I realized by virtue of this fact our experience moving through life is different and this bothers me.

I notice that my African and Caribbean friends do not have the same energetic imprinting around race. One of my friends who is from a small country in Africa recounted to me a particularly disgusting experience she had in a NYC restaurant in 2015. A white guy went up to her and said, "My God, do you know how Black you are?" I was speechless when she told me the story and just said, "What the Fuck?" Then she said, "Darling, I'm African, I don't dignify this ignorance by being hurt by it. It's so stupid it can't even be dignified with a response." Intellectually, I know she is correct, but I also know any Black American person I know would have had a far more emotional response to something like that. They'd feel something like anger and rage, something similar to what I felt when I heard the story. This rage is so complex and the wound so deep. I am very light and no one would ever insult me in that way, but in the 80s I did see them recoil and stop wanting to date me in college because my father was black. I experienced the isolation of thinking I wasn't lovable, simply because I didn't fit a Caucasian ideal.

Recently, a good friend of mine posted on Instagram that "when a man tells a black woman that she looks mixed as a form of endearment, he's insinuating that her beauty comes from the allegedly non-black part of her." All they're effectively saying is, *You're too beautiful to just be Black*. We aren't beautiful in spite of our blackness; we are beautiful because of it. Same applies when he says to a mixed woman, *"You look white."*

I like that these things are being discussed publicly and more openly, because I think this is the root of the problem in this country. It is rare that you find an honest dialogue around race. Most white people don't want to discuss it – too uncomfortable. Most Black people don't either. They live it every day, and are sick of it being a thing all the time.

Because of my own experience, I got it when she made the Post. More times than I can count, people have said to me that *you don't look mixed*, expecting me to be excited that they thought I was white. That somehow I was better or prettier or more acceptable because I could pass. And while I rarely go into a dissertation about the one drop rule here, I do acknowledge my reality as Light Bright – as almost white and then I say, I'm black – mixed with a French and African American/Cherokee bloodline.

The impact on me has been to distance myself from people, black, white, or otherwise that have a tendency to say these types of things. I have a visceral reaction to tribal thinking and I have a particularly strong one around race. I don't want to be defined by my color in either direction, be it black or white. I am acutely aware of the post-racial fantasy that many people like to live in. In this story, they like to think it's not an issue that certain things aren't happening right under their noses. It's too uncomfortable so it's not discussed in most polite conversation.

But it is there and it cuts close to the bone. My niece, who is gorgeous, brown, eight years-old and lives in Silicon Valley, gets ecstatically happy about seeing a black person. She was literally jumping up and down in the car sitting at a stop light a year ago when they first moved out there. It tells me how segregated this country can be, and how fortunate she was to be born in a city where 130 languages are spoken. While she knew she was brown in New York City, she wasn't self-conscious about it 24/7 like she is now.

She calls me to tell me that kids at her school asked her if she was the kid in the Annie remake. I think, *Oh God, that little girl is adorable also but they literally look nothing alike.* I wince and then I'm reminded that my wincing comes from my own experience. I smile when she says, "I told you, Auntie, these kids aren't sophisticated. I mean… It's not like I think all the white kids look alike." I smile and think some things have changed since she isn't internalizing the little slights the way me and my sister did growing up. But things still sting like when her teacher told her she was only allowed to talk about slavery during black history month because it made people sad. What???!!!

Many people cite black athletes, musicians, even our black President, as examples of how things have changed. When they cite the President I remind them he is mixed and has caught holy hell every second of his 8 year term, simply as Colin Powell is quoted as saying *"because of the color of his skin."* Things have changed to some degree but not as much as we'd like to think. There is still a great deal of healing to be done.

There is a sort of psychic schizophrenia in this country around race. Black culture is revered, celebrated and coopted. Yet Serena Williams is jeered at Indian Wells or accused of taking steroids. It's so difficult for many people in a predominantly white sport to accept that she is just a mentally tough, great athlete. She can't just be that because she is a black woman; there must be something else going on.

When she has an outburst around a bad line call, she is lambasted by none other than John McEnroe. Even a non-tennis fan can see the ludicrousness of John McEnroe criticizing someone for bad non-court behavior. Incidentally, when an Italian player smashed into her on the changeover no one commented in the

American press about that spout of bad behavior. So I ask, *Why is Serena held to a different standard?*

It's these little things that reveal the insidiousness of racism in this country. Of course, there are the bigger things like the black woman killed by prison officers in Texas, while her death was made to look like a suicide. The four policemen acquitted of excessive violence in the Rodney King case. Eric Gardner. Do you really need the full list? It's long and getting longer. It's undeniable that your experience of the police is radically different if you're a black male. Why quibble on this one? Even the Mayor of NYC has schooled his mixed brown son about how to not get shot by the police for walking while black. Middle class black people that I know in NYC have the same conversation with their sons, starting when they are around 10 years old. It's only prudent to teach them how to stay safe with so many police on the street. I read and hear about these stories and think, *My God, as of this writing it's 2015. How many more decades will we be dealing with this?*

I also know that being mixed has afforded me an ability to flow and be comfortable cross-culturally -- to create my own cross cultural tribe, if you will. An ability that I may not have had, if I had to fit so neatly in a racial box. A long time ago, I decided that since I don't belong to any tribe, why not use this to my advantage? I'll use it to access the best of all the worlds. And this has worked for me. Because I didn't fit anywhere, I ultimately learned to fit everywhere. I'm as comfortable in Paris as I am in Cape Town, as I am in Bed Stuy. One of my underpinnings of confidence is that I know I'm as comfortable with my doorman as I am with the people who live in the Penthouse of my building. But at the same time I am acutely aware that when I am in a place like Maine, for instance, it's rare to see someone who even remotely looks like me.

Recently, I laughed when a friend told me that on his last trip to Maine a woman ran up to him at the Portland Airport, all excited because she thought he was from Jamaica. He is from Michigan and speaks a proper English without a trace of accent. He told me that when he told her, *no, he was not from Jamaica,* and it registered with her that he was just a regular black guy on holiday with friends (click!), she looked so disoriented. It was easier for her to imagine that he was from another country than to get her head around a black American going to Kennebunkport on vacation.

So these are some of the ways that I am reminded, despite my own privilege, that race is still an open issue in this country. The most striking reminders aren't the ones that I read about in the papers, they're the ones that happen to the people close to me. The un-sutured wound is such that I see damage on both sides of the gash.

So perhaps a long time ago, I tried to not think about race at all. Today, I consciously steer clear of anyone I feel has an ignorant consciousness around race. My community, my closest people are a diverse tribe of all colors – mostly people who have transcended being defined by race or religion. They're people who know who they are but refuse to have their experience limited by category.

I pray that in my lifetime a post-racial society in the US will be a reality, not the denialist fantasy it is today. I dream big. My dreams have come true in most cases. But this is one dream that is hard for me to imagine. It's hard for me to think it will soon be a reality. But I didn't think I'd live to see a black man elected President. I was wrong. I hope I am again.

Chapter 13
Letting It Breathe on The Way to Finalizing My Divorce

No matter what gets damaged, life rearranges itself to compensate for your loss.

~ Hanya Yanagihara

Early August 2014 on Spring Street in New York City. My then husband and I are walking to the notary public. I am silently saying prayers in my head. I am praying that we get there. I am praying that he signs the 35-page divorce agreement. I am praying because that steadies me, and because I really want it to happen, and because I expect him to balk at any second.

A year earlier I was sobbing in the apartment of my dear friend in Prenzlauerberg, Germany. I had separated from my husband. It was unfathomable to me, at the time that I was getting divorced. Of course, this was a full year before I was saying prayers down Spring Street. In my Berliner friend's apartment in Prenzlauerberg, I was in shock. Divorce was something I never intended for my life. Perhaps that was why in my earlier years I always ran from relationships.

My two greatest fears were not being loved and then making the wrong choice around love. I know that it's not this black and white, but having lived through my own parents' choices and the devastation they caused for all of us, I couldn't bare the idea that I would create some semblance of the same in my own life.

My Berliner got out a bottle of her best red wine and said, "Darling, I think we're going to need this." Hell yes, we were going to need it! She has a super-power ability to breakdown and organize even the messiest stuff down to its simplest form. That night it was so comforting when she said, "Darling, really there's no shame. A lot of people get divorced. The shame would be staying in a shitty marriage." Lift a glass. Toast to that. My tears turned to laughter. Good point.

So much opened up when I got that news one January morning that the divorce was final. I was in my friend's kitchen in their town house in Brussels. I had woken up to an email from NYC from my lawyer: "You'll receive the court papers in the mail, but I want to let you know that it's finally done. You're divorced."

I remember running downstairs to tell my friends who I had known from early days back in NYC. They both hugged me and asked me if I was all right. I said, "To be honest, I'm not sure. I feel lighter. I can't help but notice that I'm in Europe when I get the news. It still feels a bit surreal. I need to integrate what I'm feeling and I can't name it right now. What I can name is how grateful I am to be here with you. I really feel so loved at this moment. Thank you." It was 9 AM, and they asked me if I wanted some coffee. I said, "I think I need a drink. We all laughed." That part was easy. There are always cases of good French champagne in their home. So at 9 am we made a toast to the end of an era.

The divorce itself took 2 years from start to finish. I had to let it breathe some. I needed to give it some time and be strategic; otherwise, it would have taken longer. There are so many raw emotions when a marriage is over. After all, in our case, we had stood up in front of our closest people and made our vows. Our ceremony was a hodgepodge. He was an atheist and I was spiritual and brought up Catholic. We couldn't get married in a Catholic church, but I did want it to be spiritual ceremony so it had a mix of Universal Kabbalah, Catholicism, Judaism and mantra playing. Multiple people had told me that our wedding was the best they had ever attended. It went on for 2 days in NYC. Afterwards, we had flown to Vieques. One thing my ex was always good at was holidays. Over the 8 years we were married, we had been on some gorgeous adventures together. Unfortunately, the problem is life isn't a vacation. We were in very different spaces relative to what it meant to make this kind of commitment.

Over the years that space deteriorated. The deterioration could be suspended on holidays for a moment or two. But even then, things would sometimes go to shit. Like the time we were in Istanbul and I found sexually explicit texts on his phone from a woman he had known in architecture school, so many years before. But I always forgave him, mostly, I see now, out of my own fears around failing. Failing at marriage felt like a big fat *F*, and I was used to being an *A* student. Over time, the F would stand for, *fuck it, I'm out of here.*

Then there was the time we were in Cappadocia, and the innkeeper who resembled a swarthy Turkish Yul Brenner in his prime. I had to use all my will power not to sleep with him. Or the time we were sailing in Turkey and my husband's good friend, saw me meditating on the bow of the ship and kissed me – in front of all five us there. My husband at the time saw it and laughed. He always thought I was not adventurous enough, so upon reflection maybe it turned him on. Who knows? What I do know is these moments were signs of a deepening fissure.

So, as I walked to the notary down Spring Street, I prayed. I just wanted the whole thing over. Honestly, I didn't know where I was going from there. I knew it wouldn't be boring, but I had no certainty.

I just knew somehow that I was starting to wake up to life again. Wake up to me again. At my core, I am strong and a fighter. I've never been willing to settle. Staying would have been settling.

For me, just getting to that walk down to the notary was a journey. The *letting it breath* in my personal life had been a good year of living in the same apartment, while being separated. People thought I was insane to live with him through this. But to this day I don't care, nor do I feel the need to explain. Those who pressed me or criticized me for my approach, lost compassion, or stood in denial or judgment have been eradicated from my life by their own hand. Good riddance.

Sometimes it's useful to take the long view in things, the strategic approach, even if in the moment it is excruciating. This was why I stayed living with him. I knew if I pushed him to move out, or if I moved out myself, all holy hell would break lose. He has never navigated change well -- perhaps because his privileged but completely unstable childhood was filled with constant upheaval and change. His default mode was always to dig in, dig into denial. And when that no longer worked he would fight to keep the status quo. That would come to include me.

So, incremental change was the way to go. Luckily for me, during this period I was teaching a lot in Europe. Every couple of months I would hop on a plane to Brussels, Paris, London, and Berlin – sometimes *all of the above* in the same trip, while staying for weeks at a time. One time even included Croatia.

But every time I turned the key in the lock when I got home, I would dread it. So I prayed for strength, and the patience to keep the long view. I took back my power in the whole thing piece by piece. I now know that following this course ultimately led in this process of divorce to serve me well. In the *letting it breathe*, and biding my time, it gave me the space to know when to strike and how to do it strategically.

Sometimes that meant playing nicely. For instance, I remember waking up to him knocking on my door and thinking, *fuck me it's 7 am. What the hell does he want?* By this time I had turned into an ice cube. My energy toward him was so neutral he told me it sent a chill through his spine. He was afraid of me but couldn't pinpoint why. But he knew his biggest mistake had been thinking kindness was weakness.

He asked me if I would go to couples therapy. I remember thinking you are beyond delusional. If you think all this is because we don't communicate you are crazy. I called a colleague in Boston to ask his advice. Simultaneously we were working on the most challenging project of my professional life. Older than me, happily remarried and having weathered a nasty divorce himself, I trusted him. I called him and said, "Chris, he wants me to go to couples therapy. I'm clear, I just want to get away from him. What a waste of time this is going to be. I have no intention of working things out. I just want out." He listened patiently and then when I stopped talking he said, "I get it. The same thing happened with me when I was divorcing my first wife. She wanted to go to therapy." Then he laughed and said, "*Just go*. It may provide some comic relief to the whole thing. It did for me. If you have a good therapist, you may even get the pleasure of seeing him called out on his shit. And Kelley, it's only an hour a week. It's not a big deal."

My ex had chosen the therapist. But the Universe works in mysterious ways, especially when you let it breathe. I didn't want to go to begin with so I really didn't give a shit about who we saw. I was disassociating from this part of the experience mostly because I was so checked out of any kind of meaningful interaction with him.

On the path to my divorce being final I learned a lot about duality -- the duality of perception and reality. We were perceived as one of the NYC cool couples by the circle of people we knew. When I asked his friend Guitar how I could have married this man, how I could have put myself in this position, he laughed and said, "Darling, don't be so hard on yourself. He can be intoxicating. He is insanely good looking and an extraordinarily creative architect. He is tall, speaks 3 languages, rode around China on his bicycle when he was 17 years old. An unusual character, to say the least. And adventure can be a powerful aphrodisiac. It just doesn't work well as the operating principle for day-to-day life."

All of that was true. I had given away so much of my power and had so much to heal when I met him that my choices weren't always conscious. Upon reflection I now know I chose to buy into the illusion, and in doing so I settled for an illusion.

So when I was in Malibu visiting a friend of mine she had burst into tears at the news. I was comforting her and saying, "It will all be okay." Then we both started laughing at the absurdity of that moment -- of me, comforting her. It was backwards just like my marriage was backwards.

My teacher had married us. After all, he was a living Spiritual Master, so who was I to question his judgment when I went to him many years earlier to say that this is what my husband was doing and not doing, and it was a nightmare. I told him that I felt like my dream had turned into a nightmare -- the exception being when we were on vacations or at parties or someplace living this external life we had created. He looked at me and said, *You know how many women come to me to me wanting a husband. You have one. You're beautiful and powerful. Make it work.*

I can see how this triggered all the dysfunctional beliefs of my Catholic upbringing, as in, W*hen you get married it's forever. If it falls apart it's somehow your fault. It's too big to fail. It'll disappoint too many people. Hurt too many people. Shattering the illusion means shattering lives. Just buckle down and keep the balls in the air and make it better.*

What a load of bullshit it is to buy into having to make it all better.

As the only one actively trying to make it better, it's not a winning formula. It's total and complete crap. My inner truths said get out of it but it was only four years later that I would file for the divorce. The experience taught me to never give away my power to anyone. Along the way, I had traded my own inner knowing to bowing before others, including my teacher's opinion and advice. I had bowed, even when the advice didn't resonate with me. As they say, *my bad*.

There were angels all along the way during this aspect of my journey, and I am grateful for them. My closest girlfriends who lived in Europe, one in Berlin, one in Surrey, England and another in Brussels rallied big time. They got me projects in Europe and held the space for me to drink a lot of wine, cry, laugh and walk around like a zombie. These powerful women didn't offer advice unless I asked for it, and this was powerful. They just held the space for me to be, which alternately meant sleeping all day, drinking a lot of wine, and crawling up in their laps like I was a child again. They were ever present. It's also a gift of this experience that I learned on a whole other level the deep sisterhood to be found in female friendship.

Unlike many people I knew in NYC, who were either being prescriptive or avoiding the topic altogether, these women just let me be. They held the space of compassion, empathy, and understanding. They also made sure I had a bit of fun along the way. They also watched over me. My friend in Surrey would fly to anywhere I was in Europe, even if that meant getting to a small island in Croatia.

I remember sitting in a beach chair and seeing her walk across the sand to me and feeling safe in the fact that I was loved. Not the love of a man, but the unflinching unconditional kind of love that at its best is the Divine Mother in action through female friendship.

She let me be, even when I insisted in getting in a speedboat dressed in a white flowing skirt and a Chanel top. Having sailed and boated a lot, I can tell you first hand that this is the most absurd outfit one can wear in a speedboat trying to catch the ferry to Hvar. But she let me be and do what I wanted. She chanted triple mantra with me when the waves were huge, and I wasn't heavy enough to stay seated on the boat. She protected me when I was a little bit out of my mind. She screamed at Luca to slow down and focus on safety, not on catching the *fucking ferry to Hvar*. Insanely, I was egging Luca on, not noticing that if he kept speeding up the boat there was a good chance that I would get thrown out into the sea. Being an excellent swimmer and slightly out of my mind I wasn't thinking that could be dangerous. I was in a James Bond fantasy of my own making. She brought it all down to earth and yelled over the wind and the waves, S*low the fucking boat down!*

I didn't get thrown out of the boat. And we didn't catch the ferry. We took a bus to Split and the ferry from there. It took a lot longer and was decidedly not glamorous. But she made sure I was safe, when I really wasn't all there. I was too disembodied and numb to be counted on for that.

Through the love of this dear friend, I started to wake up out of the numbness I had lived in during the two years before finalizing the divorce. The flight back home from Croatia helped a lot as well.

When I saw *him* in the Zurich Airport, I think it was the Divine Intelligence saying, E*nough of this numbness already. I'm going to put someone so delicious in front of you that you will start to wake up to being a woman again.*

I remember feeling his energy as I sat typing away on my computer. I looked up and thought, *damn!* There he was, all 6'5" of him talking the counter agent into giving him an upgrade. I had gotten one too. When I boarded the plane and looked at my seat I thought, H*oly shit! He's sitting beside me.*

Fragile, guarded, dreading flying home to deal with what I had to deal with, I sat down and put my headphones in.

He tapped me on the shoulder and said, "Just so you know I don't talk to people on the plane."

I thought, *dude you sure? You're talking to me right now.* I said, "No worries, I don't either."

And he went back to his book and his music. A few short moments later I felt a tap on my shoulder again. Turning to him, I asked, "Yes, what?" He asked if he could get me anything before we start taxiing for takeoff. I said, "Yes, I'd like a pair of socks out of my overhead from the fuchsia leather bag." He laughed and said, "Why am I not surprised that you have a bright pink leather bag." I laughed too. He got my socks and we both put on our earphones. A few moments later, I felt another tap on my shoulder.

I thought, S*hit, for someone who doesn't talk to anyone he's a bit chatty.* "Yes, what?" I said, turning a second time.

"Now I want to talk to you," he said.

I started laughing. "Really?" I said. "Why do you want to talk to me? Ten minutes ago you told me you didn't want to talk."

"Because I think you're the most self-contained person I've ever been around," he said.

"Why because I'm not trying to talk to you," I said.

"Yes, typically women try to talk to me," he said, laughing.

"I bet they try a lot of things, but I'm not that kind of woman," I said. We both laughed.

"I can tell." Then he said with a more sober note in his voice: "That's why I want to talk to you."

So it was the beginning of a very nice connection. Turns out he was 20 years younger than me. Before we touched ground in New York he said very nicely, "I don't give a shit about that, I just want to have a glass of wine with you when we land."

We talked all the way through baggage and customs.

He asked me out for the glass of wine as he was dropping me off at my apartment. Turns out he is one of these hot-shot entrepreneurs – a wine importer, as well as founder of five other businesses. Found out he's half Argentine, a mover and shaker, an up and coming master of the Universe. I remember thinking, W*hat is happening here*, as I recalled the wise words of another older mentor of mine, an 80-year-old man, who had told me, "I don't know what is happening to you during this divorce. But I see that it's making you stiff. You're not flowing. You're still on your game in business, but you're losing your touch as a woman. You're so scared to make another mistake that you're frozen. Just allow yourself to feel again, to go with the opportunities that get presented to you in your personal life."

As the Argentine was asking me in the cab to go out for a glass of wine, I heard the voice of the old man. Then I thought, *Fuck it. Sure, I have halitosis from traveling for so many hours and sleeping on the plane, I'm exhausted and a little gamey, but if a good-looking 30 year-old wants to carry my bags and take me out for a drink, why the hell not?*

I told him, "This is very odd but I'm separated from my ex-husband. We still live together and…"

He stopped me and said, "I don't care about any of that. I just want to go out for a glass of wine. Will you just please have a glass of wine with me?" He asked so winningly, I stopped, exhaled, and put down my barriers. I was too tired, too jolted by the typical NYC wall of reality, to not surrender to the moment.

He dropped his bags at my place and we walked to a local bar. He ordered me a Malbec. Once it arrived he sent it back, telling the waiter, "Bring her what I asked you for."

I noticed that he had a tattoo that read *Matthew 11* on his arm. "Wow, Mathew 11. Why do you have that tattooed on your arm?"

He said, slightly arrogantly, "All the women who want to sleep with me say that and they don't even know what it means."

Cheeky boy, I thought to myself. Then I said, "Let's get a few things clear… I'm not 'everywoman.' I'm not trying to sleep with you, and I do know what *Matthew 11* means."

He said kind of challengingly, "So then, what does it mean?"

A Catholic education can sure come in handy sometimes… "It means, 'What good does it do a man to gain the world but lose his soul?'"

He stopped in his tracks and said, "You're for real."

"That's certainly true," I said, laughing with some bemusement. "Now, why do you have that tattooed on your arm?"

He went on to tell me that he was very ambitious and he wanted to stay focused on his bigger reason for building his companies. We started talking spirituality. I did his Universal Kabbalah chart.

I started to wake up to being a woman again.

Walking back to my apartment, he put his arm around me and I leaned into him. When we got to my place my then husband was back home. He opened the door, holding a glass of wine.

I thought, S*hit, this magical moment could turn into a total shit show.* I thought, *let it breathe. You don't have to manage this. Surrender to the moment. Let them deal.*

I said, "Hi, this is my new friend, I need to use the rest room."

I left the two of them standing in the living room together. They did just fine. Of course, I caught a whole boatload of venom later on. But in the moment, no fireworks, they did fine.

I walked my new friend out to catch a cab, where he kissed me. We both smiled. He said, "Let's be in touch." I woke up the next day to a text and voice mail from him saying how lovely it was to meet me. He was thanking me for going for a glass of wine. He said that it was a privilege to have spent time with me. I smiled.

This fortified me for the next chapter on my divorce journey. I recalled how, initially, my then husband and I had discussed mediation. *Let's be friendly through the process.* What a lovely if totally unrealistic idea. One morning, as I was making coffee and he was walking out the door, he whirled around and said to me, "You better fucking get a lawyer."

Well, good morning to you also. I said, "Okay, no problem, I will."

To which he replied, "You better. Fuck you," and stormed out.

As I look back, I am grateful for this fit of anger, because it woke me up to how nasty the whole thing had become. I saw his sheer fury at not being able to manipulate me into staying. I needed a neutral person to represent me. It was hard for me to stay clear with the on-again-off-again realization that my then husband's words to me were meaningless. He had broken his word to me so many times that I couldn't trust anything he said. And yet when he would write me an apology letter, buy me a nice gift, take me on a trip I would forgive him. It was totally emotionally abusive. But this time, for that fit of rage I am grateful, because it was exactly what got me to my lawyer.

I must pause and say thank you to my lawyer. She knew how to fight the good fight. *Good* meaning to fight with impeccability from the beginning. I trusted her to advocate for me, but also to not prolong the whole thing. Ironically, the therapist that my ex-husband had chosen for us referred her to me. Life is a paradox and through the process, I learned on a whole new level just what a paradox it really is.

Paradox. Like the odd occasion when in the middle of this contentious process we would actually enjoy a moment of each other's company.

That's when the sadness would creep in.

He'd be mean. I'd be mean back. When emotions ramped up, I helped power the conflict escalator. It almost felt safer, cleaner. The messiness came when the familiarity crept back in.

Knowing things about each other with that intimacy of shared experience would trigger little kindnesses in us. It also had me realize that even though this was so over, there was once a bond, a dysfunctional one built on a house of cards, but a bond nonetheless.

Like when he told me *to go fuck myself* at the therapist's office. I said, "Hey mister, can you *let it breathe?*"

He said, "Hey, you're co-opting my phrase. I taught you that!"

And we both laughed.

Walking out, he said, "Come on, have dinner with me."

"I don't think that's a good idea."

"Why?" he said. "You need to eat dinner anyway. It's dinner time, just have dinner with me."

I laughed and said okay. We went to Eataly, drank a bottle of wine, and ate some great pasta — and laughed. For a moment, we were in that suspended reality of actually liking each other. It lasted all of an hour and a half.

Divorce in NY State is an interesting proposition in that it's a "no fault state." I remember saying to my lawyer, "Okay, in theory I get it. Relationships are complex. But what happens if someone refuses to give you one." She said, "Well that can be a drawn out mess." I said, "Okay, got it. I know how he is wired. I'll get him to sign it."

This would take me a year to accomplish.

I remember the day the he finally moved off the dime. I had woken up and was headed out to my ballet barre class. It was Saturday. At this juncture I was taking class almost every day. I needed the grounding and the routine to keep from going bonkers.

I walked into the large living room of our new apartment. The apartment was twice the size of the old one that we moved into two months before everything blew up. We had gotten the large apartment so that our niece could have her own bedroom. She never used it. It became his man pad.

Anyway, back to that fateful morning, following a series of visits to our shrink, the odd dinner and the awkwardness of my new friend appearing upon my return from Croatia. I walked out of my room and said *good morning*. He peered through his glasses and over the tip of the New York Times magazine, asking where are you going. I said ballet. He said, "Just so you know, I'm not going to sign it. I'm not going to give you a divorce."

I thought, *You are the most arrogant son of bitch I have never met.*

Then it was as if all the air had been sucked out of the room. I *let it breathe,* and didn't say anything for an endless moment or two. The silence was torturous, probably for both of us. Eventually, he peered again over the top of the newspaper and said, "What, don't you love me anymore?"

Ah, the gift of denial and delusion. I could not believe what I was hearing. Then I said, "Look, I married you. And in general I try to have some sort of love for humanity so I can't say I don't love you. But what you should know is I don't even *like* you . . . *at all.* As I heard him gasp, I continued, "I don't want to be your friend, and I don't consider you mine. I don't respect you. I can't stand having you anywhere near me. Your mistake is thinking kindness is weakness. Don't push me. Sign it." Before he could reply I walked out the door.

Walking to ballet down Grande Street through Chinatown into Nolita and finally though Soho to 6th Avenue and Spring Street, my hands were shaking. I was seething. How dare he try to threaten me and put me in a box. Luckily, the advanced class was so excruciatingly difficult, it gave me a respite from the vindictive thoughts swirling in my head. All I could focus on was a wide second position, plié, etc.

When I returned, I took a big breath before I entered. When I did, he was still sitting on the couch reading the NY Times. I walked in and he said, "Fine, I'll sign it. We can go to a notary tomorrow."

My sister and my niece were crashing at our place in two-day's time to spend a few days before they moved to California. I had warned them that it wasn't the best atmosphere but they wanted to be with us. Their move out West was an additional loss that I think no one wanted to fully acknowledge.

So the next morning on the way to the notary, I prayed for the ten blocks we walked to the notary the prayers of my childhood. My all time favorite, the Lord's Prayer. Our Father who art in Heaven. Hallowed be thy name, thy kingdom come thy will be done... *Please God, may thy will be that he fucking signs these papers!*

The notary laughed when he saw the papers. He said, "Really, you guys are getting a divorce? Why you seem so nice with each other." I thought, *what is it about us that makes people think that?* To this day I marvel at whatever energy it was that we gave off when we were together, *right up until the end,* that made people think we were so great as a couple.

I kept praying and breathing while he chatted with the notary. It felt like forever. Then I heard the call to sign. I signed. Then the notary pushed the paper to him. He signed, then I heard the stamp hit. I couldn't help it. I threw my arms up in the air and said YES! Both he and the notary looked shocked at my enthusiasm. I just couldn't contain myself. I was officially *FREE!* Well almost, it still had to go through the court, but the bulk was finished. The irreversible commitment had been made. It was done.

I knew the walk home would be grim. As predicted, it was. He was sad and angry and insulted by my enthusiasm. As we got home and entered the apartment my sister and my niece were there. We said, *It's done.* My ex-husband said, "Lets go to dinner. It'll really be our last chance to have dinner as a family."

In retrospect, given his state of mind I should have said no. But Ameena wanted to and I thought, W*hat's the harm. It's just dinner. We've done dinner along the way, and it's been fine.*

The four of us set out down East Broadway to Café Petisco, a long time favorite. My sister and I ordered a glass of champagne each and my niece got to have a sprite. Her own version of champagne and nearly as special, since she is typically not allowed to have soda. I saw the cloud pass over my ex-husband's face and I thought, S*hit, we shouldn't have ordered champagne.* He's drinking red wine and he's clearly pissed off we're having champagne.

The energy at that dinner got increasingly weird, culminating in a Hasidic man coming over to me and saying, "Miss, you really shouldn't be wearing those jeans."

"What are you talking about?" I asked.

"I can see your butt," he said.

A couple glasses of champagne in me and I replied, "That's your problem. You shouldn't be looking at my but anyway!" My niece and sister cracked up.

My ex-husband kept drinking more wine. By the time we concluded dinner, he was in a foul mood. Initially, he said he was pissed off because of the creepy Hasidic guy was looking at my bottom. But I knew that wasn't the case. It was because I was so happy.

So as we walked into the lobby, he turned to me in full view of the doorman and started screaming at me. "*Fuck you.* You are ruining our lives. *Fuck you,* you are a total bitch."

Wow! My sister grabbed my niece and said come on, and they left. We stormed into the laundry room and I said, "Have you lost your marbles, screaming at me like that in public and in front of our seven year old niece?"

Then I just stopped. He was enraged. I turned around and walked out while he kept pulling the laundry out of the dryer. I went upstairs to find my niece buried in a Curious George book on the couch. She looked up and said sweetly, "Auntie are you alright?"

"My love," I said, "I'm fine and I'm very sorry you saw that. It had nothing to do with you."

"I know," she said and went back to Curious George.

My sister was in my room, and when I went in to see her she said, "Jesus Christ, what the hell was that?"

"It's all just turned really bad but the papers are signed. I think it's hitting him."

Then we heard a key turn in the door. He stormed into the living room and again, in front of Ameena said, "*Fuck you*, Kelley. *Fuck you.*" Then he threw the clean clothes and sheets on the armchair and stormed back out.

I saw my niece's eyes grow big as tea cup saucers. She said, "Auntie, you can't stay with Uncle. He has become crazy." By the time he came back to the apartment we were all asleep. We were leaving very early the next morning to fly them to their new home in Silicon Valley.

The car service was picking us up the next morning at 5 AM. Little did he know that would be the last time he would see my niece and sister. I wonder sometimes if he is sorry that he never apologized to our niece. When I asked him about it, he said, "Well, the time has come for her to know that adults fight sometimes." I was speechless.

When I got back from California, it was time for me to move out. I was leaving my life as I'd known it, moving to my new apartment in the building I had always dreamed of living in.

Many miracles happened since. I believe it was the opening of a gate.

The morning of my move he stood in the doorway of our apartment and simply said, "Bye," and then turned around and walked out. I sat down and wept. I can't define all the reasons I wept. But if you've ever gotten divorced, you understand that you weep. Maybe he even wept at some point too. If he did, I never saw it.

Then there was a knock on the door. The movers were there. I took barely anything from my old life to my new. I took some of my books, and my collection of beautiful clothes. A week later I sold my wedding and engagement ring. Someone said, "Why don't you save it for your niece?" I thought, A*re you kidding? Why would I give my niece an engagement ring that holds the energy of something that failed in this way? Why would I want her to have that energy?* People said, Y*ou'll only get a fraction of the price, like 25% of it.* That proved to be true. But it wasn't about the money.

It was about stepping into a new frequency. It was about moving on.

Chapter 14
Love

We are born to love and be loved. A person without love is like land without water. Nothing can grow there

~ Dr. Joseph Michael Levry

I sat down to write about love and thought how do I even begin to speak to something so vast, so beyond comprehension, so beyond words.

It has taken me many years to go deep into myself on this one. Born on the Day of Romantic Exaltation and being a Cancer, the urge to love has always dominated my life. But I have to be careful because I am so romantic that I can lose myself, leave myself. That's not love. That's co-dependence.

Often I was in love with the idea of love, only to wake up and realize that the situations I was in were not even remotely congruent with my deepest beliefs about love. This was in turn shattering, inspiring, and ecstatically orgasmic, depending on the time, place and situation. Sometimes I would think, "Oh God, please cancel, erase, delete this one…." And at others I would feel a prayer coming on, "Please God, make this last forever." Then there was everything in between. But in retrospect, it was some version of *luscious* or contributed to future lusciousness. This is why I say it has taken me nearly all of my 50 years and many *interesting* experiences to unravel this one for myself, within my own consciousness.

Look closely, you can spot the lovers and the loved. The unloved look brittle, lacking in some primary energy that makes things tick. They are a little lost because they have disassociated from the primal source of life. They vibrate at a lower frequency and we feel it. The energy is blocked, heavy, sometimes even dark.

There are different levels of loving, maybe analogous to a peach. On the outside, the skin can be bitter or a bit sweeter, if you have the courage to take a full bite. Feeling deeply, residing under your own skin is the first gate home. Then maybe you'll vibrate at the frequency that attracts someone, who then invites you through their gates, home -- home then under your mutual skins. To arrive there is an opening into something so delicious that it's beyond the beyond.

We don't get to the third stage each time. And often, when people go without loving and being loved for a long time, when they finally find it, the Light is so bright that it terrifies them. For many, the terror of revealing to the beloved and the self is just too much to face. So they shut down by default, and go back to the living in the top layer, in the bitter skin.

I get it. It takes a willingness to risk on a level that makes you so vulnerable that you feel like you're going to crack wide open, and crack wide open you will. It's not like the fairy tales even when it is a fairy tale. But to be open to the cracking and the messy bits of the fairy tale are what makes life technicolor and *luscious*. Nothing else will fill the existential angst of being human. Nothing. What material success will complete you in the way that loving and being loved does? Plenty of people have attempted to answer that question the hard way. Deciding to have the deepest relationships with yourself and then with those around you is the key to the door to a luscious life. I think the actor Will Smith sums it up brilliantly…

> Only love is going to fill that hole. You can't win enough, you can't have enough money, you can't succeed enough. There is not enough. The only thing that will ever satiate that existential thirst is love. And I just

> remember that day I made the shift from wanting to be a winner to wanting to have the most powerful, deep and beautiful relationships I could possibly have.

The day I read this quote I set my highest intention. I'll share it with you from my heart. Every morning and night I say, "*My highest intention is to be love and have love . . .*"

It's so simple, but they say simplicity is Divinity. The morning I started to say that was the day my life became *technicolor*, four-dimensional, beyond words really.

I imagine it's because at our essence love is the most real thing about us. It's what we all long to give and receive – even when it's buried under an avalanche of walls and wounds. To love well, love what we do, love who we are, and love each other is perhaps the fundamental work of being human.

What is the moment that wakes us up enough to stop running from love? Those of us who are lucky or surrendered to love -- suddenly get real, which usually takes some major internal work in the process. And doing the work makes it clear that romantic love is only one gate to something way beyond that. And what that is appears to be is the arrival into a non-linear, undulating state of being that I can only call spiritual intimacy with the flow of life. And as anyone who has experienced or believes in magic knows… that's when things get really luscious.

Kelley Black

Chapter 15

Cinderella Makes It to The Ball

You don't have to hold on to your past - you can find a way to overcome the bad parts. Great things can happen.
 ~ Michaela DePrince

I loved Hans Christian Anderson's Fairy Tales growing up. The old hard cover versions in the Northampton, Massachusetts Public Library had the most spectacular illustrations. I found them spectacularly scary. I could sit for hours with them. I loved them. And from just as early an age, I loved to dance; I loved to swim; and I especially loved books. My favorite children's tale of all was *Cinderella*.

New York City, where I live now, is a long way from a small town library in Western Massachusetts in the 1970's. When I first came to New York 25 years ago, I fell in love with a building called London Terrace Tower in West Chelsea. The neighborhood was a different place then. There were no galleries this far west. The High Line was just a bunch of rusting old unused railroad tracks. The neighborhood was colorful, not chic. At night the transvestite prostitutes would come out a block away between 10th and 11th Streets, a block that buts up against the West Side Highway.

West Chelsea was a bit of a wasteland. No matter. I dreamed of living at London Terrace Tower facing south. I thought it was one of the most beautiful blocks in New York. I used to walk all the way west to be in the shadow and energy of the building. I wasn't on a budget then; I had no money at all. I would eat popcorn for dinner with grated cheddar cheese on it.

Even then, I invested in my relationships. I may not have had any money, but I could will myself to light a bulb inside myself and focus on what I wanted. At any given moment *what I wanted* could be entry to a club (Mars, MK, Nells, etc) or dinner at Odeon, or . . . someday living in this magnificent building I would walk across the city just to see.

To be in the energy of it meant possibility for me, something to aspire to. So I would walk west and grab dinner at the Grand Szechuan, which is still on the corner of 9th Avenue and 24th Street. The funny thing is that even then Chinese food made me feel sick. Too much oil and MSG. But I could afford it. Some sautéed broccoli and white rice would fill me up. I would take my Chinese take-out, find a seat, and look at the building and brownstones. I'd wonder who lives there, and how I could live there. I knew there was a pool inside the tower; as a lifelong swimmer, the pool was symbolic of the safety I knew I would feel if I lived there. So I would eat my broccoli, and I would dream my dream. Then I would get on the PATH train and take it back to Hoboken and my railroad tenement apartment, the one I shared with a roommate and paid $200 a month for.

So jump ahead to the Howard Gilman Opera House in February 2015: Alexei Ratmansky and the Mariinsky Ballet perform at BAM in New York. I am over the moon. I love Alexei Ratmansky's choreography which I first saw at the Paris Opera Ballet at the Palais Garnier in his staging of *Eros*. He can always be counted on to stage something sensual, novel and profound. I always cry when I watch a ballet he has staged. And nothing can make me cry like *Cinderella*.

I am mesmerized the entire time. I love the core story, focused on the central lovers. Romanticism is central to my core. But what moves me about this version danced by the Mariinsky Ballet is that it's not the usual tale. In its uniqueness I feel like it echoes my own life. I realize, as I'm weeping, that I so relate. As I burst into tears, my friend who is European says to me, "Oh my God, do you not know the story? Don't worry, its going to be okay. I know the ending. He is going to find her." This snaps me out of my weeping and I laugh. Of course, I know the story. It's just so close to my own heart that I weep every time, I tell her. I can watch it or read it. But every time it just rips into my heart.

This modernized rendition resonates even more with me. When Cinderella meets her prince at the ball, she has no immediate reason to know he's royal; and he has spotted her not because she's some magical arrival in a glass coach, but because she seems a pretty but bewildered girl needing help in unfamiliar surroundings. For me, ultimately, Cinderella is about faith and frequency.

I was that bewildered girl. I was bewildered by the energy around me. I didn't understand when my uncle came to visit and we went out to dinner, why my parents stayed home with my sister. On other occasions I was shuttled off with my Grandmother. It was only later that I realized my uncle and so many others on both sides of the family had deep wounds that surfaced in various ways as fear and criticism. This included diminishing and racist comments, emotional unavailability, and disapproving whispers about what my parents had done. I was sent to represent the outcast interracial family, because I was fair. Even as a child I knew there was something very wrong with this. It was so bewildering and pressuring, for no greater reason than that no one around me ever talked about it.

In Alexei Ratmansky's version of *Cinderella*, Cinderella's father is a drunk. He relies on her to prop him up but doesn't see her. He is oblivious to how damaging his reliance on her is. His reliance on her brings out the monster in her mother. In the ballet, her mother is bullying, autocratic, and oblivious to Cinderella's reality. The mother is emotionally closed off. Cinderella is only visible to her parents when she serves them. No level of work or service will free her. But she does have a Fairy Godmother who leads her out of this reality to a brighter realm. Her fairy godmother helps her to bridge worlds – to believe.

Growing up I was told that it was *impossible* to join the swim team. First, because I was scared of the water after my first swim lesson. Second, because *Black people don't swim*. By the time I was 9, I went on to set a state record that was only broken many years later. Bi-racial -- even worse than being black. I fit neither the stereotype of the black American of the 1970s or the Caucasian ideal. I didn't feel I fit anywhere. I felt adrift. I remember how even on the census form there was no box for mixed race. There was a box that said *other*, and for many years that is what I felt like: an *other*, a high-yellow tar-baby. The US census had no box for me – nothing simply labeled, *Cinderella*.

But one thing I realized, as I grew and grew up, is that for every slight that was levied at me, for every person that told me what I couldn't do or go there, for all the lack of emotional support, the Universe provided a counterbalance of support. It supplied it through circumstances and people that fed my belief that if I held on long enough that "unrealistic" became *possible*, was accomplished, made manifest. I developed an acute sense that universal love, often unseen and out of the "normal" construct was there for me as long as my eyes were open.

These counterbalances were always present. Even through the 1970s it was unusual to find a black or bi-racial child swimming competitively. From the beginning, my coach had recognized my steely will. As a skinny grammar-school kid, I wanted to swim. I wanted to swim because my friends were doing it. Even as a young child I could will myself into a sort of alternate reality, one that didn't match the one that was staring at me. For instance, my first swimming lesson at age 4 was being thrown off a diving board into the deep end of the pool. I marvel now at how barbaric that approach was. That's it, throw all of us off a diving board and watch us struggle to find our way to the top. Of course, they weren't going to let us drown. There were camp counselors and life guards present. But I think now what a traumatic sink-or-swim way to learn. So when my friends wanted to join the swim team, I had no idea that I could even make it as a swimmer, let alone onto the swim team. I just knew what I wanted to do.

My first swimming coach became a most benevolent force in my desire to be a good swimmer. I remember my mom sharing with me that the other parents were calling out during practice, "Someone pull her out. She's not going to cut it." In this instance, I am grateful that my mom didn't listen to them. Neither did my coach. He let me get to the other end of the 25-yard pool. After I became a force in the sprint events, 50 meter butterfly and freestyle, he said he knew from the tryouts that I could do it -- not because I had any innate skill, but because he saw I had the will to do it. Once he saw that, he said he couldn't help but get behind me.

It was only when I started studying Naam Yoga and learned through studying the Kabbalistic Tree of Life that tapping the *feeling* of what I wanted to create helped to make it all possible. They told me to toughen up, process things more rationally, learn things in a linear way. So I developed the capacity to process life through an intellectual lens. But my natural way was to feel my way through life, and I never let that go. It kept me afloat. Now 40 years after my birth, I was learning that it was actually my greatest strength.

All my life my parents and others had told me I was too sensitive. The study of Naam Yoga helped me to make sense of energy and of an ability that had helped me survive and overcome a lot of challenges in my life, that included overcoming limits of other peoples' pity, judgments, pettiness, fears, and prejudices, mostly directed my way because I was a mixed race child from an interracial marriage.

Because I was very sensitive and emotional, I was also easily wounded. But I could retreat into an alternate reality of dreams and visions. At the same time, I had a knack of drawing those who could help me, by keeping faith and believing it actually could be so. The trials and wounds helped me develop and tap into my ability to be a spiritual warrior. And why not?

For me the paradox of not belonging anywhere fostered a desire to be able to flow seamlessly between different groups of people. When I didn't have the security of neatly belonging to a group or a tribe, out of necessity, I learned how to be comfortable in the world beyond tribes and cliques. This served me well especially as I got older and was thrust into different social circles. Black, white, Latin, European, Xhosa, Zulu, Dutch, English -- I found myself focusing on our shared humanity and I learned how to listen for the opportunities to connect. Love and connection became my primary drivers.

And when there didn't seem to be any, I moved on. I stopped being overly attached. Not belonging also helped me refine my ability to derive my certainty from an unseen internal compass that I like to call my soul's GPS, my intuition and heart.

So my *It* became my connection to something that I knew with increasing clarity. But my experience of that connection, and what lay within it and beyond it, felt as beyond categorization as I was. Something I couldn't name. A vast, Divine force, a feeling, touchable and knowable in every instant. It would be what I later came to call, in more formal moments, God.

And God always came through. Over and over again there were always people who helped me move to the next level. The more open my heart has become, the more refined my listening to my intuition, the more I allow myself to feel . . . the more definitive my GPS has become. I am guided to and recognize opportunity. It often shows up in the most unexpected ways but always directly or indirectly as a result of investing in people. I am guided to the best investment, what is always people and relationships.

As part of my life's arc, the most amazing things have happened just in the last 5 years. As I became more congruent with my belief in what is possible, the more I stopped questioning my instincts, the less I relied on external evidence, the more evidence I seemed to be able to create.

Every implosion in my life was balanced by a broadening miracle, so much so that I've come to regard breakdowns as breakthroughs. Every time things have fallen apart something better aligned with the vital spirit of life has reformed a fresh pattern. I've come to believe that I am increasingly aligned to the frequency of Light in such a way that anything that no longer serves my highest good and purpose in the world is eradicated by its own hand.

While I was recovering from major surgery as my marriage fell apart, support came from the most unlikely place -- my ex-husband's good friend. He would come and play guitar for me. Classically trained with Segovia, he is a masterful guitar player. Day after day he would come and play for me. I would lay propped up on pillows while he played the guitar for hours. He also brought chocolate and flowers.

So even though the man who was supposed to love me no longer did, and I've come to believe he never actually did, another man showed me love -- unconditional love not attached to intimacy or wanting anything from me. He stood up for me, and stood by me as I got strong enough to face the trauma of divorce and my life crumbling. He stood by me, expecting nothing other than allowing him to show up for me. This was a powerful lesson in accepting love and not being attached to where it comes from. He taught me to let go of my expectations of where love comes from and just accept that it's there.

He taught me that if I cried, someone would catch me. He showed up for me, took me to dinner, listened and held the space for my rage, pain, and tears. He offered constant, unwavering support. He was and is an angel in my life.

When I finally got the divorce agreement signed after a year of cohabitating in our large 2-bedroom apartment, it was my guitarist that asked, "Where do you want to live?" I said, "I want to live in London Terrace." He said, "I hear that's very difficult to get into but call my real estate agent. He will help you." He is one of the top real estate brokers in the city. He had sold my guitarist his apartment in Brooklyn Heights. I didn't have that kind of budget, and I didn't need to have a huge place. I had that while I was married. But what I felt deeply was that I had to live in London

Terrace, and that it had to be on a high floor, facing south. So I called the real estate agent.

They say a woman in her power can move anything, that Shakti, the creative force that moves the whole Universe, can overcome any barrier, move any obstacle. That is Shakti.

Since I had gone through the surgery and the divorce, I had gotten clearer and clearer about who I am and what I wanted to create in my life. The clearer I got, the more the counterbalancing force of Light showed up in my life.

So even though everyone told me that it was impossible to get into my building, I had decided that through my faith, belief and commitment the Universe would conspire to give me what I wanted. With my whole heart I trusted this knowing. I also trust my dreams. I had seen 465 repeatedly in my dreams, followed by seeing 23. The building I live in is 465 West 23rd Street.

I connected with the real estate agent and he asked me what I wanted. "I want a pre-war building," I said. "I want to live in London Terrace. Not the Gardens but the tower. And in the tower I want the southern facing one." At the time I didn't realize that this was the most exclusive part of the building -- the tower that has the pool, the rooftop garden with the 360 degree views of the city. All I knew was I had learned long ago to trust my feelings and my prophesy dreams. The latter often spoke to me in numbers. Paying attention to that combination time and time again gave me the keys to the kingdom -- that my trust and belief in my own inner compass was what had gotten me to the ball.

As I've mentioned, when I feel myself spinning, spiraling, or feeling rejected, I put my hands on my heart with my left hand on top and inhale deeply. When I cannot inhale anymore I say "*I AM*" silently. Then I exhale and before I breathe in again I say silently to myself "*I AM.*" This powerful breathing technique immediately connects me to my heart, to my soul's truth, to my center. In doing it, I am able to be present to the lesson of the moment. The breath is one of my greatest teachers.

So I felt something else at play, even as Frank said, "I don't think I can get you that. I'll help you, but please be flexible. Look at some other buildings. There are great pre-war buildings on the Upper West Side. Please look at something near Lincoln Center. I'll drive you up there on my Vespa." I went, and not because I ever thought I would live up there. But I like riding Vespas. They're fun.

After we looked at the apartment on the UWS we got back on the Vespa. He drove me home which was all the way downtown. When he dropped me off he said, "Don't worry, we'll look at more."

I replied, "Just so you know, there isn't going to be any need to do that. I believe in you and I believe you will get me what I want. And what I want is to live in London Terrace Tower, in 465 on a high floor. Don't worry. You'll do it. I believe in you. You'll get me what I want."

I have been taught to be congruent in my speech, action, thoughts, and beliefs as a way of willing my dreams into reality. It worked when I tried out for the swim team and I had a deep belief that it would work now. I knew where I was meant to live and I believed that the Force was on my side. I believed that God had put me through the pain and trauma in my life, and that because I believed in him through direct experience, that he would help align me with this path — that the Universe would work through Frank to ensure that I remained aligned with intent. So I repeated to myself one more prayer, smiled, and headed into my apartment building.

A week later, Frank called me while I was dressing for a meeting with one of my favorite clients. I was organizing my Chanel tote bag, putting on my pearls, dressing for a meeting with the C-suite. He was electric over the phone, "Christ, you're not going to believe this! An associate of mine sent me a listing. There's an apartment in 465 on the 15th floor. It's not going to be listed publicly and the owner is really picky. *This never happens.* But you have to come now! And make sure you're *DRESSED.*"

Thanks to my Fashion Angel, being dressed is never an issue. He told me long ago that you have to be prepared and you can't be caught out. *You need to have the clothes that match the life you're stepping into, not the life you're leaving behind.*

This was one of those seminal moments when a friend's words take on another level of meaning. I could feel as I checked out every piece of what I had on, and then met my gaze in the mirror, that I was *dressed*. It wasn't lost on me that this *spontaneous* event was occurring after 25 years in a way that neatly fit into the 2 hours prior to my client meeting. Nothing needed to be shifted around to accommodate it. Life was showing up for me. I just needed to show up in return. When I arrived, I saw the way they looked at me. I was *dressed*. The Chanel bag didn't hurt either. I literally saw the owner look me up and down and say, "I think you'll do fine in this building." Six weeks later I moved in.

Moving here was some kind of perfect platform for my new life. I believe that it was all synchronized in ways I don't entirely understand. Because I study the Kabbalah, seeing the numbers is especially poignant to me. I see how the Universe often speaks through symbols and numbers. And in this regard, I've worked to hone my literacy. The numbers of this building and my apartment add to six. Six is the number of the Goddess. Six is the energetic vibration of Venus, the Goddess of love.

The day I moved in, Yasser was there to welcome me. He is the head of all the doormen and the "mayor" of this building. The first weekend I moved in he said, "How are you doing?" My eyes filled up and I started crying. He said to me, "I don't know what happened before you got here but I sense sadness and pain. I just want you to know that you are safe here. We, all of us here, are here for you. No one can get past us. You can relax now. You are safe." I wept at the magnitude of his generosity of spirit and his compassion. I wept at finally being home. I wept because I knew I was stepping through a portal for what I can only describe simply as goodness.

My sister said to me when I moved in, "You have a pool?! Kel, that's a sign. You have always felt safe in the water. Growing up, you spent most of your time in either a pool or church. You're home, mermaid. You're really home."

So much love and support is around me in my life. What I have also learned is that when dreams are aligned with the universal law of love, attached to something bigger than myself, magic happens. One of my core beliefs from childhood has shifted in such a profound way since my surgery and divorce. I no longer believe that things have to be so hard. I think the major "work" is opening and listening to the heart — tuning out the distractions of dysfunctional relationships and learning to have healthy boundaries. It includes learning to follow my own heart by taking the time to get in touch with that. This is my mode of living now, and it is grounded in the faith that what is mine is mine. I don't have to cajole, convince, or kill myself trying to get people or things. If it doesn't work for me, I'm not attached; I move on and listen for what's supposed to happen next.

The most magical occurrences happen every day in ways big and small. I guess I always knew this. I knew I would get to the end of the pool that day many moons ago, and I'm glad no one pulled me out. I'm glad I chose to step into the unknown at 47, past the space of accepting that my marriage was over, and into the calm uncertainty of what was next. And now, W*here do I want to live*? The answer comes as a feeling. I raise my hands to my heart. I breathe in and say gently to myself, *I am.*

Chapter 16

Ode to My Fashion Angel

I have always believed that fashion was not only to make women more beautiful, but also to reassure them, give them confidence.
~ Yves Saint Laurent

Since I was a teenager, I loved fashion magazines and beautiful clothes. I have always drawn comfort from the archetypal energy I found in this realm. Regardless of what was going on in my external world, I could see someone who embodied who I wanted to be, what I wanted to do, and where I saw myself going . . . and then dream myself into it. As a child growing up in the 70s, the archetypal female energies I gravitated to were based in religion such as The Virgin Mary and Mary Magdalene. Side-by-side with them sat the fashion icons of the 70s. I drew particular comfort and inspirations from untraditional beauty because these women made me dream that I too could grow up to be a beautiful and accomplished woman. Such was my pantheon.

These archetypal energies were a very powerful portal for my self-esteem. They offered a way, a glimmer, an inspiration that would lead to the grand ball.

Growing up, we did not have fashion magazines lying around our home. But there were a lot of books. When my parents were married, the Wall Street Journal, The New York Times, and PBS were ubiquitous. *And music.* With dad around, there was always music playing. And that was fun.

There was also Ebony Magazine. The intention was to make

me and my sister proud of our blackness and connected to that side of our heritage. The truth is both my sister and I were pretty self-conscious. Being raised in a homogeneous environment where no one looked like me, let alone know to cut my hair, was pretty daunting.

Then one day, I opened Ebony Magazine and saw a Fashion Fair spread. Truthfully, most of the magazine was boring to me, including both the writing and the topics. It reflected a reality that was in no way, shape, or form relative to my experience. But when I saw a light skinned clearly mixed woman with green eyes in the spreads, my attention was riveted.

Seeing this woman who had similar features, and didn't neatly fit in any category, lifted my spirits. Even though I felt like Cinderella, I could now dream of the ball. I didn't know how or who would help make it possible, but seeing her made me dream biggerShe looked confident in the photos and she had a bearing that was so authentically herShe didn't look self-conscious or too serious. I was looking at Pat Cleveland.

I became fixated with her kinetic, authentic energy, energy she carries to this day. When I would feel down or like an ugly duckling, I would read everything I could get my hands on that had her in it. Later I would discover that she was also a force for good in the world. I became even more inspired by her by the way she walked at Versaille in 1973, during the big showdown between the American designers and the French designers. To this day, the 1972 photograph of her by Irving Penn is one of the most stunning depictions of feminine power and beauty that I've ever seen.

As a 50 year-old woman, she continues to inspire me. At 61, sans plastic surgery, she represents for me the archetypal image of beauty beyond boundaries. Ironically, she was also born under the sign of Cancer, and her birthday is the day after mine.

This year, she did campaigns for Barneys and Lanvin. She is still radiantly beautiful and naturally so. She never looks like she is trying to be anything other than who she is. She is always appropriate. Unlike many women of a certain age she is never trying to look younger than she is. She just *is* herself and this is a powerful statement in an era that is completely youth obsessed. She also got the glass slipper and has been married to the same man for over 25 years.

Awareness and connection to this archetypal energy continues to help me dream bigger. It also connects me to a deep acceptance of my total being. It's a way for me to heal as needed, awaken when lulled, and will myself into the most authentic expression of who I am.

More than 15 years ago, I started my studies with Dr. Levry, Master Universal Kabbalist and founder of Naam Yoga. Through my studies with him I came to a deeper understanding of my own energetic imprint, which is strongly aspected to Venus. I was born on the day of romantic exaltation. This in large part explains the comfort I draw from harmony, the arts, beauty, femininity and fashion.

Little did I know that Cinderella was about to go to the ball. Nearly 30 years later, my greatest comfort was to come once again through the gateway of fashion.

I was in the middle of a divorce, and preparing for a four-day black-tie wedding halfway around the world in Cape Town, South Africa, when I met my Fashion Angel. His inspiration, love, and cultivation of me would literally change my life. So, minus the manipulation, exploitation, or paternalism, he is the Svengali to my Trilby and the Professor Higgins to my Eliza.

When I met him, my marriage was imploding. Eleven years

up in suffocating smoke. I was shaking in my boots; unable to see my head and heart clearly through what was happening to me. *To us.* But there was no longer an "us" in my marriage. There was only my fractured self, thick ash, and blinding smoke.

My recipe for healing emotional devastation is to travel both figuratively and literally. Crying and red wine help a lot too. Luckily I am surrounded by the most amazing friends. In the midst of this I was being pulled out of New York and given assignments to teach in Brussels, Berlin, and Le Vésinet outside Paris. My niece joked that for her auntie, *an airplane equals a car.*

The truth is that my marriage had been over for at least four years before I decided to divorce. So many people asked me, *why did you stay?* You are powerful, you're successful . . . *why?* But, the truth is, that a lot of our life worked in the practical sense. My niece who had been abused and abandoned by her own father was quite close to my ex-husband. Having also been devastated by my father as a child, I couldn't bear to do anything that would further destabilize her world.

The other mitigating factor was that I could compartmentalize and lose myself in my in my spiritual studies, my business, my niece, and my own healing. Our apartment was quite big. I holed up in the master bedroom. He stayed in the office/second bedroom. As I was recovering from the hysterectomy surgery and the marriage was falling down around us, I was *cleared to fly* by my doctor. In retrospect, being "cleared to fly" was both literal and metaphorical. The symbolism of it all was interesting when I was able to center and be neutral. And fly I did.

But it was only a matter of months before I was unable to live for a child, even one that I loved so deeply as my niece. My personal reality had become like a fun house at an amusement park. There were trick doors and mirrors that distorted and blocked the way to the exit. More than a fun house, for a time, I felt like I had been dropped into an abyss with no clear way out.

The duality of my life, how it looked on the outside and the reality of what it really was from the inside, were two opposing realities. I am a woman who is comfortable in my body. I had always really enjoyed intimacy. But the time came when I didn't want him to even touch me, and I was relieved when he no longer did. I couldn't stand the way he smelled. It was the stench of one big whopping lie.

I knew we weren't connected. But I didn't know how to get out of it because we had built a whole existence together. That's the gift of the veil lifting. As devastating as it was, the veil lifting provided me with the clarity to justify why I wanted out. In a sense I was waiting for some sort of catalyst. What I missed most was my absolute trust in my own judgment. I kept asking myself, *how could I have married him in the first place?* The answer came when I was meditating. I wanted to be married, he wanted someone who would take care of him and look good on paper. But it was never true love.

It was in the midst of this dark period of my life that I was preparing to fly to Cape Town, South Africa for my dear friend's wedding. In preparation for the wedding, I buried myself in fashion magazines. I was desperate for some connection to beauty. As I had done as a young child, I would fixate on beautiful images and archetypal energies of non-traditional women who weren't considered typically beautiful, but were recognized for being iconic influencers. I became obsessed with Gabrielle Chanel. I read the art high fashion magazines. I was going half way across the world to South Africa *by myself.* Over the course of my marriage we had always traveled a lot, so I was used to going to far flung places. But even though my husband had been invited as well, I told him to stay home.

Four days, black tie, on a continent in a country far, far away. The symbolism of South Africa wasn't lost on me. I have read every book ever written on Nelson Mandela and am obsessed with him and the history of the country. Now I was going there. Somehow I knew this trip was both the door and the key to a deep healing of the break in my confidence. It was a chance to center, create, and feel my way back into a new life.

When I meditated I would ask God for help. I asked him to make manifest a guide for this literal and figurative journey that lay ahead of me. I asked for help getting dressed for this wedding. I knew this wedding was going to be beyond posh. My friend had pointedly asked me and all of her friends to really dress. Out of respect for her, out of respect for the sacredness of true love, I was determined to show up for her.

I knew that if I could, in some way I would be showing up for myself. Showing up on my own was significant, since my dear friend and my then husband had known each other for years. In fact, it was because of him that we had met it the first place. There would be many people there who knew us as a couple. My presence, on my own, was a way of signaling to the world that I was willing to let the past be past, and step fully into my new life. Cinderella was going to the ball.

One day, midsummer in 2013, I walked into a jewel box of a store in my neighborhood and burst into tears. I couldn't handle preparing for the wedding. The end of a marriage is a death, and to be stepping into a wedding was really overwhelming. I was shattered, unsteady, and could no longer find solace in my compartmentalized comfort zones. A single crack had run through them all and shattered my whole reality. I surrendered, and wept. This is when I first met my Fashion Angel, when he walked up to help me in his store.

My Fashion Angel is so much more than a stylist. He is a creative force of nature. His emotional intelligence is off the hook and he is also a very direct man. For him and me, fashion is about so much more than the external. He immediately understood that this was about something much bigger than buying a designer dress. It was about block-by-block regaining my center, rebuilding my confidence. This required both coddling and pushing me out of my comfort zone. It was about surrendering, and allowing myself to receive help. It was also about regaining my ability to trust myself, and my choices around who I let close to me.

Working with my Fashion Angel, who had been style director of Bloomingdales, and was also a top stylist and designer gave me something to focus on. It shifted my focus to the future, and moved me from being a victim to being a powerful creator.

Not surprisingly, every time I met with my Fashion Angel, he pushed me out of my comfort zone by dragging my focus back into the present moment. He was supporting my rebirth, something that required me being fully present to the moment. He had me trying on things, including Japanese designers, Commes de Garcon, Junya Wantanabe, Issey Miyake, that I would simply never have imagined I could wear. He gracefully pushed the envelope putting me in the avant garde and then balancing it with vintage Yves St Laurent, Sonia Rykiel, and Loewe, balancing the Japanese avant garde with French louche chic. Feminine, but not trying too hard. I found it both grounding and expanding in the discovery of my full and true self.

We rebuilt my confidence block by block. This incredible man, and his eye for my untraditional beauty, helped me clock my energetic frequency from one of contraction and despair to one of hope and creativity.

While I still had to navigate a messy divorce, magic started to happen. I went to South Africa, and returned steadier than when I left. I dressed to the nines out of respect for my own journey, and that of my friend, who had vowed she would never get married. Putting 100 percent effort into my outfits for the wedding was an extension of me showing up for her. It was also my way of showing her the deep love and respect I have for her. It was also the beginning of me going out into the world in very high circles on my own as a single woman. Cinderella had a seat at the ball.

As the numbness wore off, through the magic of working with my Fashion Angel I woke up to and opened up to life again. The numb, shut down dead feeling went away. I started to trust myself again.

I began to relax and align with my true, highest self. I became more awake to life and to love. I opened my heart. The truth to this day is that I only wear what I feel great in, including my lingerie. I suggest that my clients do the same. How I look is secondary. It's about feeling safe, reassured, confident and centered. It's about me staying aligned with my true self.

When I returned home from South Africa, something deep had started to heal in me. I felt stronger and more ready for the battle to get divorced which despite having no property or children would take two years and a lot of negotiating. But meeting my Fashion Angel and the work we did for Africa had made me stronger, more in touch with being a powerful, sensual woman again.

When I got back, I continued to work with my Fashion Angel. One could say I'm a bit co-dependent. I don't buy anything except lingerie without consulting him. We collaborate constantly. It is so much fun and with each season, I have become stronger, more open to life, more receptive. And I continue to flourish both personally and professionally. My business has grown exponentially since I connected with my Fashion Angel. Yes, our work helps me get out of my comfort zone on multiple levels. It gives me the confidence to hold my own with a CEO client who is on the world stage and frequents Davos.

Building my wardrobe means continuing to clock my frequency higher and higher. As Einstein says, "everything is energy." Having a wardrobe that works creates an ease in my life and helps me to be focused and more secure in my own skin.

I remember a top photographer I was dating said, I can't compete with him. He sees you, he knows you, he is propelling you forward in ways I cannot. That is, even though I'm the one who is literally inside you. We had a good laugh over this. But still, he was threatened by my Fashion Angel. I understand because there is some cosmic, dharmic soul connection between us.

All this also taught me about another layer of being intimate. My work with my Fashion Angel had opened the door to me calling sensitive, creative, successful men into my life. This helped me let go of old beliefs around who I am supposed to be with, and the type of man who could hold space and hold me safe in an intimate relationship.

When I met my photographer, he had seen me on a bus. He didn't know who I was. He is something of a global citizen who works with and knows a lot of renown people. To this day he tells me that his attraction to me was something intangible. "I was so drawn to you I couldn't help myself. I had to have you," he told me. We loved each other for a time deeply and profoundly. I would never have felt safe or confident enough to let him in, to literally receive him, without the help of my Fashion Angel who not only rebuilt my confidence, but also shepherded me through the waxing and waning of my love relationship with this complicated artist. Wearing what feels good creates a receptivity to love and to life. It helps take down the armoring and opens me to playfulness, creativity and more. It helps me to relax and embrace my life.

But the experience gave me the confidence to love unconditionally.

Through my Fashion Angel's guidance, I am taken to another level of understanding of myself. We continue to work together and our work continues to raise my consciousness. He keeps me focused and clear about who I am in the world. It is a spiritual, heart opening experience. He is a gift from God. His guidance has been as healing and expansive as the spiritual work I do. Working with him is a transcendental spiritual experience in and of itself.

My fashion Angel helped me see myself clearly. He also helped me see my future. He dressed me to meet my future.

People may think fashion is frivolous. But, of course, all of us get dressed. What we wear is an extension of who we are – part of our interface with the social matrix. Unless one resides in a nudist colony, dressing cannot be avoided. It's not about how much the clothes cost, labels, or trends. It's about understanding yourself, who you are, and deeply connecting to that true self. It's about having the courage to express that self in order to contribute to the world.

Like everything else, clothes hold an energy, a frequency that is either filled with light or not. From my perspective, getting dressed is about showing respect for the world, for yourself. When it works well, it moves you closer to the Light. This has been my experience.

Clothes make a statement about who I am in the world. Since people and social cues are so often visual, the statement matters.

Clothes magnetize or repel. It has nothing to do with being a size or a body type. It has to do with aligning with true self. It is evident when someone feels comfortable in their clothes. Mine are selected with intention, care and love and that vibration surrounds me when I put them on.

When I get dressed I feel loved. I also feel the powerful energy of creative people who influenced the world through fashion. Yves St Laurent, Ann Demeulemeester, and Gabriel Chanel all in their way liberated women. Liberation, freedom and expansion I correlate to the energy of love. Love is such a powerful thing. This love keeps me attuned. Being well dressed is a layer of being comfortable in my own skin. Clients have remarked that they feel respected and appreciate the effort I put into my appearance when I meet them. It's part of showing up fully, placing how I look, my heart, and my intellect all in the service of supporting them. Being comfortable in my own skin helps them to relax also. When they relax then we can really dive into the business at hand.

From the day I met my Fashion Angel, I have not made one false step. My clothes work for me. My life works for me.

I have been told that I am beautiful, but the truth is I am not conventionally beautiful. I'm not an easily accessible type of beauty. My beauty is more a Modigliani beauty that is reflects an intellect's or creative person's choice in a woman. I'm hard to pin down which appeals to a certain type of man – mostly high-powered entrepreneurs or creative types.

My fashion Angel magnetized this frequency by making my outer image congruent with my inner self and values. What does this mean?

Knowing that I never make a misstep in my wardrobe choices makes me more confident. It's amazing what opens up when you don't have to think about getting dressed. When you know that everything you put on works to maximum impact and benefit.

Fashion matters. Style matters. It's not about trends, being a certain size, or being something other than myself. On the contrary, it's about being exactly who I am. It's about expressing who I am on the inside on through to the outside. It projects a congruence of self, and makes me confidently happy. Priceless.

Chapter 17

Ambition, Money & Success

There are people who have money and people who are rich.
~Coco Chanel

Recently, I was on the phone with an associate from the yoga world. We were discussing an upcoming retreat in Mexico. She was giving me the selling points: private room on the water, all inclusive resort, classes all day long, a chance to evolve, people from all over the world. Recharge. Contribute to raising the vibratory frequency of the earth by chanting mantra. And last but not least she said, "I'll give you the early-bird pricing."

She's a lovely woman and as she hit the selling points I had a couple of internal responses. Private room on the water — *sounds good to me, check*. But the phrase, *all inclusive resort* sent shivers down my spine. I pictured being trapped in a pastel paradise surrounded by hundreds of my "closest" friends – *sounds cont*rived. And tending toward the introverted side hundreds of people in one place feels slightly overwhelming.

Evolving, well, I know where she's going with that word. But I feel like I'm already in a constant state of evolution. Since 2012 my life has actually felt like one of accelerated evolution. Major surgery and divorce, seemingly rent the spiritual fabric I'd been weaving, since I was a child. I had come to an evolutionary crossroads. I had exhausted all alternatives, but transformation. Yes, I experienced major life-altering events. Like it or not, I am *evolving*.

I embrace evolving just by living life, enjoying life, and fully opening to life. This is my next evolutionary practice. Life is continually raising my consciousness. I feel I am working with the most amazing high-frequency clients and being blessed to have the most amazing, kundalini sacred sexual exchanges with my beloved. The latter has been something quite profound, because after the surgery I wasn't sure that I would ever be able to open myself to that degree again.

As for the yoga retreat, the meditating sounds amazing. I'v seen the powerful effects of mantra in my life, in my clients, and in my city. The block where the first Naam Yoga studio was on 24th Street went from being rundown to being one of the poshest blocks in the city in the span of ten years. It's not an accident that mantra was also being chanted around the clock on that block. An energetic shift seemed to take place even in the immediate area.

Then there is early-bird pricing.

I appreciate a deal as much as anyone, but getting a deal isn't my primary decision influencer. If I want something, an experience, a piece of jewelry, an item of clothing, I am happy to pay for it. I guess I consider it an investment in myself and I think I'm a good investment with a high rate of return.

Something being cheaper doesn't make me want it more. In fact, if I wouldn't buy it at the full price then a cheaper price won't change my mind, unless, of course, it's an airline ticket. When I have been in Europe, I've been known to switch my flight to route through Paris to get a cheaper ticket. But really that was about Paris first and the cheaper price second.

The truth is my relationship to money is different than most peoples. I am very ambitious in the sense that I want whatever I engage my energy in to matter to me. What matters to me is to be a complete woman who knows how to live fully awake. When I am living in alignment with this intention, I feel most secure, centered and grounded. Financial security in the traditional sense is not something I've strived for as an end in itself. Perhaps that's because I'm born under the sign of Cancer, the Divine Mother and a cardinal water sign. It is perhaps the most emotionally sensitive sign in the zodiac. I feel my way through life aided by intuition and emotional intelligence and the merging of projective, protective intelligence with the first tow.

Having said that, I also have been blessed with the energy of Jupiter on my destiny line. Jupiter is the lord of material and spiritual prosperity. This blessing has probably also given me the imprint of knowing and believing that I will always be provided for. This belief has been born out.

My hyper-awareness of time passing quickly has also probably contributed. Knowing that the clock is ticking is something I have been acutely aware of since my mom first said to me, "Who will take care of you, if something happens to me?" Seriously, I don't think this is something to ask an eight year-old. But I'm grateful, even though I experienced it as something pretty scary. My thought at the time was also *God, I hope it's not Dad. He's a workaholic and he drinks and smokes too much.* He was also never home. Later, I would find out he was never home because he was a functioning addict and one of the Pioneer Valley's greatest womanizers. So from my mom I got the idea that her time and mine and everyone else's was limited. So better make the most of it.

When I was younger, making the most of it became defined as being the best I could be at whatever I engaged in. Today that means *whatever I engage my energy in.* Even then, I would rather be by myself than with people I didn't find interesting. After all, I could always find something interesting in one of my books, or looking at a painting in the Smith College art museum, or just lying on my bed spacing out to the Rolling stones, the Beatles, John Coltrane or Rick Springfield.

I applied myself but was very picky where and when and with whom. But when I chose to participate I was all in. I'd get up at 4:00 in the morning to be in a pool training for 2 hours before going to school. Sure, why not? But the Massachusetts winters are long and cold, and there were definitely chilly mornings when my mom woke me up long before dawn, such that I thought, *What the hell am I doing this for?* But I would grab a can of Diet Coke *(eeeewww)* to get my caffeine hit and head off to the Smith College pool. I wasn't allowed to have coffee but I was a Diet Coke to give me a caffeine jolt, enough to get me in the pool. Have you ever seen what's in a diet coke? A coffee would have been a lot better.

Later in life, I quit the 4:00 a.m. bit after one year of competing in Division II college swimming. Fast forward to adulthood, and I started to get a deeper awareness that for me ambition was synonymous with passion and excelling. I realized that I am incapable of doing things half way. I am either engaged or not. My greatest ambition is to have a Technicolor life. To fully open to life, to fully love.

To fulfill this ambition, I have gotten a lot more comfortable being out of my comfort zone. *Out of my comfort zone* was imprinted in me from the beginning of my life. The very nature of my existence, the year I came into the world, 1965, was out of everyone's comfort zones. The country was in the middle of social upheaval related to race. Many states still had miscegenation laws on the books. In many places in the country it was literally illegal for my parents to be married, and in most places even where these laws didn't exist there were rigid social codes that essentially equated it to the same thing. My existence, by virtue of my parents union, put me *out of my comfort zone* from the very beginning.

I believe that when I was born the fact that I was light and bright softened the blow. I have green eyes. These green eyes of mine seemed to mystify people and hold a currency all their own. People would say, *Where did she get those eyes?* It would seem that green eyes are as uncommon as my existence.

From the time I was a child, ambition and excelling were loaded. They were tied to something bigger than money. Being the best, excelling would prove everyone wrong. Excelling would prove that to be bi-racial wasn't a curse. It would disprove anyone's notion that being bi-racial meant that you were screwed up and lost without an identity.

So I applied myself. The fact that I have Mars in my chart as my primary planet gave me the strength and determination to overcome a lot. Much emotional abuse and abandonment in my home life left some gaping wounds that took considerable deep work to heal in life. On the upside, however, it gave me the fire in my belly. Whenever anyone suggested that I couldn't do something, it was as if a switch went on and I would think, *Watch me.*

It also gave me the determination to win. I refused to give up or give in. Even in the most absurd situations. I remember my mother's brother, one of the most racist people on the planet, asking me to run with him when we were visiting him in Maryland in the summer. As an adult now, I ask myself, *Why were we even there?*

I was an athlete/scholar and I thought, *Why not?* So I ran with him. I hate running to this day. As an ex-military man and NSA egghead, the guy was missing a heart, especially where his "black" niece was concerned. He was merciless on that run. I knew, as children know in an unfiltered way, that he didn't like me and was trying to make me quit. Well, I finished that 5 miles, and collapsed from exhaustion when we finally reached the house. But I didn't quit. I refused to give him that satisfaction. I remember my mom beaming at this accomplishment. As a grown woman, I would never allow my niece or any child I love to be targeted by that kind of energy.

So the ambition and excelling imprint started at a young age. Money, of course, came along with it. First, it came to me in NYC as a young advertising executive. I was hand picked by the president of the Agency to pitch a new piece of business with him. I was 23 years old. And as luck would have it, my "mad man" of a boss who routinely had 3 martini lunches didn't return to the office that afternoon. Even though I was shaking in my boots, I killed my piece of the pitch and we won the business. Plus I got a raise I didn't expect, even if I'd only expected to win.

It was different from my boyfriend's ambition. He was a banker and also a former competitive athlete. He wanted to win and he wanted to make a lot of money. For him the two were interlinked. For me the money came as a logical extension of excelling and being my best but it wasn't my primary motivator. I realized when I was in that business that my "ambition" wasn't winning. My primary motivator was that I hated losing.

I liked money and intuitively knew it made things easier. But even at a young age when I was new in NYC and just beginning my career life, I couldn't just do things for money. I had to connect with the energy and feel it in my heart; otherwise, I would space out and ultimately fail. This is what happened when I worked for L'Oreal corporate in marketing. I was passionate about being in a French environment but I couldn't connect to the products. They were, and still are, loaded with chemicals. *Just Crap*. Their corporate culture was equally polluted.

It was when I was working there that I started to ask myself the bigger life questions like, *What is success anyway?* Is it really just a resume, benefits, a consistent paycheck, a house in the suburbs and two weeks off? It was clear that I didn't want a house in the suburbs or a country club lifestyle. The routine and predictability, not to mention the associated isolation of housing tracts, made me cringe. Meanwhile, commuting back and forth every day on the LIRR, Amtrak, Metro North or NJ Transit equated to hell. Not for me. I loved New York and Paris. I liked being respected professionally and the nice paycheck that came along with it. But I wanted more. The external trappings of *success* weren't enough to make me feel *successful*. Everything I had been conditioned to believe was success didn't feel like it. I had left my fiancé, so I knew having the good-looking successful guy in and of itself wasn't enough either.

So I set out to define success on my own terms which indirectly turned into defining who I am. Then it became aligning life to fit my true self. What I discovered was that my relationship with money was very different from other peoples', including people who had a lot more success than I did.

I didn't seem to worry about it, and I seemed to always be able to manifest more of it when I needed it. Granted I wasn't reckless.

I saved money. I had a 401k. I never bought an apartment. But I think that was because of my fear of committing to the responsibility of a mortgage without a husband. It wasn't a clear rationale for a successful single woman but that was the space I was in. Later on, when I got divorced, I was so grateful that there was no property to split up.

What I also realized was my own power regarding money. I trust my ability to provide value in the world and I trust my internal compass to reveal opportunities. A fair exchange is about energy exchange. It's not an accident that I am compensated well for what I do. I see it as connected to an open heart and traditional feminine traits, including receptivity, playfulness and healthy boundaries. I require and allow myself to receive proper compensation and I have fun doing it. My clients would say that we play and have fun even when we are birthing something difficult. Somewhere in our meetings we laugh at least once.

Perhaps this is what is different about my relationship to money. I view money as an exchange of energy. I don't apply much more importance to it than that. That's still significant, since everything *is* energy. But I've learned not to buy into a lower frequency just because it has money attached to it. I am comfortable with the exchange of energy in both directions. I continue to like to win and to intend to excel. But that's not just in business, it's also in love. What does it mean to exchange energy in my relationships? I intend my exchanges to be at a high frequency of light, exchanges that are bi-directional and balanced. I will release or block energy (read *money*) that doesn't serve me without blinking an eye or looking back. High frequency energy is my primary currency. When I move in a high-frequency economy, it all feels clean and clear. Energy is abundant and it flows.

Chapter 18

The Lost Girls

You open your heart knowing that there's a chance it may be broken one day and in opening your heart, you experience a love and joy that you never dreamed possible. You find that being vulnerable is the only way to allow your heart to feel true pleasure that's so real it scares you.

~ Bob Marley

Fourth of July, 2015. I am meeting my Jackie O for dinner. My Jackie O is a global citizen based in Manhattan also. An art consultant and curator, she is chic with a capital C. She lives downtown but has a decidedly uptown vibe. Oscar de la Renta and Carine Gilson are two of her favorites. She also wears Chanel. I wear the latter also, but I lean toward Fifi Chachnil for my lingerie. Over dinner, we both lament and laugh about the lingerie famine in this chic city of ours. Lingerie is something NYC doesn't do very well. It may be the only thing. This is a city that prides itself on being the best. Now my client and friend from Calvin Klein tells me that they have just hired a lingerie designer from Paris. Great news, my Jackie O and I laugh over the prospect at dinner. Yes! Keep hope for a great, sexy black bra alive!

An uptown girl and a downtown girl. My Jackie O is decidedly uptown, and I'm decidedly downtown, but we both are global citizens with fathers who abandoned us. We share those scars, and we've both shared in their healing. It's something we understand about each other, and not just each other. Our radar is sharp to recognize the energy in others. This father wound stuff is a tricky one that leaves its mark in subtle ways under the visible surface. On the up side, it makes me hyper-aware of staying close to the Goddess -- of vigilantly honoring her within myself.

I don't chase anything or anyone. That's a mantra that we both share; the same perspective on being a Goddess. Maybe it's the case because all the praying, pleading, and primping didn't make our fathers stay. It didn't save them from choosing the darkness.

I have learned to hold a little back until the intimacy's earned. I think of it as staying close to my soul. I let a few people into my inner life. I talk to *God/Goddess* before bed. My heart doesn't conform to shadows. I stay close to the Light. My Jackie O and I have opinions about what it means to be a certain kind of woman. And those shared opinions bond us. We share a properness coupled with irreverence for the ironies and complexities of life. Both of our lives have been odysseys.

We are going to a party in her prewar building. We both live in iconic prewar buildings -- the kind that are occupied by a certain sort of person. The kind that is hard to get into, lived in a long time, and rarely left. Proper doormen are the sentries of these buildings, and they are considered part of the community in the building. Our buildings don't have lots of turnover or craziness.

The party we're heading to tonight is in the penthouse of her building. The host, a man in his 40s, has invited the tenants. They are welcome to bring friends. We think, *why not?* After our dinner, we arrive later than we expected. That night's fireworks have passed, but that's ok. They were shot over the East Side, and we are West Side girls. We heard the boom over dinner, but didn't see the sparkles.

We grab a bottle of Pimm's and head up to the penthouse. This is where we find the lost girls. The energy of the lost girls is so jolting that we feel disembodied. They are women, younger than either of us by far, everywhere. They are most likely educated and from a certain background, but they are depleted. They look at the two of us like we are aliens. When my Jackie O asks for the host, they just shrug and say nothing. We try to pass into the large sitting room. They stand. We repeat, *excuse us*, as we walk through. They don't move.

The lost girls have the desperate vibe that women, regardless of age, have when they are seeing themselves as not enough -- seeing themselves into *objects* to be desired or not desired by men. They have commoditized themselves. Now I feel like they're standing around like furniture to be used, or moved, rolled, repositioned, bumped into, or walked around.

Out of the corner of her eye, my Jackie O sees the host taking a lost girl into the bathroom. He looks like a predator and she looks like the prey. Her lost-girl friends seem excited that she is going off with him -- going off with the older *penthouse* guy. The energy is so dense and heavy. The energetic field feels muddy. The men look drunk and the women look depleted. They have lost their radiance. I want to tell them there is a difference between "trading" and "connecting."

There is also a smell we both pick up on no one else seems to notice. It is one of the most disgusting smells we've ever smelled. It's dank, depleted, and devoid of Light. Kind of shocked, we go up to the roof for fresh air and we see the Empire State Building dressed in red, white and blue for the holiday. She is beautiful and a striking counterpoint to the lost girls.

We go back down into the penthouse and see more lost girls. What are they wearing? -- Desperate looking expressions in outfits that are cut way too short on the bottom and way too low on the top. Their eyes look dull and their auras seem depleted. It's depressing and jolting.

We look at each other and say, *let's go*. My Jackie O puts the Pimm's on the countertop. We turn to go.

"Wait," I say. "Why are we leaving the Pimm's. They are drinking Coors Light, and won't even know what it is."

"I already put it down," she says, taking a step.

"Well, I'm picking it back up," I say, taking it with us on the way to the door.

We go back to my Jackie O's apartment, which always feels like an elegant, spiritual refuge, but even more so now. We are both a bit shell-shocked. We want to rescue them and at the same time are repelled by them. The overriding feeling, though, is shock and sadness.

The day after I'm sitting on my roof with a friend of mine, a French African and former model. She tells me that she too sees the lost girls all around this city. She is also 50 and says to me, "What the fuck. The girls of this generation, they think they're so powerful but they are so *gone* — they are so *lost*. Do you see the way they behave. Do you hear the way they speak?" And then we both shake our heads. Something is happening with Gen Y…is it exclusive to Gen Y? Is it all the internet porn, the celebrity obsession, Kim Kardashian getting famous with a sex tape? We can't pinpoint it but there are so many lost girls.

Every now and then one makes her way to my Wednesday class and I feel hope for her. If she makes it to a Naam Yoga class, her internal candle is still lit somewhere in her. But the lost girls who want to stay lost never come back to the class. Truth is, we all need to respect free will. Plus no one can save any of us. To be luscious we need to *choose* to heal and save ourselves. To walk freely to the temple of Light.

As I reflect on the lost girls of the Fourth of July, I want to take all of them home with me, if only for a moment. I want to invite them into the energy of love and compassion to help them know they don't have to settle for crumbs -- that they are children of the Goddess. That they are loved.

But it's not our place to say anything to them; and we know that if we tried, they couldn't hear it anyway. If they couldn't hear me say, *Excuse me*, they certainly couldn't hear me ask, *Why have you abandoned your Goddess?* There was nothing to be shared. So, we said goodbye to the lost girls up there in the predatory mood of the Penthouse, and we walked away with our Pimm's — returning to the Goddess vibrations of our own realm.

Chapter 19

No Sleepwalking

I was told I was different and I felt out of place. And then one day I realized something I hope you all realize. Different is good.

~ Angelina Jolie

I have always loved how God sends his Divine messages through people. I see the unseen and have prophesy dreams and powerful visions. I also notice how the Higher world continually works through people sending Divine messages through people.

Over the past few years that I've taught Naam Yoga for Women every Wednesday night on the Upper West Side, I've noticed a pattern. My students tell me that messages often come to them when they get out of class, following the closing meditation. I have repeatedly heard that they feel lighter, experiencing a clearing and a clarity. Something tangible shifts for them and their lives change in big and small ways.

It is the power of the teachings, and we are all deeply grateful for the gift of this powerful wisdom. By design, the class has distilled a vast spiritual science into the tools and techniques that best serve women by helping them rediscover and merge with their true selves. If that wasn't enough, the Dalai Lama and other living spiritual leaders have said that the Western woman will save the world. No pressure, ladies.

Women who come to the class, connect to the potential of the Divine Feminine Goddess energy within themselves in a way that is both sustainable and practical. This is a powerful time to connect with the Divine Feminine energy, as it's been said that since December 21, 2012, this is the energy that will guide humanity to its greatest healing.

I like to think that the Wednesday class is a portal for magic and the unlocking of the great mystery of what it means to be a fully alive and aligned 21st century woman. It feels like we are emerging into an era of enlightenment. It is a time where we can heal anything that blocks the heart connection to each other and higher worlds. From the darkness to the dawn. The class is one of the spiritual portals that supports women going out in the world centered in their Shakti – the creative primordial force that is said to move the entire Universe.

Many students have had remarkable blessings following the class. One woman set her intention to create a phenomenal love relationship. Intending to *"Call in the One."* She came to the class religiously, every week, sitting in the front row for a month. Following the fourth week, she went to Communal, the organic restaurant underneath the studio. Communal's owner also practices Naam Yoga and meditation.

I always clock the class to the unseen energetic forces that are at play, including the moon cycles (waxing and waning); the energy that rules Wednesday is mercury and when combined with a waxing moon (the energy for expansion and manifestation) we can unleash the power of the world to make dreams manifest. Typically, the class has 10 to 20 people in it.

This particular night to close the class we invoked the powerful mantra, *Har Haree Hare.* That night, everyone left floating. Our said student, a woman in her late 50s, floated out of class and into the arms of the man who would become her Beloved. They met after the class while she was drinking a green juice. She never came back to the class, and that doesn't matter at all. What matters is that she was able to open to life in a way that is much bigger -- to have a deeper reverence for herself as a child of God. She shifted her consciousness from playing small to playing big. She clocked her frequency to the frequency of what she wanted in her life and she manifested it.

I believe she manifested it because the class put her in her body, connecting her with her radiance and creative power. She connected deeply with her true self and her energetic field expanded.

Many moons later, I was sitting with another woman, who I had mentored through my work with WorldPulse. She was visiting from Washington, DC and had just gone through a lot in the past few months. Over that time her mom had come down sick with cancer, and she'd had a hard break-up with her boyfriend. Even though we don't see each other that frequently, when we do it's as though we're picking up a thread from yesterday. Our bond doesn't skip a beat. She opened up about her ex-boyfriend. It was clear that she was still shaken, so much so that she had become a bit disembodied, and all up in her head. Analysis paralysis often occurs when we are afraid of being hurt, rejected or just unable to make sense of things. The trouble is that many of the great mysteries aren't unraveled intellectually; they are deciphered through what I call heart wisdom.

She was spinning. This is the space that women can go to when they are hurt -- the all-men-are-*fill-in-the-blank* space. All men are dicks. All men are out for themselves. All men are afraid to commit. Etc. The cliché moral for women hurting like this everywhere: I don't need a man, I'm going to focus on my *fill-in-the-blank*.

I know this space well. I've lived it, and witnessed it many times with my female clients. It's the default, defended position. It's born out of a pain that is so deep that it is almost unbearable. The trouble is that remaining in this place isolates us in a mindset of control under the guise of independence. Living there is more than cutting us off from our feeling nature. It neuters us. Maybe we achieve status and professional success from this hyper-focus on the internal dialog, on the internal chatter of the social mind, but we won't achieve peace.

We were sitting at Communal talking, and I was encouraging her to not take it personally -- to use the experience of the break-up as a wakeup call. I was encouraging her to ask the Divine Intelligence to explain to her what had happened, so that she could make sense of it all and heal.

They say that if you ask the Architect of the Universe, you will be shown. It's a proven intention: ask and ye shall receive; knock and the door shall be open. In that moment she did ask, and then the owner walked over. He and his wife own Communal together. He is a great guy. Great looking, global citizen, fun, and deeply spiritual. He is also a MAN with a capital "M – A – N."

The polarity dance between men and women is always interesting. There is something so powerful about a man reminding a woman that she is a Goddess. That she is seen, valued, and respected.

He came over and started talking to us about how heartbreaking it is for him to watch how women behave in the restaurant. They have walked so far away from their essence, he was saying. He spoke of how this contributes to "sleepwalking" in the world. How he felt so strongly that when women are disconnected from themselves and settle for crumbs, how it contributes to the world being asleep. Then he spoke of how *"men need to step up, and women need to wake up, and everyone needs to stop sleepwalking!"*

He encouraged her to hold her center and not take the breakup personally. He reassured her that her work was to get really clear about what she wanted, but at the same time to never close her heart to love.

He spoke with such reverence about his wife. He also confessed to having been a sleepwalker himself. *He asked, How many women can you sleep with and how much money can you have, before you wake up and realize that you are a vampire surrounded by vampires? That was eventually the question I had to ask myself.*

From his perspective, it wasn't a woman's job to save men or "make it better" for them. He felt that a woman's job was to hold the frequency that inspires men to "wake up" and stop sleepwalking. He said if someone isn't ready to wake up, walk away. He spoke of how he believed that women hold the center of creation. When his sons were born he connected with this profound truth. He referenced what happens to societies where women don't hold men to a standard for being better men. He said that men dishonor themselves when they lower themselves to the level of the sleepwalker, becoming sleepwalkers themselves.

"Stick with the light of being a woman," he said, "and don't worry about losing a boyfriend. The right man will come, the one who will choose the Light. He is already looking for you, I guarantee it. Every man is looking for this Light – the Light of the Divine Feminine frequency." (Even in same sex couples there is typically one person that holds this frequency). "Just do your spiritual work and stay in your heart."

This man married a woman who is so connected to the Light of the Divine Feminine Goddess. He spoke eloquently about how she inspired him to wake up to being a better man. At 44, he spoke about his younger years. "I used women who didn't have healthy boundaries -- women who enabled and put up with my nonsense."

He said, "Stick with Kelley. She has so much Light that all the men want to take her class too. Seriously, I'm telling you, she holds the frequency that makes us all want to do better, be better. She holds that Light and you can too."

And then he looked at her and said, "Do you get what I'm saying?" At that moment she looked so inspired and so much lighter. And I laughed and said, "I'm going to have you teach the women's class. I think women need to hear it from a man who is straight, good looking, and married with children." I wasn't kidding. His message was powerful, healing, and resonant. When he was done he moved on to chat with other people in the restaurant.

A man had spoken. But this moment was the power of the word in action. This was a moment that had transformed someone's life. He spoke the truth from a very high level, with such conviction and power that it was evident that an energy much bigger than all of us was working through him.

Chapter 20

The Tooth Fairy is Real. She Cleans my Teeth.

Just let awareness have its way with you completely.

~Scott Morrison

When was the last time you put a tooth under your own pillow? I trust it's been a while. As a child there was always some magic to the expectation of it all. Even the act of exchanging something for a tooth under a child's pillow has something of the same magic. I remember as a child being a bit awestruck at the transformation of the missing tooth. But where did they go after that?

I remember one day while my mom and I were at the grocery store she opened her wallet to get change and there I saw a bunch of small white teeth. I asked, "Mom, what is that?" She said, "Darling, they are your teeth and your sister's." Heart reeling, I felt some seven-year-old version of *WTF*! How did they disappear from under my pillow only to be found in my mom's wallet? Did that mean the tooth fairy and mom had a relationship of some kind? Were mom, the tooth fairy, and I all interconnected across the cosmos? How was it all connected? It wasn't like the gig was totally blown for me at that moment. But I did start to wonder right then and there, *Just how deep does this rabbit hole go?*

Fast forward to adulthood and a real live tooth fairy appears to me in the flesh. She is leaning over me, cleaning my teeth. I came to her through a Harmonyum Healing client I worked with to help her ease her anxiety. She would come once a week to see me for healing energy work. After a few treatments she started talking about what she called her *Tooth Fairy*. At the time, I had been looking for someone to clean my teeth since the hygienist who had cleaned them for 20 years had recently given up her practice. On my last appointment with her she had confided with me that she had finally had enough. She had decided, now in her late 70's, to retire.

I am a relationship-based person. I invest in people and it's challenging for me to do anything or engage in any activity unless I feel connected. I'm really sensitive to energy. For instance, on the road to the Tooth Fairy I tried a hygienist in one of the fancy practices here in NYC. I walked into a posh practice on Madison Avenue between 57th and 58th.

The office was gorgeous and the energy was bad. First, they kept me waiting for 45 minutes. Not a winning start with a new patient. Next the woman who was cleaning my teeth was asking me questions while she had the metal hooks in my mouth and, as she asked questions, she simultaneously said, "watch the television, it will distract you." I didn't even know her, how could she presume to know what would *distract* me? That was nearly as irritating as the blood pooling in my mouth, and the drum-like repetition of "you have a lot of tarter and plaque." I wanted to say, "No kidding! Don't you think I know that by all the blood I'm spitting out of my mouth?" But between the blood and the hooks and her incessant yapping about watching television I just tried to breathe. I thought, This too shall pass. Then the dentist popped in to tell me how much cosmetic dentistry I needed, and how my jaw was in the wrong place. Okay, I think it's nice to have a relationship before being told everything wrong with my teeth, jaw etc. It felt like scare tactics to get me to sign up for a lot of unnecessary dental work. I left feeling annoyed and uncared for. Who cares that they were written up in the "best of New York" pages of NY Magazine . . . Grumbly, I thought, Best at what?

So when I left I knew I was never going back. That moment coincided with my client's visit for her Harmonyum treatment. Harmonyum causes a shift in consciousness, an opening to elevated perception. So in answer to that frustration over who was going to clean my teeth a messenger delivered the message, *Go to the Tooth Fairy*.

My client was delivering the message waxing poetic about the Tooth Fairy. I was intrigued by the moniker. But even then, you couldn't have told me the Tooth Fairy was real. I knew better. I'd seen the teeth in my mother's purse.

Then, bam! Instant inspiration when I met the Tooth Fairy -- 72 and stunningly beautiful! I felt like she was looking right through me. We had a knowing smile exchange and a natural familiarity from the beginning. I had to give her a hug right in that moment. I knew we were connected.

From the beginning the Tooth Fairy had insights, "You have men around you and you just left your husband. He wasn't good for you anyway. No big loss. Actually a gift." This made me laugh. Then she said, "Am I right? I'm right. That's why you're laughing. Good you're laughing. That means you're healing." Then we both laughed and she said, "Rinse."

My first visit to the Tooth Fairy was just following my return from Europe. I was still in the last stages of finalizing the divorce. I hadn't gotten the final decree from the courts, but her saying what she said steadied me. She got me laughing about something that had been devastating. I was still trying to ground myself from the fall out. I felt like the Universe was speaking through her, reassuring me.

There is something powerful when someone I know well gives me an insight that resonates. But there is something particularly intense about someone I don't know at all seeing into my soul and calling it -- nailing it in a way that makes me know that God is working through people to support me. All I need to do is stay awake, pay attention, and listen. These moments I call *universal love and law in action.*

Next visit to the Tooth Fairy another message comes. With the suction hook in in my mouth she says, "Do you watch the Hallmark Channel? I don't usually. It's schmaltzy stuff, the Hallmark Channel. But last night I felt drawn to it. So I watched and there was a show about a man and a woman who met when they were in transition. One was separated and the other finalizing her divorce. In the movie the man had a small child. A daughter around 5 or 6 who was praying for a good Mommy and someone nice for her Daddy. She prayed on it. This little girl in her small body and powerful soul was longing for them to get back together. She wanted them back together and the Universe was listening. Now rinse." I rinse and I'm on the edge of my seat because she's speaking to my situation. She continues, "So anyway, the daughter kept wishing for them to be together and guess what. They ended up together. Maybe you should watch the Hallmark Chanel every now and then." I gasped. Rinse, please.

I gasped because just a few days before I was in my teacher's master Naam Yoga workshop. At one point he asked us all to pray for someone we loved. I settled into the mantra *ramadasa* with the full intention of praying for my sister and my niece. But a man I knew and his young daughter kept bumping them out of my field. Every time I closed my eyes to meditate I saw them. So I settled in and prayed for them. The man and his five-year-old daughter came to me every morning during my meditation.

As it happens, a woman I met in the Hamptons asked me unsolicited one day about who I was seeing. I told her that the man and child I loved weren't with me. I told her that he had freaked out and had to leave because his life was chaotic. I told her I had to let them go. She said, "They are your family and that by the middle of August you'll reconnect. By fall you will be together again. You can't stay apart. You're soul connected. Divinely connected by something bigger than both of you." Overwhelmed, I ordered another glass of wine and knocked it back.

The next day my friend asked me, "What happened with you guys? I told her and she said, "Don't forget about him. You love him. Don't close the door on miracles. Life isn't black and white. Let him know the door is still open."

The Universe sends us signs. I had been thinking about reaching out to him. We had not spoken for two months. My soul kept saying to me to reach out to him. But I was scared so I didn't'. But God has a way of not giving up on us even when we are scared to be vulnerable or feel like giving up. I had always felt that we had a contract that came from above. The way we met on the MTA bus, the way I could write after we made love, and then got a publishing contract. There was something bigger than the two of us at work from the beginning.

And while I know the Light respects free will, I also know it doesn't give up on humans so easily. It keeps leading us to where it wants us to be. I know that my internal system doesn't work so well when I don't listen. I get constipated, moody, unsettled, until I finally heed the call of Divine Intelligence. Since I am typically someone who is peaceful, that feeling which is not my usual state of being signals to me that something is going on that needs my attention. Guaranteed, I will get and stay "itchy" when this happens. I see that the messengers were there to shift my consciousness around the situation.

So I reached out to him and we reconnected. It was beautiful and still is. But I did need to listen to the messengers.

As it turns out, The Tooth Fairy is a Mermaid like me. Did I mention that I'm also a mermaid? Well, I am. We speak the same mystical language and we both pay attention to the signs. We both feel a heart connection to the moon and its cycles.

The Tooth Fairy tells me stories, and like me, many of her lessons come through men. Such is our life experience. I told her recently, "You're like me. You're a Goddess and men will always be around you. But you need to pay attention to your side of the fence in the sense of allowing them to care for you, and choosing wisely who you are going to receive. But allow yourself to receive and stay away from assumptions."

She asked me, "What are you?" I laughed . . . that has been the ongoing question of my life. A question I've been asked since I was a small child. I have an exoticism that is hard for people to pin down. Depending on my mood, I either welcome the question, get annoyed by it or just sigh and think here we go again.

The energy behind the Tooth Fairy's query was different though.

"I told you when we first met," I replied, "my bloodline, my lineage is Black and French."

The Tooth Fairy laughed and said, "I know that. I mean *who are you?*"

Then it dawned on me she was asking me where I got my superpowers – the prophecy dreams, the visions, the heightened intuitive capacity – all of that came from my fathers side.

Before I could say anything she said, "I know where you get IT. IT's on your father's side. Is there something else in there?"

"My Great Grandmother was a Cherokee Shaman," I said. "My dad used to always say to me, you're like Phoebe. You're going to help a lot of people . . ."

Then she said, "I knew it!" We both were silent. Then we both smiled. Then we both laughed. We both laughed a lot.

"Tell that publisher the book is going to be huge," she said. "There's going to be a movie deal. It's going to be a best seller. Mark my words. Rinse."

"What?" she said. "Why that look on your face?"

"He called me earlier and told me the same thing."

She said, "*See*, we know." Then she asked, "What did you do to your foot, to your right big toe?"

"Why do you ask?" I said, pressing back into the chair under the lights.

"Well," she said, looking into my mouth with a little mirror. "Your right molar is screwed up and it was totally fine on your last visit. So that tells me that you messed up the right side of your foot — most likely your right big toe."

So how was she supposed to know that while wearing a closed structured shoe, despite it being August, I had smashed my toe on a piece of concrete during my recent visit to Silicon Valley.

"You're not grounded there. It's not good for you. I bet every time you go out there something weird happens and you hurt yourself," she said, grabbing a suction hose.

She was right. Right after my last visit, I made a vow not to go out there again. I wanted my niece and sister to come back to New York for our next visit. Every time I was there it was like I left my body and something weird happened... I had insomnia which I never had in NYC; I stubbed my toe; I woke up in the middle of the night, vomiting with diarrhea. Something about the energy there didn't work for my system and psyche. This reinforced what I already knew, that we have relationships not only with people but with places, that everything holds a vibratory frequency.

A few visits back, the Tooth Fairy looked into my mouth and said, "Stop pushing so hard at that ballet barre class... you're left knee is not into it. It needs a rest." Keep in mind, I had said nothing about how I'd stressed my left knee at ballet. It was killing me.

"How can you tell?" I asked with a bit of a gurgle to my voice.

"Well, it's right here in your tooth. See. Well, you can't see. But I can see. it's plain as day in your left bicuspid."

It's nice to have a tooth fairy with a knowing beyond ridding my teeth of tarter and plaque. It would be good enough for her to do that well, which she does. But what I've realized is that even something as mundane as a teeth cleaning can be a magical experience. When I look at how I got to the Tooth Fairy, I see that the portal was open to something much more magical than good oral hygiene.

Shortly after my appointment with the Tooth Fairy, I got a note from a friend of mine who owns a jazz club called Club Rayé in Paris. He emailed to say he wanted to throw my book a launch party with press. The machine was in motion. I was thrilled when I also got word that a fashion photographer who'd worked regularly with Vogue was in for shooting my author photo. It was all synchronizing and tomorrow I'd visit the tooth fairy for another teeth cleaning. Who knew tarter and plaque could lead to magic and revelations?

But I've come to know in my heart that this is how the Universe works. Divine Intelligence speaks to us this way. You have to pay attention to more than just your own agenda. If we care to listen, the layers of sound in this life emerge as language. What you hear and see on the surface is the least of it. I've discovered that even a teeth cleaning can turn out to be something of a Divine revelation. Even as I write this chapter, I receive an email attachment from the man and his little girl. It's a photo of the two of them smiling. She's just lost her first tooth.

Chapter 21
Reflections on Spirituality

Many people think that being spiritual means being positive, but being spiritual means being conscious and aware. To become conscious is a much different thing than to become positive. To become conscious and aware we must become authentic. Authenticity includes both positive and negative.

~ Teal Swan

I was just out in the Bay Area with my sister and niece. My sister is doing her masters in spiritual psychology and I was out there taking my niece on adventures while Mommy was in a 4-day retreat in Petaluma. Every time I am in California it strikes me how different it is. When I travel to Europe that feels closer to my everyday reality than California. There is something about the energy there. Maybe it is the incessant positivity that I encounter in my interactions with people. Everyone is so nice in a way that is different than in the Northeast. It's more than laid back, as everyone just seems so smiley in a way that can sometimes be slightly irritating to this New Yorker. Okay, I've said it. There is something about California that feels less real to me. When I land at JFK, after flying on the red-eye home, it's like being slammed into a wall of realness.

Terminal 4 Delta at 7:30 AM, already there are so many people in motion. My phone is ringing from the moment I step off the plane. I pick it up and the car service driver says, "Are you here?" It makes me chuckle to myself. Where else would I be? Perhaps it's funnier to me, because I'm completely overtired. I can never sleep on flights and I don't like to take sleeping aids. I want to say, "I picked up so clearly, I'm here and not 30,000 feet in the air." But I refrain. That would be snarky. So I politely say, *"I'm here.* Just have carry on luggage and I'm almost outside." Five minutes later my phone rings again. Same driver. Where are you? It's a déjà vu. I'm walking toward the driver, being asked "Am I here?" Regardless where you find me, that's where I am most days. I'm here.

This time I want to say, *"Not really.* I feel pretty disembodied to be honest, which is true. Not snarky or sarcastic in the least. That's how I feel. I choose the "sane" response though, and say, "I'm almost to the C area, where the drivers wait." But honestly, I'm not really here in the way that I consider "being here." The red-eye has me wiped out.

Everything is moving so quickly and a traffic attendant is barking at me to walk on the other side of the median. In my exhausted state, I laugh to myself and realize I'm giving her a dirty look. She keeps barking at me to walk on the other side. I am so tired I want to tell her to piss off and stop barking at me but I refrain. I stare straight ahead and float on by her.

Yup, I'm home and despite all the barking and the crowds and the traffic I smile. Because NYC is real. And *I AM HERE.*

Spirituality is becoming more and more mainstream every day. When I first integrated it into my coaching methodology, people thought I was crazy. What spirituality and leadership? Spirituality and business? Spirituality and communications? Those were the sorts of questions I was asked when many years ago I explored the idea of merging practical spirituality with coaching. I felt that this is what was missing from the field at the time. Now it's everywhere, including the Buddhist Monk who works with tech leaders in Silicon Valley, the Shift Network, and Wisdom 2.0 for business. I could go on and on. Talk of spiritual growth and development is mainstream aided by Oprah's Spiritual Sundays. My clients routinely ask me to do their charts to map out the energetic cycles and the best time to initiate projects according to the laws of the unseen world.

I guess I always believed that this would happen. Otherwise, I wouldn't have been able to embark on launching my business in a sea of naysayers. But I did, and here we are. Truth be told, I cannot separate my spirituality from who I am, or from my work, because it's the leading vector of who I am. It informs my approach to everything. Even as I write this, I feel weird putting that on paper. Because I just can't stand it when people walk around telling everyone how spiritual they are. For me, it's kind of like money. If you have it, it just is. So it's not necessary to talk about it all the time. But maybe that feeling I have about it is a remnant of my New England upbringing. There are certain things I've been taught not to talk about…. Religion, politics, money… and even though I'm 50 this conditioning is something that has stayed with me. No matter how I might name it, I have to acknowledge that my spirituality is beyond the religion I was brought up with.

Spirituality has gotten me to an embrace and acceptance of the moments of transition and rapid change that have spurred growth in my life. I've grown to see change as an accelerator toward greater expansion and possibility, even when it felt like a sledgehammer to my heart.

I believe to truly be spiritual you need to know acceptance. Acceptance of a Higher Intelligence at work ordering things: acceptance of intuition as the soul's GPS, acceptance of allowing for the totality of life, acceptance of the inherent uncertainty of life and the possibility each moment bestows. I also believe that being Spiritual is to make peace with the past and have the courage to leave it behind, while honoring its profound gifts.

When I am able to stay in the space of acceptance I experience a powerful inner peace. Transitions become blessed moments. Life then undulates and flows rather than being linear. In the process, I drop the punishing judgments of myself and others, to open to the experiences, all of the experiences, I'm having -- to know and cross the chasms within myself, to connect with my own infinite potential for change, and to honor that capacity in others as well.

Without the faith to believe in some purpose bigger than the tragedies of my life, I don't think I could have withstood them. Just in case I wasn't getting the message, miscarrying and never being able to hold a baby to full term, plus a partial hysterectomy made it clear to me that I would never birth a baby out of my own body despite having loved children my whole life. I started babysitting when I was 13, such was my pull toward the energy of children and babies.

Devastating events were some of the greatest teachers of my life, but they're not important in a way. All lives have their own dose of tragedy and triumphs, and I would not presume to say that my life has had any more or less than anyone else. I do know that being spiritual has helped me own the totality of my experience and release any shame or feelings of *less-than* that I may have accumulated as I moved through my life. Spirituality reminded me that I am worthy and deserving of goodness and that there is always a bigger purpose to the events that happen -- a purpose bigger than my names and descriptions for people and things. When my eyes are open, I am reminded in each moment that Universal Law and Love are always present… all I have to do is engage.

Spirituality helped me to take all the grief and anger related to various events in my life and use them to break my heart open. To be a better, more conscious person. To transmute loss into creativity and to a deeper opening to life. Without it, a long time ago I would have shut down and been one of the walking wounded. I also understand that all of it was working to wake me up to a more luscious life.

My life has never been *normal,* whatever normal means. It's a relative term. It's been a windy road, and through the twists, turns, and tragedies, I've passed through enough fire that I feel like it was the Universe, in its most ruthless way at times, compelling me to wake up to my true self. Here was the Universe compelling me to accept my true self fully -- to live in the truth of my life and not deny any part of that truth.

So the challenge became to develop the consciousness and awareness to really be honest with myself. That was the challenge, to match the internal and external. Ultimately, this has empowered me to believe it is safe to be vulnerable, truthful and open. My experience has reinforced the view that it is from this space that the greatest magic happens.

Owning all of myself, the light and the darkness, is something of a mission to become a better person through simply accepting an honest view of myself. Spirituality helped me face my shadows… and pour them into a cup of tea.

My spiritual path has evolved beyond any form of organized religion. I don't like rules or dogma, and I've never been capable or had the inclination to follow anything blindly. But I have been seeking to have a deeper understanding of my human experience to know why I am here and to make sense of the prophecy dreams, visions, and the seemingly unexplainable synchronicities of my life.

Having an awareness of energy and fields is innate to me since childhood. But it was only through a deepening of my spiritual studies and journey that I learned how to really walk back in a whole way to that place I knew as a child. This in turn gave me a chance to make sense of all of it in a practical way and then help others do the same. To take the esoteric and apply it to daily life has been one of my greatest blessings.

I also don't believe in any one people being "chosen." I remember as a child being told that we, the Catholics, were the only chosen people, the only ones getting into heaven. It was unfathomable to me then and now that the many remarkable people I know who were neither baptized or brought up in any organized religion would be damned. It just doesn't make sense, and never did to me. I remember laughing hysterically with my childhood friend at the absurd aspects of our religious education. You see, she was Jewish and I was Catholic and we were both being told that we were "the chosen" people. We used to laugh about it. *I'm chosen. No, I'm chosen. No. I'm chosen. No, I'm chosen. Ba ha ha ha.*

Children know the truth, and we both innately knew that this didn't make sense.

Having said all that I don't believe in throwing out the baby with the bathwater. Thich Nhat Hanh is known to have said that if you were brought up in a religious tradition that tradition is the initial portal to your spirituality, and to deny it is to deny an essential part of yourself. That is why I cannot deny my Catholicism or Christianity. I am perhaps what is known as a cafeteria Catholic. You will find me at midnight mass on Christmas and in a church on Easter Sunday. And on an odd Sunday I just might show up spontaneously in Church. I feel safe there. The smell of incense and the ritual of the Homily feels like coming home to me. Growing up I really did feel the most safe in a pool and in a church. This has stayed with me. I visit old churches in Europe when I'm there to light a candle and say a prayer. It's my lineage.

But I also feel happy in a synagogue, a Buddhist temple, a mosque. While the rituals are not as familiar to me, the feeling of Light and peace is. The longing to expand spiritually has been deep within me. I liked Catholic school and chose a Jesuit University when all my high school advisors were telling me to go to an Ivy League or 7 Sisters university. They were all very disappointed when I didn't. I grew up in a college town and intellect was valued above most things. I just never understood why they thought my choice was so diminishing. To me, intellect and spirituality were not separate things. Even then I felt that the two are not in opposition. Nor do I think science and spirituality need to be in opposition. I guess on some level I've always felt that science proves what spirituality has always known. It makes evident that which those who bear witness to the unseen have always known and felt.

My spiritual journey has also included growing beyond the constraints of my Catholic upbringing by necessity, as I'm not a tribal person. I long for more and that led me to study yoga.

I laugh when I think of my yoga journey, because it was so unlikely. Truth be told, 20 years ago my sister tried to get me into yoga. At the time, I couldn't relate to it. The people in the classes we went to didn't seem grounded to me and they didn't seem real. I was an ad executive and perceived it as too *woo woo*. The kicker was when an ashtanga teacher flipped me into a position I told him I didn't want to try. I thought, *I am so over this*. All it's doing is annoying me. Little did I know that in really a few short years I would find myself deep in the study of Kundalini and Naam Yoga as well as Universal Kabbalah. Once again I learned never to say never…

Seeking, I went back to church this time to Marble Collegiate Church in NYC, which is where Norman Vincent Peale had famously preached. This felt better to me, and I liked how progressive it was. The community was very diverse and included openly gay people which was not something I found in my Catholic tradition. I'm not gay but I liked the acceptance of different people and lifestyles. So I went there pretty regularly. Still, something was missing. None of it was connecting me to my heart. I was processing it all in my head.

I came to realize that what I wanted was to crack the code, understand the mysteries of life and church wasn't doing that for me. Neither was reading a multitude of books – books by medical intuitives, the Gnostic Gospels, the Bible, the Kabbalah of Sex, Toltec Wisdom; my search went on and on and I still wasn't cracking the code of my own life. I now know what I was seeking couldn't be cracked by my mind. The portal in was through my heart.

When I lost my job and my boyfriend, my life was resembling that line from the Talking Heads, "How did I get here?" I decided to give yoga another try. By God's Grace I was lead to a limb of yoga that could open and heal my heart.

I met Dr. Joseph Michael Levry in 2002. I had returned from Stockholm and London, and my facialist, who was located at a Kundalini Yoga studio near my apartment, said to me, "The really big gun guy just opened a studio on the other side of Madison Park. He is a master kabbalist and yogi known for the accuracy of his predictions. He also is an industrial engineer and comes from a long lineage of spirituality in his family. He is a Rose and Croix Kabbalist. They say his wisdom is the mathematics of spirituality. Go see him. He will help you make sense of all of it, if you're interested."

To this day I feel like the Universe was speaking through her and the simple moment with her changed my life. In turn, this moment has taught me to have a reverence for everyone who crosses my path. "God works in mysterious ways" is a living, practical truth. This moment was an act of Divine Love and later on in life I would point to it as the moment when I understood that Universal Law is always looking out for me, as long as I keep my eyes, ears and heart open. I now recognize that Victoria ultimately was there to deliver a message from the unseen world. Go across the park . . .

This moment is how I was led to my spiritual mentor and teacher Dr. Levry. When I met with him the first time I was so defensive. It was hard to be vulnerable, but I knew I needed help and church, therapy, books, as none of it had helped me heal on the level that I needed healing. So there I was in his living room telling him how I wasn't going to be a vegetarian, and how I had no intention of not drinking wine and how I liked to dance. I vomited out a series of defenses, all the reasons why I thought that yoga was not a good fit for me. He listened intently and then said to me, "You have to forgive them. You need to heal, and to do that you have to open your heart. And when you do you are going to be a leader of women in the age of the Divine Feminine." This stopped me in my tracks. I knew I was damaged, and that I didn't know how to effectively channel how powerful I was. I also wasn't completely comfortable with my super powers – the visions, the dreams – all of it was always with me but eluding me at the same time. So when he said this I started sobbing. Then I said just tell me what to do and I'll do it.

I was promptly given an hour of meditations for the morning (to be done between the hours of 4 to 7) and before bed. He later told me that he knew I would stick to it. He said that he knew I had the discipline to really do it.

And so one of the most pivotal moments of my life occurred, the game changer. I later learned through my studies with him that everyone has an imprint, and that mine includes Mars in my heart center and Venus on my Karmic Lesson point of my Pentagram. Decoded, the first part means that I was destined to become and/or meet a great Spiritual Master in my lifetime. The second, that my greatest lessons come through men, and that I am destined to have a deep and profound love in my life. I am fortunate to have been gifted with this twice so far in my life. Other aspects included Jupiter on my Destiny line, indicating spiritual and material expansion. The emphasis of the moon explained my deep desire for children and family. A successful career and spiritual path are not enough in and of themselves for me. This I now accept and embrace. But I can lovingly integrate spiritual Light, family, and being madly in love with my man. Acceptance and integration of love across my life is the fabric of who I am as a human being and as a woman.

Knowing that this is in my field helped me to make sense of our meeting and to understand our deep connection. He has always referred to me as his sister, which has been humbling. It is only now that I grasp what this really means in my life. Through the years he hasn't spoon fed me but rather dropped pearls of wisdom only when I was ready for them, when I could decipher them. He was also often tough on me — pushing me to be the bigger person, to see the long view, to be compassionate when all I wanted to do is point a finger and tell people to fuck off. This approach to my learning created the internal circumstances by which I could refine my own abilities to read the numbers, the cycles, and better support other people through their journey. It also taught me to listen with purpose, rather than just hear. And to meet people where they are.

Little did I know this meeting would open the portal for me to cross the chasm and walk back to my true self. It gave me the courage and strength to feel again, to fully face the shadows and trauma. It opened the gates to a deep understanding of my personal history and to reclaim the elemental forces that would give me keys to realizing my own destiny.

Having the courage to do this work is the biggest blessing of my life, and the one that allowed me to receive the biggest blessings and lessons of my life thus far. To cross the chasm, I had to really commit to knowing myself. That meant all of me, both the shadows and the Light. This is far from an easy task. I say that because there is so much talk about "spirituality," so much window shopping for a quick bite. It's as if we are living in an age of the spiritual checklist. Become a vegan or vegetarian, *check*, I'm spiritual. Stop caring about material things, *check*, I'm spiritual. This is the easy part, if you choose to do it. I never wanted to do either, but was rather seeking to feel more connected, integrated, congruent, and safe in the world. I wanted to overcome the internal, mental, and emotional churning and anxiety. I wanted peace.

The substance of my practice doesn't come to me by not wearing high heels anymore or by not eating meat. If it were only that easy, anyone with a little discipline could do that. Here's the rub, though; real spiritual work requires a shift in consciousness and awareness to the world being a *sacred place*.

Dr. Levry taught me that the world is kept together by love and that starts with loving oneself. With his unwavering support I embarked on the process of really facing myself. To make myself better I had to wake up to loving myself and understand the role I had played in everything that had occurred in my life. Through this process I raised my energetic frequency and shifted my field from one where I had been the victim of circumstances -- the circumstances of my birth, the circumstances of my parents choices and wounds, the circumstances of my own limited consciousness based on what I had experienced. Over time, and with a lot of deep and often painful spiritual work and growth, I got to a place where I could create my circumstances.

This required me to open my heart. When my heart was closed and armored, my soul was asleep. To find Light I had to open my heart. Essentially studying Naam Yoga was a walk back to my heart and to the truth of my heart. Ultimately, my heart then became my biggest teacher.

It was through the teachings of Dr. Levry that I learned how to read the cycles of the moon, to clock the timing of beginning and ending things to position me for optimum success. This is where I learned to unravel the great mysteries, and perhaps the greatest one in the social order being to not to be pushed around by the social order, but to bow to nothing other than the truth of my heart.

What I love about the teachings of Naam Yoga is that these profound teachings provided me with an inclusive portal to raise my own energetic frequency while still honoring my own history. It helps me see the Divinity in all teachings as it contains Hebrew, Latin, Hindu, Gurmukhi. It feeds my soul as well as my intellect. I feel that it is spiritual nourishment for my whole being. It has also taught me the hard lesson of not giving away my power to anyone, not even to a spiritual master. This was a tough pill to swallow, since once I did this I accepted full responsibility for all my choices.

I remember early on being taught to do the math on my life, tracking the timing of all the biggest events of my life to the energetic cycle I was in and to where the moon was when they were initiated. I did a timeline on it and observed the accuracy of this, what we'll call spiritual technology. Every time I had gotten the timing right I had a measure of success. When I had started intimate relationships, or chosen living spaces in an inauspicious time, inevitably my life was made harder than necessary. Things unraveled. Time and time again, as I mapped my own life to the patterns that needed correction, they revealed themselves to me.

It was through these teachings that I also came to accept that the real chasm to cross was the one I had built within myself. The deepest spiritual awakening for me wasn't seeing the unseen or having prophesy dreams and visions when I was meditating. The deep awakening for me was realizing that all the problems that I perceived in my life, all the situations that I faced, were the result of some deep healing that I needed to experience. All the upheavals and changes that occurred in my life were happening to remove the false structures and lies that were detrimental to my life and blocking what I was intended to create in the world.

Once I got this lesson on a deep level then my resistance to change began to fall away. I stopped fighting with myself. As I did this, my definition of spirituality also began to change. It was no longer some abstract concept of heaven and hell.

Over the last 15 years I grew to redefine spirituality as consciousness and self-realization. I also began to believe deep in my heart that self-realization, walking back to who I really am, and allowing for the expression of that, is God realization.

Through the study of Naam Yoga and Universal Kabbalah, I was given the tools to balance yin and yang within myself and to notice when they were out of balance. When I was too far in yin, I was an out of control emotional being driven by the wounds and emotions of the past. When I was too far in yang, I would shut down and become armored and hide behind work and wine. My life was controlled by my emotional state. I experienced that when I could really sit with my emotions, be with them in my body, as opposed to disembodying as a coping mechanism, that I could vibrate at perfect frequency of unconditional love, which supports me in both joy and sadness. I can be with all of it and not be taken over by any of it. Being with all of it enables me to make fully formed, conscious decisions.

I also realized that there is a big difference between containing my emotions and denying them, in which the former contributes to an expansion of the Light and the latter to darkness.

I have to emphasize my spiritual journey has not always felt good. In fact, about half the time it hasn't. At times, facing myself was a really hard lift, and the more I got real the more unreal some aspects of my life got. Also, the more real I got, the more my heart opened, the more memories came back to me of trauma that had happened to me in my life, and all the stories I had told myself as a coping mechanism. This included stories about my father, who I had told myself was a genius who really loved us more than life itself. But the reality is he had both an unnatural attachment to me and a complete inability to show up for us. He abandoned us to women and alcohol, and like most addicts when he did show up in my life it was to take something.

When I was recovering from major surgery and he called to ask me for money, and to tell me to get back to work, it all became starkly clear. All of it. Keep in mind I could barely walk and was loaded up on opiate painkillers. But even through those, I could finally see my patterning around pushing myself to the limit and beyond to feel even remotely worthy. I could see the pattern around not acknowledging my need for intimacy, my pattern of trying to make it better for everyone even when it was at great cost to myself. It all came together when I received this one phone call from my father. And then the layers around my choices in friendships, relationships with men, and relationships across the board, all became clear as well. With my next step I had to summon the courage to walk away from the past. To drop it like it's hot. Doing this also felt like shedding a false identity. Emerging from the shedding was like learning to walk again.

It took courage. As I reordered my internal conversation, I said a lot of goodbyes. I released the past attachment to my father and then set about healing the residual pain around that and his abusiveness. Then I had to get to the place of forgiveness.

Through the releasing of the past, including seeing both my parents clearly I came face to face with the levels of abuse that I had grown up with. Just stomaching this and not running from the memories took every ounce of discipline I carry. It was not pretty, and there were layers upon layers of associated grief with each revelation.

It's been said that the kingdom of heaven is here and that it requires that the inner child in all of us be reborn. This rebirth requires the courage to see the truth about our own lives. Until I was able to really face it without allowing myself to be a victim or to blame other people, including my parents, I couldn't make sense of where I had been. This is why I say that doing spiritual work is not a feel good proposition. It's painful until it isn't anymore.

Through the teachings of Naam Yoga and a daily spiritual practice, I was able to face the truth of my life, feel the grief, pain and anger around certain experiences and choices and then restructure my inner dialogue around all of it. But I must emphasize that my spiritual journey was not a process of being positive. It was about getting real and having the courage to be authentic.

Chanting Mantra is my chosen form of rewriting my inner dialogues. I remember when the day came when my mind was blank and stayed blank. No worrying, not spinning or second guessing, just a deep listening to the truth of my heart and soul. When this happened I forgave myself and also gave myself permission to make an evolutionary choice to really stand for my own self. I started having healthy boundaries.

As I allowed myself to be with all of it, the emotions, anger, grief, sadness, frustration cleared from my body as well as my psyche. I moved from belief in God to Faith, the eye that sees God in everything. And when I shifted to this space I aligned with a completely different energetic field and frequency.

As my inner world shifted my outer world shifted. My health shifted and my ability to create shifted. I had always applied myself and through discipline and hard work I had come a long way from the reality I grew up in. So manifesting wasn't new in my life. What became a new experience was how it manifested. I was vibrating at a different frequency, one that is more alive.

As the duality between what I was really thinking and feeling was erased, I became congruent and integrated. Everything became more harmonious and what I attracted to my life became a series of blessings.

For me, a spiritual path meant healing the oldest wounds and patterning within myself in such a way that all forms of self-abuse ceased. As my consciousness expanded, I also became aware of the subtle and not so subtle ways I was abusing myself. Not being clear about what I needed and wanted in intimate relationships is a form of self-abuse. Running myself into the ground trying to make everyone feel better isn't services. It's a form of self-abuse too. Not allowing myself to be receptive was a form of self-abuse. Not being playful is a form of self-abuse. Not allowing myself to be vulnerable was a form of self-abuse. Denying the truth of my heart and not sharing that I loved someone is a form of self-abuse.

I am grateful to have met a living spiritual Master and being guided through my deepest healing and ultimately rebirth. I am also very grateful that through the process I have never been asked to renounce the lineage I grew up through or to give up things I love including red meat, wine, champagne, making love as well as a love of beautiful clothes, art and beauty in the name of being more spiritual. Rather, through these teachings I learned to decipher the deeper meaning of the prayers I had grown up with. Decoding the Lord's Prayer was quite a profound moment for me as this had almost been my spiritual mantra since I first learned it at the age of four.

The teachings also helped me honor the complexities of my own life while also decoding and simplifying life. As I got clearer I found that the portal was opening to a vast capacity to love unconditionally both myself and others.

The teachings of Universal Kabbalah say that people with Mars aspected where mine is either become spiritual masters and/or meet a great living master. So perhaps it has been my destiny all along to deepen my understanding of the great truths and mysteries and also to meet and study with two living spiritual masters – to be graced with a living spiritual mother and father.

The difference it has made for me is beyond words. So it is I hope this translates into being a presence in the world that also makes a difference – a difference that is maybe, just maybe, also beyond words.

Chapter 22

The Silver Chord, True Self, and Being a Mermaid

Be yourself, everyone else is taken

~Oscar Wilde

The Silver Cord

One of the most challenging things for me in my life and also for many of my clients and yoga students is to keep a handle on the true self. When we are children, through the silver chord we connect our physical experience in matter to the astral realm – to the unseen world. When you hear young children talk about friends that you cannot see it is a mistake to dismiss their knowing. Most likely these are not mere imaginary friends, but guides and friends from the Astral world that are guiding them.

Sutrama, or Silver Cord, is, in metaphysical literature, a term referring to the link between the physical body, the astral body, and the Higher Self (*the Monad*). The Silver Cord is mentioned by occultists and mystics, especially in contexts of dying and of near-death experiences, but actually it is the cord that feeds the personality (*the Ego*) with the energy that maintains the life influx inside of the body. In some schools of Spirituality it is also called *perispirit*.

The silver cord is often described as a long elastic cable made of light or energy. It appears to be approximately one inch in diameter and sparkles much like the tinsel on a Christmas tree. It facilitates astral travel and insight.

The silver cord is akin to a leash—albeit a very long one. It keeps humans tethered to our physical earthly body while we roam about on the spiritual plane. Some mystics also refer to it as a sort of spiritual umbilical cord that keeps your soul and body connected. Whichever way you view it, it is comforting to know that you have a lifeline between these two bodies.

The silver cord is known in many religious circles. You'll also find it referenced in the Bible.

> *Or ever the silver cord be loosed...Then shall the dust return to the earth as it was: and the spirit shall return unto God who gave it. (Ecclesiastes 12:6-7)*

Ecclesiastes is a reminder that life on this earth is empty and pointless in the end, if we are living without a connection to the higher realms of Light.

When the silver chord is severed, death occurs. It is connected to the heart chakra in each of the subtle bodies. It keeps us connected to our body when we astral travel.

The soul's truth comes from the highest realm, the true self that is in all of us and connected to Light. Some would say this is why our greatest work is to walk back to the truth of our heart; to reestablish that connection and then support it by our intellect.

A fair description of the physical body is that it's a sensitive electromagnetic vehicle which filters and grounds spiritual energy and consciousness. By filter, I mean that higher, subtle energy is stepped-down by chakras through each subtle body until it manifests in the physical body. Denser matter is the most restrictive, so energy and consciousness is more limited when we are solely relating to life through our physical body without a connection to our subtle bodies.

Google the *silver chord* and you will see that much is written about the disconnection happening at physical death.

I believe prior to our physical passing a "death" occurs when we distance ourselves from our connection to our spiritual nourishment. Without a spiritual connection we cannot be fully conscious of who we are and our purpose here. Without that connection, life is lived solely plugged into the matrix of matter and the physical life to be informed by day-to-day events rather than informed by the higher worlds.

For me the duality, the *trouble*, started when I was around seven years of age. I say the trouble started because this was when I started to be influenced so strongly by external forces – by the Matrix of *should*, *have to*, and *societal conditioning*, in which I started to believe that those forces were more real, more true, than the guidance of my heart and the unseen world. The duality began for me when I started reversing my processing, meaning that I began believing that the unseen is a fraction of my experience, when, in fact, if you deal in such facts, all my experiences on the physical plane had first come through the Astral plane. With this reversal came a morphing into what I thought *I was supposed to be* rather than who, at heart, I really was. It would take a lot of emotional pain and a health crisis before I was able to walk fully back to my True Self.

When my false self, my *should* self, became dominant, I moved to trying to merge my beliefs and behaviors with social validation in order to survive or even thrive in the world as defined by the cultural norms of the community I lived in. This was often at fierce odds with how I really felt.

I shifted away from being a powerful little girl who made no apologies for what I knew. I had moved through life according to my childhood extrasensory capacity to sense what wasn't seen yet. Even when I was told that my imaginary friends weren't real I knew they were. They felt more real than anything that was going on around me. I would have prophesy dreams most nights, and then I would watch them unfold in front of my eyes. The dreams included my father's affairs when my mother was pregnant with my sister. These were strange dreams for a four year-old to have. Bearing witness to my father's affairs through dreams as a child, I didn't know what I was seeing. I just knew it was leading to a lot of pain for all of us.

There were his long absences. I remember asking my mother, who are these ladies I'm seeing in my dreams? And she would shake her head and smile a sad smile and tell me I'm the only lady in our house. I would hug her and go inside myself. I knew differently. I had been shown what was really going on.

Simultaneously, I was excelling at Montessori pre-school. Mrs. Whalen told my mother that I would come in to school and tell the other kids I was a Queen. And then I would ask them to do things for me. My mom, while amused, did her best to condition my Queen out of me. She interpreted it as being bossy and selfish. Now today Sheryl Sandberg and others would say I was exhibiting leadership potential early on.

Then it was time for kindergarten. I went from the progressive Montessori school to the more structured Catholic school. Rules were ever present, but I liked it mostly because I got to spend a lot of time in church with the incense, stained glass, and rituals. And the big cross with JC felt comforting, despite it being a crucifixion. And there were all the candles. I wasn't so keen on the uniform: red plaid skirt, white shirt, patent leather shoes. It was a bit boring for me. Creativity was nonexistent, getting dressed in the a.m. Same thing, day after day. Economical for the parents, yes. Equalizing, yes. But still *boring*. There was one day in the year that this all changed. Picture day we got to wear what we wanted to with one caveat – the girls had to wear dresses.

I had just been introduced to *Grrr Animals*. I had a delightful pantsuit and a white shirt with a matching top. It was colorful, cheerful, and I could move in it in a way that I couldn't in the regular daily uniform. I could play hard without worrying if my underpants were going to show when I twirled around or bent down. Undies are not allowed to show if you're a good catholic girl.

My heart's desire was to wear my *Grrr Animals* outfit. I was so proud of it and I took very good care of it, refusing to wear it unless it was a special occasion. On picture day I put my stake in the ground. I staged a protest which was actually a full on fit; refusing to wear a dress, I dug in. On this one, I applaud my parents. This time it was different. I wasn't told to tone it down. I had the backing of both parents. I remember feeling so validated as I put on my outfit. Pants—YES! And the three of us marched into school. Dad was even there and not at the office. I usually barely saw him as he came home late and went to the office early. I had back up.

At this moment, I felt safe in a way that I hadn't most of the time. We were the three musketeers and my needs and my perspective were being validated. I wasn't backing down and I had support for my position. We marched into Mother Superior's office – a daunting prospect even on a good day. This was 1970 and this was going to cause a situation. The head priest was called in. The one who sat with all of us kids in the picture. He was Jesuit and I remember him nodding and listening – with a twinkle in his eye. When everyone was done, he laughed and put his hand on my head and said, let her wear what she wants. It's only once a year. A wave of euphoria washed over me. Victory! To this day, when I look at my kindergarten picture I feel ecstatically happy. And I look ecstatically happy too, grinning ear to ear in the photo with my two pigtails and pants. It is the grin of alignment with my truth, combined with victory. I felt empowered. My first major victory had happened at age five.

This feeling was short-lived. I was five when I first remember being called a "nigger" and told I had a "nigger" Father. I gave that boy a concussion with a basketball that I slammed into his face. I didn't know what the word meant but I knew it wasn't nice. This is where I started to become increasingly self-conscious about being bi-racial.

I fought back but I also felt increasingly isolated and different. Before then the same biases may have existed, but I believe that my connection to spirit and the unseen world was so strong that it didn't register in the same way. I was buoyed by my Guardian Angel Gabriel and his pals from the unseen world.

So around the age of seven my defiance and spark started dimming. I knew I was different but that didn't feel safe. I started people pleasing and trying to make it better for everyone else. It didn't help that my parents' marriage was really falling apart. It's true that there were only three places I felt safe: church, a pool, and my Mimi's home.

Church was a sanctuary, because it was quiet and mystical. The pool was where I excelled. I relished training and the fact that I often won the sprint freestyle and butterfly events. I think somewhere in me I also liked proving that someone adrift in the sea between tribes could not only swim but win. I am very light. But this was 1970s Massachusetts and in that place and time I stuck out.

I still had prophesy dreams and an acute sixth sense, but as I channeled more energy into being accepted and fitting in, my antennae got rusty. I shut down and focused on swimming and studying. I was all in my head and being rewarded for it. The externals were in place, ribbons, medals and records for swimming and A's on my report card.

Fast forward to fall 2001. September 11th and the city I live in is in crisis. I'm in crisis also. I've lost my job, my boyfriend broke up with me, and I feel very alone. All the makings of a spiritual crisis. For years, I felt that something was radically wrong with my life. Having struggled on and off with depression and eating disorders I was scared and tired. I didn't want to go through another dark night of the soul. Now I realize it's not really a choice but at the time, having done it repeatedly over my life, I knew I didn't want to have that experience again.

Lucky for me a former client and dear friend encouraged me to go to a yoga studio. I was pretty anti-yoga at this time. I was still in classic type-A over achieving mode. *Being* was pretty far from how I lived my life. It seemed like I never slowed down enough to simply be. More often than not, I filled my schedule to the brim until I was so exhausted that I went into hermit mode and watched lots of movies and slept in. Also, trying to be what I wasn't was confusing and exhausting. I had hit a wall.

So I took her advice. After all, she is German, a Fulbright scholar, and an MBA – someone who I respected and admired for her intellect. I thought if she can stomach the place, there may be something in it for me.

I had a private session with a kundalini yogi around healing a broken heart. I had a longing to heal but the session felt like crap. I thought, *look at this guy, all in white, speaking in some language I can't decipher* (later I learned it was Gurmuhki which is the root language of Sanskrit and akin to Hebrew, Greek and Latin). I could relate more to the spa that was part of the studio. The woman that gave me facials there suggested that I go to another studio across Madison Park that had just opened on 24th Street. She said a famous Mystic, Universal Kabbalist and Yogi had opened it and that she thought he would be helpful to me. She said he was different. Skeptical but broken up, I thought, *why not? What do I have to lose?*

So upon returning from my holiday in Stockholm, I walked into the studio. I was told that the founder, Gurunam, *aka* Dr. Joseph Michael Levry, would be teaching class on Wednesday evening. I attended the class and while there were many people there who fulfilled my stereotypes feeding my then judgmental streak, there were also others who felt like me: *type A, professional, broken, and looking for help healing their deepest wounds.* His style also resonated with me. Sitting before us was a man who clearly embraced being a man. And he had an irreverent streak that made us laugh. I felt that he was simultaneously beyond all of us but also part of us. I also liked that he emphasized that he wasn't looking for followers, but rather was dedicated to helping us walk back to our own hearts. That made a lot of sense to me. Accessible, loving, but also real and not trying to be better than us or stand as some oracle. He struck me as devoid of spiritual arrogance and full of unconditional love. He reminded me of the best of what I had experienced with the Jesuit priests I knew. I felt safe. I wanted to meet with him.

I got an appointment to meet with him privately and when I walked into our meeting room, he said to me, "You have to open your heart. You have to forgive them. You are not wrong. They did not give you what you needed from them growing up and they didn't protect you. Your home looked a certain way but it was also one of the most emotionally abusive environments you could have survived. It decimated your sense of worth but it also made you strong and courageous. Now you have to have the courage to forgive them and open your heart. Open your heart to life and who you really are."

I started weeping.

This great man, Dr. Joseph Michael Levry, became my spiritual mentor teaching me directly and honing my walk back to my connection to Source and myself. He also became my spiritual father. Like the Jesuit priests who had influenced me growing up, he recognized something in me that I had long forgotten and he watered the seeds of what he saw. He told me that one day I would be a force in the world for leading women for helping them heal in the age of the Divine Feminine. This was more than 15 years ago and at the time I thought, "He has got to be kidding. I can barely lead myself around."

A deep spiritual awakening and journey is profoundly difficult and challenging. Yes, it is, at times, comforting. But it's in equal measure comforting and disconcerting. It brings you face to face with yourself – the dark, wounded, angry broken parts. It was terrifying for me most of the time, especially when the capacities I had as a young child began to surface again. All of it came flooding back. All the painful experiences, as well as the prophesy dreams and visions. They came back with a vengeance and it became increasingly difficult for me to deny who I really am.

Through this process I realized it was ludicrous to think I could go back to working in an ad agency. I took time to myself to heal and just do things that I was called to do, including multiple Kundalini and Naam yoga trainings, healing certifications and classical Pilates certifications. I got deep into Universal Kabbalah and accepted again that my true way of being was to feel my way through life -- to follow my instincts and intuition. I started to listen to my heart without questioning its guidance. I did what I felt, including starting my business. Incidentally, the name came to me while meditating and most people told me it would fail — fast forward and it not only didn't fail but turns out it was ahead of the curve in bringing resilience and mindfulness to the field of leadership development. As I got deeper into my spiritual awakening, I got closer to myself and understanding who I really am – again. By this time, I was 36 years old.

Fast forward to 2012 as my journey to my true self accelerated with my surgery. It was following my partial hysterectomy that, well, everything fell apart. Literally, my body shattered, and my life as I knew it shattered, but what came out of the rubble has been like a fairy tale. Now I know that all my spiritual studies and everything that came before prepared me for the final leg of the journey to self-acceptance and true self-integration.

My True Self

I started this chapter quoting Oscar Wilde, "Be yourself, everyone else is taken." It wasn't until my whole life shattered, and I had done a lot of deep spiritual work to heal my mother wound and other emotional scars, that I was finally able to claim my true self I separated from at age seven. It had taken me this long to realize *that everyone else is taken*. There was no one else to be.

When I reference my *True Self*, I am lucky. I had a remembrance of it. Many people never know it because while the Spirit works to reveal it to us all, unless we do our work to heal our body of pain and karmic influences, our current state of mind will oppose it. I am fortunate to have been guided by two living Spiritual Masters – one a woman and the other a man. I am deeply grateful to both of them. They are essentially my spiritual mother and father. By being graced with the esoteric or great knowledge, I was able to seek and find my true self. It is this deep spiritual study that gave me the courage to lose my conditioned ways of thinking and behaving, combined with a radical personal crisis that gave me the vision of my life as it is meant to be, as created by my true self.

Once I settled in and integrated the shock of realizing that my life as I knew it was an illusion, all the things that held sway over me, keeping me tethered to my conformist self, suddenly had no substance, no value and no lasting quality. When this happens it's like waking up from a long deep sleep – both terrifying and thrilling – but ultimately the key to a better life.

In my experience, as my inner essence of who I really am was revealed to me, the culprits of my pain and frustration were revealed as well. I had a choice whether to leap into the unknown or stay in the illusion. Scary as it was, living a lie was scarier to me, so I leapt. When I leapt, the only thing that was certain in my life was my deep connection to who I really was. I needed to trust that connection. Everything else in my life, as I had known it, had collapsed. It was over. I was 47 years old and emerging from the remains.

More than once during this process I prayed and surrendered to my highest self and then did exactly what I was told from that place of connection. Even when it didn't make sense to my intellect, I did it. This process is both liberating and terrifying. To discover *true reality* and the *real me*, I had to dare to see things anew. I dared to restructure my value system. In retrospect, I realize that while I was waking up to a new reality, I was also seeking what I could not immediately know or understand. Three years later, I am 50 and the odyssey of this part of my journey now makes sense.

I believe opening and embracing my true self had opened me to life in a way that I could never have dreamed of. Having the courage to let go of anything and anyone that was aligned and supportive of my false self created the space for all that has since come in. My business expanded, my love life expanded, my heart opened and I felt safe – finally safe. I asked the higher world to release any old patterning of attachment to anyone or anything including my own beliefs and behaviors that contracted me or weighed me down. Then anything and anyone who was not aligned with creative truth was removed by their own hand.

The alignment with my true self gave me what could appear to be super powers in terms of being able to manifest easily and effortlessly. When I leapt into the unknown my capacity to create – to think something – and have it then manifest, to be able to see the signs and synchronicity, to recognize the messages of the Universal Divine Intelligence became acute and has never left.

I am guided to where I am supposed to be and I no longer question it. If my intellect can't immediately accept what is happening, if it doesn't "make sense" I know how to stay aligned with my intuition and guidance, knowing that my intellect will catch up.

Living with a Mermaid Consciousness

I recently returned to New York from Kennebunkport, Maine, one of the most beautiful places on the Eastern seaboard. It is the land of lobster, oysters, fishermen, sea porpoises and boats, rocking, clinking, boats. Lots of boats.

As the plane made its descent into Portland Airport my heart felt instantly happy. I heard the nasal accent, saw water everywhere and felt peaceful, expansive. It also brought back memories of sailing in Turkey, swimming every day growing up, and time at the beach in various locations around the world. My profound deep truth is that I am watery and feel happiest close to and in the water.

I have known this for a long time, but being in Maine woke me up to it on a different level. There is a picture that my childhood best friend's husband took of us on the bow of his boat that weekend. At 50 I believe it is the most sensual picture ever taken of me. In my white flowing skirt, and bikini top snuggled up to my best friend from childhood, holding pink champagne with the sea behind us, the picture radiates peace, happiness and alignment. I've been told that the picture is photographic evidence that I'm a mermaid.

Something happens to me when I am near the water. I become instantly happy, instantly at peace. And all I want to do is eat shellfish – lobster, peeky toe crab, clams with bellies, oysters. This was my breakfast, lunch and dinner for 4 days straight. Having a pool is one thing but being near and in the sea is quite another. It's magic – I even love the smell of the sea and the feeling of salt caked in my hair and on my skin.

In Maine I started dreaming about Mermaids and when I returned to New York I longed to learn more about them. Archetypal energy helps me lock into expanding my thinking and energetic frequency. So most times, if something is revealed to me in a dream strongly, I will heed the call and try to discover as much as I can about the archetype.

So my mermaid dreams and the mermaid picture sent me on a quest for the mermaid in myself. What I found out is that she is the archetypal energy of Venus, Aphrodite, and the Divine Feminine Goddess. I have been told that my cosmic imprint, the numbers say my energy is dominated by Venus and the Moon. True, I have a strategically placed Mars that I am deeply grateful for as it is what gives me strength. But the Venus and Moon are where the mermaid sits within me.

I know that it is from her energy and imprint that my intense bonding to water comes from. Also, there is my dominant way of feeling my way through life. Reading about mermaids awakened another level of self-acceptance in me to my highest intention to be love and have love. Far beyond success, my primary drive is *love* in all its manifestations.

In Divine Spiritual Wisdom, Universal Kabbalah as taught by Dr. Joseph Michael Levry, we are taught that we all come in with a cosmic code or imprint. This wisdom is an essential part of my walk back to my true self. It is said that Divine Spiritual Wisdom is the mathematics of spirituality and that the Universe, while seemingly chaotic, really isn't. The Universal Laws of Nature – the unseen cycles – are said to always be at work influencing us.

My chart happens to be filled with Venus and the Moon as well as a strategically placed Mars and Uranus. As it turns out, Uranus contains the Sun and Venus. Also, I am also born on the day of Romantic Exaltation.

All of the seven creative planets have a positive and negative influence. Knowing them well, befriending them, enabled me to embrace and integrate the totality of me – both the shadows and the Light, ultimately moving me to a very high consciousness of truth around who I am.

The notion *The truth will set you free* predates the Bible. Embracing who I really am has set me free. I've realized in the process that one of my archetypal energies is a mermaid.

Mermaids are aligned with Aphrodite and Venus, the love Goddesses. I have four Venus aspected in my Universal Kabbalah chart. The Mermaid is legendary for only allowing herself to be seen by the true of heart. There are those who experience me as warm and others who experience me as aloof. I now accept that it takes me time to share myself with people and to really reveal myself to others.

Water is a dominant quality of my soul. I feel my way through life, what can be challenging for others to accept and understand. If I am not feeling it, I won't engage. If I feel it, I see it all the way through — sometimes beyond what seems rational. Once I am engaged, once someone or something has got me on that level, I'm in…all in.

I now know that as I've aligned with my true self, water finds its way to me in all aspects of my life. I live on an island that is flanked by the Hudson River on one side and the East River on the other. I see the opening to the sea at the bottom of the island from my apartment.

There is a body of water in my building, and it is here that on many days I find my solace in the same way that I once did as a child. As someone who found refuge in water as a child, I realize that this still holds true in my adulthood. Close to the sea is where I feel safe and at home. It is my womb.

I also understand why I am able to draw many men to me, but only a few are and have been capable of staying with me. The way I love is uncommon in the sense that I have a sort of uninhibited sensuality and innocence that is one hundred percent in the moment aware of the possibilities of exchanging energy with others. I cannot exchange energy with someone unless I can feel them connected inside me at a place where "I" disappears.

With the exception of two men to date, most cannot reciprocate this natural way of interacting. My journey back to my true self has also included a deep respect for the primal capacity within myself that has never left. Deadened for many years, at 50 this primalness has reawakened my freedom with regard to sexuality, sensuality, and love that is beyond most men's comprehension. It takes a man who is powerfully connected to spirit to merge with the energy of my mermaid. Only this type of man warrants my complete surrender to his manhood.

I love with my entire being. I don't understand why humans must try or work at loving each other. Through my mermaid archetype I am able to further ground into my true self. Maybe this is what the personal archetypes and energetic imprints do for all of us. They ultimately connect us to them as they reveal themselves. So you are your archetype, even as you become your archetype. One day you honestly answer the question for yourself, *What is my archetype?* Through your archetypal energy you stop running from yourself and begin your return.

Returning to the heart is no easy challenge. But in this life, what are your other options?

Chapter 23

I Love NYC
(And Here's Why)

Just be true to yourself, and listen as much as one is able to other people whose opinions you respect and look up to but in the end it has to come from you. You can't really worry too much by looking to the left and the right about what the competition is doing or what other people in your field are doing. It has to be a true vision.
~Anna Wintour

Anyone reading this of a certain age has seen the *I love NYC* advertising campaign – the tee-shirts hawked on the street, and at one time the television ads. The campaign began in 1977, 12 years before I landed here. Those tee-shirts are a global icon much like the city itself. Think Lennon in front of the Statue of Liberty.

So much of the city is iconic. Like the skyline etched across the horizon, you can't miss the Empire State and Chrysler buildings coming into Manhattan from JFK. After living here for 26 years, the Manhattan skyline is all the more meaningful to me. Every time I see it across the dashboard of the car service bringing me through the Manhattan tunnel on 38th Street to take me home, I get emotional. This emotion hasn't always been happy but it's always been there.

In fact, when I was going through my divorce, I was so grief-stricken, so angry, I ran away every chance I could. I was in flight for two years, flying back and forth to London, Berlin, Brussels and Paris. Before that for two years, I was going to Mexico City every three months. I was in flight from something more than geography.

When I would come home from Europe, it was like returning home to a parent who was being tough on me. Those returns and the view of the skyline shifted me to a position where I felt no other clear choice but to be the authority and driving power behind my own life. I knew, in those returning moments, I had to make peace with the choices I had made.

Ultimately, I love NYC because I feel as though she raised me. My most formative healing experiences have occurred while living here. I guess most of all I love her because she accepted me.

NYC has never been shocked that I had a black Father. Why would she be? She doesn't care about pedigree. But she cares about chutzpah, strength of vision, and being your best self. She doesn't suffer fools easily but she proved to me that if I showed up for my own life she would too. And so far she has.

Where else would I get to unpack all of who I am? I couldn't run from myself here. I had to figure it out. And in the figuring it out, she supported the totality and accepted me at every twist and turn. This is the city of reinvention, and she helped me move from a career in branding/advertising, to marketing, to starting my own business. She also provided the challenges that made me step up. She is expensive, exacting, and filled with a global community of high achieving people. Mediocrity is unacceptable here. Everyone who comes and stays here regardless of race, religion, or profession, comes here to *do* something. This makes for an unrelentingly high bar. No worries. It's just there, part of the weather system.

The city is also a spiritual vortex. All of the great spiritual masters at one time or another have passed through NYC. Maybe this is why the city reminds me that life is a jewel: honor and integrate all its facets. You can run, you can try to hide, but ultimately NYC is so tough and so high frequency that she demands that I not hide from myself. And like a lover or a parent who is determined to bring out the best, she is unrelenting. This has worked to my benefit.

NYC has tested me more than once. There have been times when I fought against her demands. She also set traps, sometimes subtle, in order for me to see what I'm made of. She demands creativity and discipline. I consider myself lucky to be gifted with both. Combined with a deep spiritual practice, I have found what I needed in myself to succeed here. I had to fully access all three aspects of myself, since I landed here 26 years ago. To do so, I needed to access and accept the full scope of my life, even the dark messy bits.

Like many people, I came here with not much money in my pocket. Once I got out of college, my parents made it clear that I was on my own. I am not a trust-fund kid. I never had parents who paid for my apartment or supported me financially. I realize now that they did me a favor. From the beginning, I had to find my way. To navigate the city, I had to perfectly align my inner compass.

I also was lucky because in 1989 the city was a very different place. The meatpacking district sill packed meat. I would walk through there with my friends after clubbing. I'd see the butchers hanging carcasses from hooks in the wee hours of the morning. This was a magical time in NYC, when all the worlds crossed. Bankers hung out with artists, hung out with musicians. No one demanded that you pay $1,500 for bottle service at a club.

Here was where I first realized that a man could love me. Really love me. I knew it after I said to him 3 times, "But I need you to know that my father is black." After the third time he laughed and said to me, "What do you think I'm not getting? I mean, I'm Polish, but I'm not stupid. You know, I got it the first time, and I don't care." *She* delivered us to each other, and I believe with my whole heart that it wouldn't have happened in any other city in this country.

Why? Because there is no other city like NYC in the US. It is where all the worlds meet. It's where 130 languages are spoken. It's where immense wealth bumps up against immense poverty. Somehow it's all side by side. But NYC is not segregated the way many places in this country are. It's too densely populated. So by the sheer geography of the city I am faced everyday with layers of humanity on the streets, in the subway, in my building. Not a day goes by without hearing another language spoken or seeing/meeting someone who speaks a language that is different from my native English. It's a daily occurrence to see someone who looks different from me. But because we live together inside the vast humanity of this city, it often feels so easy to see how none of us are that different at all.

NYC brings you smack face-to-face with the brilliant, tragicomic, fairy tale, and magic of being a human being. She smells alternately great or horrible depending on the time of year. She is messy and chic all at the same time. She is not PC. She wears her emotions on her sleeve without pretense. She doesn't have time to make you feel comfortable about your dishonesty or illusions. She is real. She will make me feel something whether I like it or not.

Sure, sometimes this is exhausting. And when one of my clients says to me, "Get out of my head. Why can't you be mediocre ever?!" We both laugh because we know neither one of us can. This city won't allow it. My client didn't land on an executive leadership team by being mediocre. I didn't land in the same room as him as his trusted advisor by being mediocre. It's not possible here. *She* doesn't tolerate mediocrity well. That demand makes me better. I would bet that most of the people I know would say that it makes them better too. Because of this demand I have found it vital to stay connected with the source of my personal power.

I said to a friend of mine who moved here from Denver, "You'll get along just fine here if you clock your frequency." NYC has energy and an expectation of her children. For instance, I remember this woman telling me once how she was going to a gala. She was planning to wear a dress with a big bow in the front. She told me that she always got compliments on it in Denver. I thought to myself, *Oh my God, she can't do that here.* My student from a major fashion house, who also knew her, said, "Look, let me help you plan what you're wearing." Gracefully, we helped her shift her frequency. She had a great time at the event, and found herself genuinely complimented on her outfit.

People make judgments here based on appearance. It's a place where it's important to have style, whatever that means to you. It's a place to be conscious of how that style will play in the rooms of life here. I found out how important clothes are here. Luckily, I'm pretty vain and so that aspect of life here just fed a part of me. Here I learned that personal style matters. Autopilot is the kiss of death here.

NYC polished me up into the person who I am. She taught me how to evolve into the woman I am and also to continue evolving. She taught me to never get complacent.

NYC is the mother and the father who taught me that my dream of creating a community of diverse accomplished people – entrepreneurs, artists, and creators from all over the planet — is possible. This is, and always has been, my circle of people here.

She satisfies my curiosities. She lets me explore all the aspects of the ever-changing canvas of my own life. I get to do ballet barre class every day. It's my sorority. At 9:30 AM most weekdays you can find me at that barre, laughing and sweating and sometimes in excruciating pain from pushing my limits. It's a metaphor for the extremes of this intense city. That hour every morning is a metaphor for daily life here.

She has introduced me to the most amazing people, some of whom are back in Europe and others here. People who have the biggest hearts and the biggest minds. People who speak at Davos or start companies that are mission-driven with a double bottom-line. This city is where I can end up being mentored by Russell Simmons, meet Sade Adu, or connect with my childhood idol Pat

Cleveland, all while feeling perfectly comfortable in my own skin being exactly who I am.

People who refuse to be mediocre and who bring the totality of themselves to the world surround me. These are people who push their limits and boundaries. They create, inspire, and impact in ways that leave me breathless.

There are magical moments everywhere in this city, but the most magical of all is how we all coexist together, most of the time peacefully. Today, I saw a Muslim street hawker cover his wares and then unroll a prayer rug, praying on the sidewalk in Arabic, in front of a protestant church with a stream of people washing by. It was midtown at lunchtime and the streets were packed. I marvelled at how no one bothered him or his wares. Everyone just seemed to merge around him and keep going with his or her business. This level of tolerance I love about this city.

Which is not to say that some of the human ticks don't exist. In my old neighborhood, traditionally Jewish and now quite mixed, there was a stir in my building when a woman walked into it with a full burka on. The doorman freaked out and looked at me and my ex-husband and niece and said, "What do I do?" We started cracking up and said, "What you always do. Why is she any different?" Then he laughed too, and she rolled her eyes before getting in the elevator.

There was also the time about seven years ago when my ex and I were cycling through Bed Stuy. On our way to see my sister and niece, some naughty teenagers threw rocks at my husband while saying *hipster, go home*. This was at the height of gentrification there, and people who had long lived in the neighborhood were being priced out. So again, like the human experience, it isn't perfect. But it is real.

I'd like to think that those of us who live here for any extended period of time are real and marching to our own drummers. We're coloring outside the lines. This is so apparent to me when I'm in Los Angeles and Santa Monica. People do not cross against the light there. Even when there is no traffic, people stand politely waiting for the light to change. I don't. I feel only slightly subversive when I dart across the street against the light. I've been warned that next time I'll get a ticket. Uh huh, it just seems ridiculous. I just have to laugh

I come from a city where just a week ago I saw a guy face off against a bus. It was the most insane, hilarious and outrageous moment. It was New York. 11 AM, 8th Avenue and 23rd Street. I came up out of the subway after ballet class into drizzly rain. We had the light with the countdown. We all started walking across the street and then an MTA bus turned. It was a lot bigger than us. We looked like a pack of ants compared to the bus. But the guy, sturdy and athletic with a lacrosse t-shirt, whirled around and faced the bus waving his umbrella and screaming, F*uck you! I have the light.* Then the bus driver leaned out and said, *fuck you, I know! I see it!* They proceeded to scream at each other and I thought, *Man, Mr. lacrosse player, just keep walking.* What he was doing was idiotic but, at the same time, he was fully feeling his moment. And so was the bus driver. I called my sister who now lives in Silicon Valley to give her the blow-by-blow. She laughed and then sighed, *God I miss NYC.*

Quite the opposite. NYC has a tolerance for difference that is rarely found in other places in this country. Barneys shoots ad campaigns with women in their late 50s and 60s and another one with Transgender models.

It's a tough place, but it's also a limitless place with a wide range of social codes. For this reason I feel like it's an easy place to live out the third act of life. People here don't shrink away from life just because they aren't numerically young anymore. They stay geared up. For instance, some of the most iconic New Yorkers work energized right until the end. Diane Von Furstenberg is going stronger than ever — and in her late sixties. Diana Vreeland worked and was relevant into her 80s. Then there's Gloria Steinem, Pat Cleveland, Barbara Walters, Jackie Onassis.

I also feel like being a New York kid gave my niece the ability to withstand being the only black kid in her school after she moved to Silicon Valley. Rather than get down on herself for not being like the other kids, she told me she felt sorry for them saying, "Auntie they can't help it if they don't get me. They don't even know about Chanukah or speak another language. Isn't that boring for them and kind of sad?" I smiled and thought, T*hat's the New Yorker in her*.

For the most part, no one cares about your differences here. I often think the whole city marches to a different drummer. *Weird* is just an abstract concept here. Living here we are surrounded by weird and chic; loud and graceful; rich and poor, and everything in between. Living here is *being* in the unrelenting harmony and cacophony of life. In this cacophony of life I am busy. Life is rich. Luscious.

The whole city is full to the brim. The city here is busy being alive. Fully alive, which I admit can be somewhat exhausting. There's no coasting here. So when I need to coast, I go away. I go to Croatia, to Maine, to Gocek, to someplace that has a lot of water or some good lingerie shopping like Fifi Chachnil in Paris. Or I just make the choice to sleep in, curl up with a book or watch a movie. I don't feel like I'm missing out when I stay in, because there's *always* something interesting happening here. It's the city that never sleeps. It's perhaps the primary reason that I love NYC. She is not asleep. She is fully alive. Thanks to her, I feel like I am too.

Chapter 24

Everything is Energy

If you want to find the secrets of the Universe, think in terms of energy, frequency and vibration.

~Nikola Tesla

Since January 2015, I have been pulled to ride. Every morning while meditating, I would see the same image of a chestnut thoroughbred with his forehead on mine. Morning after morning, that image called to me until a long-buried memory from childhood came back. This memory was calling to me, leading me somewhere.

When I was a child, we moved from the center of our small New England town to a house on the outskirts in the country. Western Massachusetts is a lot like upstate New York, rural, mountainous, and when I was growing up there were farms and stables. Heritage Farm was walking distance from our new home.

I can't recall my exact age when I was first introduced to riding lessons. I know I was small compared to the horses. I think I was eight or nine. I remember how tall the horses stood, the ring, the smell of hay, horse manure, and the exhilarating feeling of merging with the movement, the motion. The freedom of riding was exhilarating for me.

Fast forward to New Year's (2015). Following my meditation I was flooded by that memory and this feeling of freedom. I put a picture of that chestnut thoroughbred on my vision board. Day after day, while meditating, I see the same vision: the same horse with his forehead on mine.

As the memory of the first horse I rode returned to me, I realized I was being led to ride again. I felt my heart soften at the simple memory of that horse, so many years ago. I am fifty at this writing, and I can't recall the name of that horse, but I recall the rich smells and feelings. Life experience has taught me about my heart. You could say that my heart has taught me about living from my heart. Once I feel deeply in my heart, I know the truth, the undeniable truth that precedes or transcends any rational thinking. Through the gate of my heart, it's my soul's GPS calling me.

Morning after morning, I felt my heart soften and open as the image of this horse returned to me. I've learned two things over time that go hand in hand. The first is to trust the visions in my meditations. The second is to trust the feelings of my heart, even when none of it makes rational sense. So I called my friend MC, who owns the Horse Institute. I felt an energetic portal open up.

MC picked me up from the Rhinecliff train station. As I was getting in the car, MC asked me, "When was the last time you rode?"

"I think 20 years ago." Then I remembered that I'd be 50 within a month. I started cracking up. I said, "Wait. Double that number." It began to sink in. I was going to ride for the first time in 40 years.

I can't even explain why I wanted to do it. There was no linear explanation, except that I kept seeing the horse in my meditations; I posted him on my vision board, and that had soon led to arriving at Ancramdale at the farm. I'm excited and a little nervous.

MC encouraged me. "Don't worry," she said. "Even after 40 years, It'll still be there waiting for you." She seemed to have so much faith and trust that it all would unfold perfectly. Her speech was decisive and clear. She spoke with a knowing. "Riding," she said, "is an imprint. It's an energy. You'll feel it. It'll all comeback."

Her encouragement helped me steady myself. I breathed. I connected with my pelvis and my heart. I intentionally shifted my attention back in to my body.

I know when I am disembodied, and when I need to center. To get there, I used a simple breathing exercise from Naam Yoga. I put my right hand on my heart and my left on the center of my pelvis. I breathed in and held it for a 10 count. I exhaled and held out for another 10 count. Boom. I was back in the moment. My anxiety had left me. I was good to go.

MC and I kept talking about energy, how it includes muscle memory, soul memory and energetic imprinting. She assured me that it's like getting back on a bicycle. I laughed because a horse is A LOT bigger than a bicycle. MC's confidence in me and the horse I'm to meet steadied me. Then I met Henry. He really was the horse that I'd been seeing in my meditation. He was chestnut with a long white mark on his face.

He snorted while I brushed him. I felt tentative around him, when MC said, "Those are his happy horse sounds." I relaxed. *L*, MC's husband, was equally encouraging. There was a knowing between all of us that I felt was going to unfold into a magical, mystical couple of days. I felt a sense trigger in me; riding a horse was going to be a profoundly spiritual experience.

Riding is an exercise in trusting and in partnership. It requires that you're in it together. Henry felt everything. When I held the reins 1/16th of an inch higher in my left hand, Henry leaned to the left. We began communicating in a powerful way through energy exchange. I felt something like a powerful, circular flow. Not one moment of force. But I felt a sense of subtle power. I felt something exquisite happening.

I laughed, because trying to force Henry would have been like trying to move the animal version of the Titanic. He was really big. MC's husband Larry asked me if I rode motorcycles. I told him, "No, but I've ridden a Vespa." He reminded me that I was riding a horse, not a Vespa. Larry told me, "Stop leaning when

Henry turns. Find your center. Stay balanced."

This is a metaphor for life. Balancing yin and yang. Staying in your body. Finding your center. Balance. Being present to the moment. I felt the quality of the energy exchange make all the difference for me and Henry, much like what happens between people.

We all began laughing. I thought Henry was laughing in his own way also. He kept making his happy sounds. At one point I got really relaxed and laissez-faire in a spaced-out, unfocused way. For a moment, it all went to shit in the ring.

Henry began wandering aimlessly around the ring. While he did this I simply patted him. I shifted into a *pleasing* space and out of myself. I stopped upholding my side of the equation. For the moment I was so blinded by being in love with this horse, I couldn't see that I was doing us both a disservice. What a metaphor for human interaction.

MC spoke up. "*Why are you rewarding him?* He is behaving really badly because you are not clear with him. When you aren't clear, Henry, he doesn't feel safe. He doesn't know what you want. Tell Henry what you want."

Wow, I thought, isn't that a metaphor for my life? How often have I not communicated clearly about my feelings, especially in intimate relationships, because I was afraid to upset the apple cart? This isn't a safe space for anyone. I don't feel safe when I'm not clear or when I am on autopilot making default unconscious decisions. People get frustrated or don't feel safe when they don't know what I want. When I'm expecting people to read my mind, while at the same time give out unclear cues, things can rapidly go to shit. Henry reminded me that it's unsettling to misunderstand where people are coming from, when their cues and actions aren't aligned with their intentions. Henry wakes me up to this on another level. To express my intent clearly in the moment I need to express my awareness in a direct and simple manner.

In a flash, I go focused. With clarity of intention and a deeper understanding of the energy dynamic, I *"told"* Henry to trot towards the letter C in the ring. I shifted my gaze, and I saw the picture of us moving there in my mind. Suddenly, we were trotting towards C. Henry started making his happy sounds again. It was the beginning of a beautiful relationship.

Those two days contributed to making me more confident about my ability to shift old patterns. I opened more, became more present, more trusting, and loving. I began to see how this opening and clarity were clocking my field to my calling in my Beloved. Partnering with Henry opened my heart, deepened my understanding of the nature of energy exchange.

Henry reinforced my own integration with my true self, the one that is clear, focused, heart-centered and able to ask for what she wants. Being at the Horse Institute made me a more open and engaged person when I returned to New York.

Everything is energy.

Now how attuned am I to the quality of the energy being exchanged?

Chapter 25

The Power of Dreaming

Without leaps of imagination or dreaming, we lose the excitement of possibilities. Dreaming after all is a form of planning.

~ Gloria Steinam

I woke up today from one of my epic dreams. Since childhood I've had them. I've faced and healed my shadows. The 15 years of dedicated deep study with a living spiritual master have made them more powerful than ever. Two powerful living spiritual masters have confirmed something I feel deeply, that I heal myself in my dreams. Dreams are also where I get powerful messages from the higher world. My dreams mirror my real life, and often foretell what is to come.

I have also prayed before bed since before I was four, praying on my knees reciting Our Father and Hail Mary. Throughout my formative years, I would have dreams showing me Cinderella going to the ball, the Eiffel tower frequently in them. I'd also dream of Kuan Yin and white tigers and white lions. Elephant and pine trees often come to me in my dreams.

Sometimes they are so epic and intense that I wake up completely disoriented and I stay that way until I write them out. I make an effort to decipher the codes, because they speak to me in codes. Like the time two years ago when a pentagram was drawn in my dream with various numbers at the points. This was sometime before I went to South Africa. Reading the points I knew I would meet someone there with the birthday indicated in that pentagram. Turns out that I did. When I told the man his birthday, the color washed out of his face. I don't know why I've been experiencing this ability to see things before they occurred for as long as I can remember.

It was these dreams that showed me where I was going at the height of my childhood isolation. I would be shown night after night something so much bigger than the reality I was experiencing. In my dreams, I was shown cities around the globe. Twenty and thirty years later I found myself in those cities, experiencing the phenomenon of knowing where to walk, where to go, even understand languages I had never studied or been exposed to but in my dreams.

There was the time I was in Provence outside Avignon. I was staying with friends who lived in Paris. We were trying to find the famous market at L'Isle Sur La Sorgue. The small town is famous for its many antique shops. It hosts antique markets most Sundays. We were driving and got to a juncture where Michael said, "Angie, look at the map and see if we go left or right." This was 1990 and before the age of GPS and cell phones. We were just old school with a paper map of the area. While she was looking at a map, I said, "Michael go left." Then we all started laughing.

"Wow you sound so sure except that you've never been here," he said.

"Only in my dreams," I said, smiling.

"Well, let's go left then," he said, signaling left.

I smiled. Inside, I had a knowing. I trust my dreams and what they show me. By the way, a few minutes later we arrived at the Sunday market.

There have been other synchronous moments, and many nights of epic dreams. Maybe this is why I'm not certainty-driven in the conventional sense of certainty and security. My certainty and security come from what is revealed to me from the higher world.

This isn't woo woo. It's become more real to me than anything else, because I'm always shown where to go. So I learned a long time ago to go where I'm led. For instance, I had a dream once that was reinforced again while I was meditating the following morning. I saw the phrase, *Balancing the Executive Life*, repeated in the dream. I learned a long time that the messages spoken in dreams are not linear in the way that, let's say, a lesson is conveyed in school. Sometimes they arrive in dreams literally, at other times through symbols. The higher world often communicates in symbols.

So it's important to learn how to spend time with dreams. I write them down when I wake up, because they can be so fleeting. I don't want to miss the gift. When they give me an idea or a road to walk, they will also reveal to me the steps to take. So as it turns out, this phrase, *Balancing the Executive Life*, and the accompanying dream symbology were telling me to start my business -- to use my spiritual power and business acumen to develop a methodology to help leaders lead from a more centered, mindful place.

Then the pieces came together. I met a woman, who I am not close to, nor still in touch with. She told me that I should meet Andrew Neitlich. So I arranged for us to have a conference call wherein I rather audaciously asked this former McKinsey consultant and Harvard MBA for his birthday. I said I needed to do the numbers to see if his coaching program made sense for me. He said, "Sure, here's my birthday." He then laughed and said, "I don't know of any data that proves what you're about to do, but go for it."

Then I did the numbers and prayed for guidance. The numbers told me to do his executive coaching program. I got on a plane to Tampa Florida, drove to Sarasota and sat in a hotel conference room for four days of intense study with him. Then I went back and got my masters training with him. At one point he asked me, "I asked for your best thinking, is that your best?"

I replied, "Yes. Yes, it is." He responded, "I don't think so." Ouch! But that kind of demanding approach ramped up my business game.

By now, I have coached scores of clients who have made a big footprint in the world. People who speak at Davos, others who are global brand ambassadors, women who are profiled in publications like Glamour, women who have been on the cover of Forbes. I fly under the radar for the most part. My job is to support them in being their true self -- healing and achieving in a way that positively impacts people in the world. When they do well, I exhale and feel like I have done my job well.

This all started with a dream.

When I teach my Wednesday class we usually do postures which open the Daath point on the back of the neck. This point is the unseen 11th sphere on the Tree of Life. It's said to be the door to the unseen world. Many women in my class tell me they have dreams after the class and I encourage them to spend time with their dreams -- to take them seriously. There is a healing, a reconciling of the conflicts of the conscious and unconscious. If you're blessed by the higher world, prophesy happens also. If even one woman exits my class trusting this guidance, I know her life will change. Awareness of dreams make life technicolor.

Sometimes for no reason at all I will get exhausted and have to take a nap. What I now understand is that when this happens, there is an urgency to the message I need to get, one that can't wait until I go to sleep that night. So now that I understand what is happening, I just take a nap and get the message. I am lucky that my life is structured in such a way that I have the space to do this. I believe the Higher World has a hand in this being the case as well.

I had a dream recently in which someone who means a lot to me was calling me on the phone. In the dream, an older woman is saying, "Just talk to him. Pick up the phone." When I do, I listen and he is telling me he *got it*. He tells me that he listens to the Universe too and that it took him a long time, a year, but he is saying, "I know what's right and I'm doing it." In the dream I take a big inhale and say nothing. Then I wake up. Falling back asleep, the dream shows me in a white dress with red epaulets on it. I start walking up a lush red velvet staircase in the long white gown. A year ago, I had dreams of the same man and the two of us surrounded with red velvet.

Two days after I had the dream my phone rang in my apartment in NYC. I picked up and heard the same man I'd spoken to in the dream telling me verbatim what I'd heard him say in the dream. And like in the dream, I just took a big breath in and listened. Truth be told, sometimes it takes me a bit of time to fully integrate my dreams. The power and impact of these synchronicities can be beyond comprehension at times. Following the dream I am gleefully happy and in surrender mode. I know that between this dream and the one I woke up from earlier filled with elephants and pine trees that it's going to be a tremendously magical time. It already is, and it's going to get even more so.

I still pray before I go to bed. I have my own conversations with God each night. Making love is in itself a prayerful act – a direct connection with the divine. It may not happen every night, but when it does, it brings me closer to divinity. I also pray the prayers of my childhood, Our Father . . . Hail Mary, plus I've added to them. I also say, *By the Grace of God and the Luminous Beings may the great Architect of the Universe reveal to me, through the Archangel Gabriel, what I need to know at this moment in time and space for the Glory of God on earth.* And he does. They do. I keep my end of the bargain and I listen.

Chapter 26

Ameena and Michael's Relationship Lesson

For one human being to love another; that is perhaps the most difficult of all our tasks, the ultimate, the last test and proof, the work for which all other work is but preparation.

~ Rainer Maria Rilke

My niece Ameena is eight. When she was very little, my sister and I used to laugh about her being what we called "the oracle." She has the most soulful, deep-brown eyes with a self-contained way of looking not only at you but through you. Since she was a baby, she came with us to Naam Yoga and meditation classes. You might say that the teachings imprinted her with a certain frequency. But I also believe that she was born with an innate connection to the unseen world and to the immediate truth of her soul.

During her pregnancy, my sister would chant high frequency mantras. She also followed the teachings of the Kabbalah of birth. Ameena also carries our spiritual lineage. By lineage, she is imprinted with the mystical side of Catholicism, namely the Gnostic teachings. But she's also imprinted through our blood lineage with shamanism and psychic abilities. She is blessed to be born of a mother who not only embraces spirituality, but has helped her cultivate and maintain her connection to the unseen world. She has a profound sensitivity and empathy without losing herself or over-identifying with other people.

For better or worse, like all of us, Ameena feels her way through life. That sensitivity can also turn to fire and fits, if she is pushed the wrong way. Her Mother and Aunt have those qualities as well. The energetic imprinting of lineage runs deep.

    I believe spiritual grounding has given Ameena the capacity to hold her center. She knows and honors who she is. For instance, she doesn't take most things personally. Things that would royally piss her Auntie and Mother off seem to roll off her back. For instance, when the kids in her new suburban, homogenous school asked her, if she was Annie, played by Quvenzhané Wallis in the recent remake, her response was, "Auntie, I told you these kids aren't sophisticated. I mean, I'm brown like that girl in Annie, but we don't look anything alike. Her hair is really tight and I have loose curls. We both have small noses but… well, Auntie, I told you they aren't sophisticated. I mean, it's not like I think all the white kids look the same."

    Talk about perspective. I marvel at the way she doesn't internalize slights or stupidity around race. While these things really piss me and my sister off, Ameena Grace just thinks ignorance is ignorant and moves on. She misses New York, where she was born. Silicon Valley has been a culture shock in many ways for her. She still gets excited when she sees a black person, but she seems to have an ability to not dwell on what doesn't serve her. Instead, she focuses on what works for her, like hiking in the park, Karate lessons, or swimming at Half Moon Bay and in her pool at home. These activities all work for her and bring her joy. Not to mention, well, she has a "boyfriend."

    Michael is another one of the few brown kids in her school. Like Ameena, he is growing up in a single parent household. Ameena is with her mom and Michael is with his dad. Michael is crazy about her, over-the-moon crazy about her. My sister sent me a picture of him staring at my niece while she read her book and I thought to myself, *We are in so much trouble.* She has mesmerized people, especially boys since she was a toddler. They become fixated with her in a way that can be obsessive. People stop and tell us how beautiful she is but we know that it's not just the physical. She has a command of herself and a radiance that people are drawn to. She also follows her own compass, much to the chagrin of adults; she knows her truth and stands by it.

She likes Michael. The intensity of his devotion, however, can overwhelm her. So they have had to make agreements. One of them is if he comes for an all-day play date, she needs breaks to do her thing, meaning play with her dolls, quiet time with her books, drawing . . . things where she can retreat into her own little world and recharge. The two of them seem to be in harmony when he can flow with that. She in turn can flow with him. He is a boy's boy. He's very active, wanting to swim and run and do what a nine year-old boy likes to do. Most of the time they have a lovely give-and-take, and are sweetly responsive to each other.

But sometimes things are more sideways. Recently, Michael's father saw my sister at after school pickup. He said Michael really wanted to see Ameena for an all-day play date. My sister said, "Okay. Let me check with Ameena, and I'll reach out to you to arrange things."

In turn, Ameena told my sister, "Okay, but he needs to know that if he is at our home all day then he has to respect my space. Sometimes he is all over me and I can't stand that. Keep in mind she is eight years old so "all over me" has a different connotation than it would for an adult.

My sister doesn't want to get caught in the role of rescuing Ameena from Michael, if he won't give her her space. So instead she tells Ameena, "Remember Ameena Grace, *he can't read your mind*. So you have to use your voice and *tell him how you feel*." Ameena nods and rolls her eyes. Because like most of us, she sometimes doesn't want to deal – especially when she's tired. Ameena loses patience with Michael at times, especially when she's told him the same thing over and over. So my sister reminds Ameena that people can have a lot going on, and that sometimes they need a reminder.

Michael arrives for the play date and sleepover. First time. Monumental.

Things are going swimmingly. I get sent a photo of them jumping into the pool together, which is beyond adorable. After a few hours of swimming and being in the sun Ameena needs her "downtime." He is a little pooped too, so they go upstairs to the apartment. Once there, he is all up in her space and she freaks out. Yelling at him, "We had an agreement and you broke it. Now you have to go home." Then he freaks out and up the conflict escalator it goes. She storms away from him and he starts crying and saying to my sister, "I like her so much, why doesn't she like me more." Ameena overhears this and says, ""I would like you better, if you respected me and weren't so annoying."

As my sister related the story, I was wondering what happened next. Did they have a time out, nix the sleepover, break up? None of the above. They worked through it. She told him how she felt, and he gave her more space. One could even say they compromised. So now when he comes over for a play date, he occupies himself during her breaks. But she takes shorter breaks.

Ameena has a classic creative personality. She needs time by herself to connect internally and express herself through her creations, whether she is making a new outfit for Barbie or drawing or dancing in the living room. She is like me and my sister in this way. We all tend to put on our favorite songs and dance around our homes. We all did it as kids. Even today, as I write this, I was listening to the Bee Gees' *More Than a Woman* and dancing before I went out to my lunch meeting. My sister and I like to retreat into our books as a place of inspiration. When we come up for air, we can connect with people again.

Michael feels to me to have a more linear personality. He's goal-directed and singularly focused on playing or on her. And he's cool with that. He doesn't seem to need as much the solitude. But he increasingly understands that Ameena needs her downtime. So he doesn't take it so personally.

Observing all this, it seems that these two eight year olds are getting a good rhythm. One thing that stands out to me is that I never hear them attacking each other personally. Even Ameena's tirade was, well, about how she felt. Both of them seem to stay in this space. They don't go into character assassination mode. I'm proud and inspired by how she stays away from attacking him with name calling or insults. She sticks with what she feels. Uncensored, she expresses how she feels to him. Maybe she hasn't yet learned to overthink things, second guess herself, or come up with contingency plans. She just *feels* and *is*. Ameena is in touch with her "I AM." And above all, she's practicing expressing it – by just expressing it.

What I also notice with them is there are no hidden agendas. Michael is clean and clear. He wants all day play dates, and he asks for them. She wants to spend time with him but she needs it structured so that she has some space. They aren't afraid of losing each other, if they express what they want. Fear of abandonment hasn't lodged in their hearts yet. But maybe that's because they're practicing being in the space of putting words to what they feel.

Like him she is clean and clear about where she is. When they fight, they don't chew on it. They freak out, talk, and move on. And neither one of them throws the argument in each other's face days later. Why? Because when you're eight or nine, days later is a lifetime.

I am learning a lot from the little dynamic between my niece and her friend. She speaks her truth and she stays in her heart. She is detached from the outcome and she's just herself. She inherently knows how to be — be in the moment, be herself, and be congruent with how she feels and what she says.

So now the question becomes, How do we help her stay in this space? — this space of simple alignment with herself. She is all heart. But, then again, that's all she knows. Her fearlessness is rooted there. She is integrated and in her true self. And perhaps one day, she'll learn fear. Even then, I suspect she'll have the wherewithal to measure and weigh fear within the lightness her own heart.

Sometimes her truth is a little intense for sure. She is pretty uncensored and in adult life we are not often privy to such naturalness. Like when she tells us things like:

"How can you listen to that old music?! It just makes my ears melt!"

"Mommy, you wouldn't understand because you're from the old school and I'm *new school*."

But we do our best to support her staying in her heart. And maybe it's a bit selfish of us, but no matter. Because it inspires us to do the same.

Chapter 27

Hogwarts & A Night in NYC

There is no elegance without grace, and no grace without ease. There is no ease without naturalness.

~ Jacqueline de Ribes

I am finishing up a meeting with one of my favorite clients. She is on an executive team and seriously one of the most amazing people that I've met in my life. She has heart combined with business acumen and empathy -- a total trifecta. I just love her for that.

It's a fall day in NYC. The sky has risen into that deep October blue. The trees in Central Park have turned golden, ochre, and terra cotta. The air feels so crisp. Fall is perhaps the loveliest time in this city. Everyone is back in town, the social schedule is full with interesting parties, dinners, art openings and, of course, there is ballet barre class in the a.m. As I walk across town after my meeting, I feel grateful for all that this city has opened up and given me.

Tonight is no exception. I have the privilege of going to the Guggenheim opening of *Alberto Burri: The Trauma of War*. As I walk home, it strikes me how this Italian artist painted just after World War II using the rubble of war, burnt plastic, broken brick, bent metal. He is historically significant, and I'm excited for the show. Although I'll rely on my dear friend who is a top art consultant to give me the historical context, I've done some background reading on Burri before the opening, because not only do I love to drink champagne with beautiful, interesting people, but I have this romance with knowledge and art. I can't help myself.

Getting dressed is a whirlwind. I'm starving, as I've not had lunch. So I quickly try to eat some soup before I get picked up. My apartment looks like a tornado because I have no time to get ready, and I'm trying to be independent on my outfit choice. This is a problem of the privileged, art openings, outfits, cars arriving to pick me up. These are not only first-world "problems." But they're uniquely privileged problems within a privileged city. I'm aware of this. I've had my problems, and I can live with problems like these. In this case, I want to make sure I feel good in what I'm wearing, because what I wear impacts my whole experience.

In a social world, clothes are a second skin. What the eyes open to, they touch. Optics are important to me as I'm a very visual person. I feel like they are part of my relationship with the artwork and the social milieu that surrounds it. I feel like my clothes make my internal and external life congruent. They also connect me with the provenance of the work itself. In a public space, the ownership of the work is for all those in attendance. I feel the artwork doesn't end with the frame; it ripples to the circles around it and into the eye. It becomes you. Why not dress with a little of this in mind?

Arriving at the Guggenheim with my friend, the ritual begins. First the ground floor with the open bar. Here is where it starts. Champagne, really good wine, mixed drinks, it's all there. Even though I've been here since 1989, every time I go to something like this I feel ecstatically happy and grateful. Once you clock into the frequency and the field of NYC, there is something so expansive that it is breathtaking. Maybe it's the scale of this beautiful museum, maybe it's 5th Avenue on Central Park or the multiple languages overheard. And on top of it, there's the connection. Everyone there is in some way part of the same portal and field.

Then we notice the *Cat in the Hat*. The two of us love the *Cat in the Hat* . . . This is the guy that we see every fall at the Guggenheim opening. He is seriously a human version of the *Cat in the Hat*. He is a cool Cat, a regal black man – Caribbean, African American, African from the continent, I don't know. But one thing I do know is he is awesome, if only for his regalness and style. Every year he is there at the precise time that we are. Year after year we all nod, acknowledge each other. My friend and I excitedly whisper to each other, look the *Cat in the Hat*.

The *Cat in the Hat* feels like a Hogwart. It is clear that he has magical abilities. After all his hair is three-feet high in a head wrap, and all heads turn as he walks up the famous circular ramp. The *Cat in the Hat* is a magical juxtaposition with these paintings. Thank God my friend can give me a context. I say to her, "These paintings make me feel like I'm going to have a nightmare. They look like bombed out buildings. Now Seventy years after WWII and we have Syria, Israel/Palestine, Iraq, Libya, Afghanistan, Yemen, the Sudan, the Ukraine, refugees flooding across borders, sinking in ships." I take a breath and stop. "It feels so intense that so many years after he finished them, the paintings make me feel like the war hasn't ended. Their experience is ours."

As we view the paintings they serve as a catalyst for a deep discussion. I look around and there are groups huddled all along these famous Frank Lloyd Wright ramps. I ask my friend who is a curator how they come to decide on what to show. I'm struck repeatedly how uncanny it is that these paintings done just after WWII reflect what's happening today. Maybe the renewed power of great art is its continued relevance. As we walk up the ramp of the museum, the talk moves back and forth between the Italian palazzo's in Venice that my friend has visited, to the amazing shows she's curated, to me telling her that she will always be my art consultant once I have the money to buy "real" art. We laugh. We talk about fashion, which we both love. We discuss the connection between art, fashion, authenticity, having a point of view, and the near impossibility of seeing your own culture.

But the show is intense, and so as we descend back down we agree that we need another. This isn't the type of event you just go home from afterwards. Like all profound experiences that spark deep feelings, it needs integrating, digesting. My friend asks me, after standing on these hard floors with four inch heels, "Do you want to go somewhere we can sit down?" I vote for sitting too. So we hop a cab. Then the question is, "The Mark or The Carlyle?"

Heck, we could get out of our comfort zone and try The Mark. But for me, it pales in comparison to The Carlyle. I am a downtown girl but on the odd chance I find myself on the Upper East Side, The Carlyle is my go-to. I've had some wonderful experiences there. I saw one of Eartha Kitt's last shows there. She was close to 80 at the time, and still had everyone mesmerized. The Carlyle is a slice of old New York. It exudes old money, subtlety and a level of service that I can't help but relish. It's the perfect place to head after an uptown event. It's classic but not stuffy. We opt for the Carlyle. It's old romantic New York, a holdover from another era.

We sit down in the lustrous light of the Carlyle with the energy and the power of the paintings still around us. The conversation we started at the Guggenheim continues. We talk about how astounding it is that people get so polarized around who is right and who is wrong -- that somehow compassion and empathy gets lost in the struggle to do what's right. Who is right or wrong when a school is bombed, a city leveled, or a fresh war explodes a new refugee crisis. We both consider how all of that is so beyond the ensuing strategies of right and wrong.

I mention how I cannot believe that people are so opposed to the US helping refugees from these types of conflicts. We helped after World War II. Then and now, refugee quotas remain. Still people object as though forgetting that this country was built on the backs of immigrants and slaves. Populations of people fleeing the horrors of war, religious persecution, and poverty are the polar opposite of forcing people to travel here as slaves. Yet, slavery and war remain with us. The world's legacy is not far from any of us.

I share my family descendants with peasants, mill workers, and fur trappers. On the other side I share my line with share croppers and slaves. Every generation contributed to doing better than the last. As we're talking my friend shares with me her family emigration history.

I say to her, "I look around, and I see the world at war, so where is the empathy and compassion for these people?" Then I share that I was recently at a Sunday dinner with a group of Brazilians. Here I met a UN Security Council member from Spain. We started talking about Syria. Granted I had a bit of wine, but as we talked I started getting teary and I said to the man from the UN, "As human beings we have a responsibility to help these people. It could be us in a different time and space. You could have been running from the Spanish civil war and I could have been running from slavery. Both of our ancestors fled, and someone along the way helped them." My friend and I sipped more wine and grew silent and I continued telling her what I had told him, "I would want someone to help me if I was in that position," and he said, simply and respectfully, "Me too. My life depends on it. War never leaves us. But compassion seems always in jeopardy."

This conversation revolves over the course of the night across the globe. The question of the Palestinians and the Israeli settlements comes up. Always a fun one, especially in NYC – which is to say, not fun at all. It's serious. The topic can be particularly charged. Our voices grow hushed. And yet the thing we're trying to describe seems to take the same shape no matter where in the world you look -- the same provocations, armaments, techniques, and repercussions. As for the civilians, no matter where you seem to look you see the same makes and models of burnt-out cars, the same tee-shirts, jeans, and blown off shoes.

We talk about all of this spurred on by the paintings, where there's a central theme across geopolitical lines. It's that, globally, fear coupled with the determination to retain control, is resulting in the civilian populations being killed in numbers greater than the fighting forces themselves – killed by authorities, by armies, by drones, by proxies, by mercenaries, by nations, and state-sponsored terrorists.

Perhaps it's all becoming so acute so that it can be healed – so this cycle that repeats itself over and over can stop.

It's a topic we're not going to solve. We feel the depth of it and take a breath. Just after our second glasses of wine come, we switch to the topics of healing, spirituality and fashion. My friend suggests the paintings are so frightening and so ugly that in their state of provocation they move us to see beauty in the ugly. I say, "Perhaps but they might just as well give me nightmares."

Then, seemingly out of nowhere, amidst all this seriousness and splendor, we have a Hogwart moment. There is a woman standing beside my friend, gazing over the rims of her wire glasses. She looks me dead in the eye and says in a posh English accent, "Those pearls around your neck are astounding. Fantastic, in fact." I say, "Thank you" and she continues, "How long are they?" "65 inches," I tell her. She asks, "Who makes them?" I laugh and say they are costume, no Mikimoto. And she says, "No, they are special. They are strung on gold wire." Now I know she is a Hogwart. The room is very dimly lit, and even a 10 year old with perfect vision wouldn't be able to see what they are strung on. She says, "Yep, strung on gold wire." Then she belly laughs and says you're not fooling me, those are by Chanel. "You like your Chanel." I tell her that I do like Chanel, but mostly I like Coco Chanel herself. She was a remarkable woman. She belly laughs again and says, "Well, you're both remarkable women."

Silently I think to myself, W*hat is remarkable is your being in the Carlyle in running shorts and a turquoise windbreaker at 9 PM on a Thursday night.* There is no dress code here but people are dressed. It's not the kind of place you walk around in yoga pants. It's The Carlyle. But this woman is magical and beyond charismatic. We are hooked and want her to join us.

I say, "Please, sit here with us." And my friend seconds, "Yes, join us for a drink." Even as we invite her to sit, I wonder where the hell she came from. I am facing the only entrance, and yet I didn't see her walk in.

And so commences an ascent into a Hogwart vortex, where time seemingly stops. Turns out she is friends with Pamela Harriman who is one of our favorites. She tells us stories. Stories of being a woman in the *Firm*.

I sit there thinking, *which law firm?* She says, "Darling, not a law firm, *THE FIRM*." Incredulous, I ask, "The firm? As in the British Royal Family?" She says, "Yes, I work for Prince Charles. Have done so for the past 20 years. Look, I'll show you some photos. She pulls out her iPhone. Poof, there she is with Charles, and then Diana's brother, and then . . . She regales us with stories about all of them and makes a point of saying how much she cannot stand Kate Middleton's mother or any people who are "*climbers*."

We are laughing so hard. We don't like climbers either. In fact, we both are slightly introverted and tend to pull back, observe, and merge with the energy at hand. We all agree on this.

Then the conversation turns to Paris and London. My friend says that she spends a lot of time in London and that my book is launching in Paris. The Hogwart whips out her golden rolodex sitting right there in her mind. She says, "Tell your publisher that you must have a reading at Shakespeare and Co and also WH Smith in Paris. That is if you actually want to sell lots of books! Do you want to sell the books, or is it a vanity project?"

I am laughing and tell her, "I do want to sell a lot of books. It's definitely not a vanity project. I'd like to think it's my love letter to life, my gift to the world. It's about connection, synchronicity, Hogwart experiences. It's about the magic of life."

She is very serious, pushing. "Get him to make sure you have readings at those bookstores. You can sell this book. This book is going to be big. I know." And I smile. It feels like another message from the Universe.

Then she switches to Chanel and begins to tell me all the places in Paris that I absolutely must visit in Paris while I'm there in December.

The talk shift back to London. It turns out that our Hogwart and my dear friend have the same neighborhood in common. And we all love Scott's. It's funny how sensuality stays in one's system.

I reflect on this. We all wax on about the seafood and champagne at Scott's – memories of oysters, shellfish, and multiple glasses of champagne. We share memories of the times spent there apart but doing the same thing. Now here we all are together.

Then out of the blue the Hogwart, who is also wearing a lot of turquoise, leans in and says to me, "I want your necklace." I say, "What?" and my friend echoes, "What?" and we both start laughing, because we think she is kidding. Then she says, "No, I'm serious, I have a bag a of cash. How much do you want for it?" I say smiling and a bit amused, "No it's not for sale." She says, "Come on. I have to have it, and everything is for sale."

We are belly laughing now but I'm clutching my hamsa necklace, and I say, "No, it's not for sale." But she presses, pushes and cajoles. Then finally she says, "Why won't you just sell it to me like anyone else most certainly would? You're American. Just name the price."

"It's not for sale," I say.

"Come on," she counters. "Now it's getting boring. Just let me buy the necklace."

"No, it's from Israel," I insist. "It was a special gift for my 50th birthday. It's a special Israeli opal. It's priceless to me. I never take it off. I would never sell it." I think then she realizes that it's not for sale. Something deeper is being said within all the smiles and laughter of the moment. I'm telling her that I don't have a price.

And with a twinkle in her eye our Hogwart tells me, "I knew I liked you."

Chapter 28

Keep The Goddess on Your Side

It's all about flexibility, about not knowing what's going to happen next. Listen and stay in the moment. Play with people who will support you. Get comfortable with being uncomfortable. Be willing to risk.

~ Amy Poehler

So much has been written about the Divine Feminine since December 21st, 2012, when *She* began to blow in as the new prevailing energy of a new era. This is why the Egyptian and Mayan calendars stop on this day. The old energetic order is a dying era. Something magical is being heralded, even as the old order battles to sustain its historical controls.

At cocktail parties, yoga circles, dinners in business circles, and everywhere in between, people, especially women, have been talking about *HER*. Sometimes, they talk like she's some magical fairy who's coming to rescue us. There are magical, mystical creatures all around us, seen and unseen. Just as mysterious remains the question, W*ho and what is this Universal Divine Feminine, Divine Mother Goddess energy?*

Fast forward from 2012 to Wednesday July 1st, 2015. I'm talking about *Her* in my Naam Yoga Class for Women. Not only have I been talking about *Her*, I talk to *Her*. I've done this ever since I discovered that she dwells in my heart. Even as I held the energy of that class, that same night I attended the birthday party of a dear friend, former client, and student of mine, a woman who epitomizes the Goddess energy in positive, global action. She's Global Brand Ambassador and founder of the *African Literacy Project*. As part of the party she was throwing a *Goddess Gathering* in the appropriately named "jewel box" penthouse in Manhattan.

Parallel that night to my Naam Yoga class and the Goddess Gathering was the full moon in Capricorn. From our spot in the Penthouse, looking out from floor to ceiling windows, *Her* radiance shown. Ms. Moon was watching over us, looking in at us as we drank champagne and relished being part of this amazing powerful circle in this amazing space.

There was a cake with a polka-dot high-heel shoe on top, set as the centerpiece of the table. Champagne flowed, laughter filled the room. I thought, T*hese are my people.* These are powerful, sensual, global women, real women, having authentic discussions -- not just talking about what they do for work. These women know how to be *women*.

The radiant gathering reflected the beauty, poise and magnetism of the hostess. Water seeks its own level and the Hostess had a magical Cancerian ability to bring the best people together – both men and women. It was a global gathering, almost all of the continents represented. As I looked around the room I smiled to myself and thought *SHE*, the Divine Feminine Goddess, the Divine Mother is here…

Our Hostess tapped her champagne glass and asked me to speak about the Goddess, and the significance of the full moon and the Divine Feminine. She asked me to bless the room and everyone in it. I spoke from my heart and was surrounded by women after I spoke, women saying that I had profoundly touched their hearts.

I am told I hold the energy of the Divine Feminine, that I am one of her ambassadors here on Earth. One of the great living spiritual masters of our time Dr. Joseph Michael Levry told me this 15 years ago. The unseen world, which visits me, often has told me that this is my mission on Earth -- to be a portal and a voice for this energy. It feels like a tall order most of the time. But I reflect often on what this means, not only for me but for all of us.

I don't think *She* is a magic fairy who lives outside of us, although I do believe she is everywhere – which is to say that I experience Her everywhere. Look around and without digging too deep, you'll see She is evident. Pay attention and you'll see *Her* energy is making itself heard in all sectors. The social, political, spiritual and business shifts that are occurring at this time reflect her presence. *Keep the Goddess on your side.*

The Goddess, the Divine Feminine, is a potential that is within all women. She is not something outside of us. Her potential is within us. She is our greatest light, wisdom and ability to love. Every time we choose to stay in the temple of light; every time we choose to heal our wounds, every time we have the courage to grieve and feel everything fully and authentically, every time we choose to walk away from the darkness of default behaviors, patterning, and illusion, then -- every time, she is making herself known and heard.

She's there every time a CEO decides that gender parity is something that can't wait 80 years, because for purely business reasons it needs to happen sooner. She's there in the boardrooms and the multinationals. She's there in the hearts of men who seek conscious women to partner with. She's there for those men who seek to integrate all aspects of themselves and move beyond the old, outdated patriarchal codes. She is reflected in their actions and the ways they wield masculine power.

She is not something outside us. She is within us and she is calling to us to wake up – to raise our consciousness, to do the great work and then express it through our vocations, passions, our intimacy and connection with each other. She is calling our hearts to be open to receive LOVE — loving each other and loving what we spend our lives doing. Calling us to live fearlessly, to move from "working" to answering a calling. *Keep the Goddess on our side.*

LOVE is the ultimate truth, and when we have the courage to choose it, we express the potential of the Divine Feminine Goddess that lives in all of us. Love is the purest expression of the Goddess. She is always on our side. But when we leave the temple of our hearts, we step into the world of shadows. Yet even shadows are an extension of *Her*. An honest acceptance of our shadows offers us a path back to living within the temple of the heart. Light casts a shadow, and those shadows are sometimes needed to point us back to the central flame. Bear witness to both your judgments and your faults. Don't cast out your shadows on others. Recognize them from within, with love. If we are wise, and learn how to be, then abiding with our feelings, even our darkest feelings, gives us what we need to walk back to our hearts – to return to the Temple of Light.

The Goddess is on your side. Have the courage and the compassion to express *Her* potential. Stand for compassion and spirit. Take a stand for what is morally right. Collaborate and rethink our notions of power. Expand beyond controlling each other to wielding power working side-by-side. Have the courage to share in the healing of our emotional wounds. We all have them. They come with the school of life.

Allowing yourself to be with the totality and the granularity your immediate experience keeps the Goddess on your side. Dropping your defenses and being vulnerable keeps the Goddess on your side too…

During the Goddess Gathering and my Naam Yoga Class for Women, the Capricorn full moon had brought up a lot in me emotionally.

I realized I was grieving the loss of a good man. Until now, I knew I had a deep affection for him but I don't think I realized how much I loved him and his daughter. After all, when I first met him, I was in the middle of a divorce. My heart was in Berlin via Cape Town South Africa. I was sorting through so much in myself. I wasn't even present to being in NYC, let alone to what he would come to mean to me.

But I would come to know.

It's the first week in September. I've been in my new apartment for a week. It feels like such an amazing gift to be living in this posh, prewar, romantic NYC building -- this building that I've dreamed of living in since I came to New York City in 1989. It's the sort of NYC building that is rare now in a city increasingly filled with glass and steel. I believe with my whole heart that the building is a portal to my greatest happiness. All the numbers for the building, my floor, and my apartment add to six, the Kabbalistic number of Venus, Harmony, and Love.

I am still in the middle of my divorce but I've landed well. The location is the perfect gateway to rebuilding my life as a single woman after being married for all these years. Moving here has set the bar higher and supports me in meeting it. I'm no longer who I was. My facades have fallen away. I've clocked my frequency to who I honestly am. I am living my life now, not someone else's.

But it's a process. I'm still getting used to the distance between spaces. For over a year now, I've been running away from New York, flying to Dubrovnik, London, Paris, Berlin, Brussels, Cape Town . . . *anywhere but here* has been my governing philosophy. I've been running away from my collapsing marriage, and running back to myself via these cities. Now I'm back to mine — my life, my city, myself. I'm no longer in the energy of *make-it-better-for-everyone-else*. I'm focused on making it better for myself. I'm back to fully healing and unifying my energies.

Even back in my home city, I've been walking around a bit disembodied. Time has become surreal, in part because most of the time I'm jet lagged. I haven't been fully in any one place. My heart has been in Berlin, my physical body is in NYC, and my energy . . . well, it's felt scattered across the globe. I know I've been fragile, so I'm being gentle with myself.

The first week in my new building I see Yasser the head doorman. I consider him an Egyptian angel in human form. And it was Yasser who put me at ease when I first moved in. "I don't know what happened to you but you won't always be sad. It will pass and we will help you," he says. As I start weeping, I feel this wave of gratitude. I realize just how safe I feel in this building. It's a feeling I haven't felt in such a long time. I'm relieved. I'm grateful. I'm also totally exhausted.

Yasser has been seeing me walk out of the building for the last week and jump into cabs. He says to me, "Kelley, Take the bus. It's right across the street. Everyone in the building does. It's so easy. Take the crosstown bus. Save your money for more Chanel," he says with a broad smile. He insists. I feel like a force bigger than both of us is talking through him. I say to myself, *Okay, why not. I'll try it. I'll take the bus.*

I'm headed to my client on Park Avenue and 21st Street. I'm dressed for my meeting. I have my huge sunglasses on with my earphones on. This is how I roll, as I run around the city during the day. Headphones on, and sunglasses -- sunglasses even when it's overcast. Both the sunglasses and the earphones buffer me from all the disparate energy that buffets me across the Manhattan streets and transit systems.

I'm spacing out and I feel an energy beside me. I turn my head and there's a really handsome man sitting beside me. I think, *This is the Swiss Air flight all over again, only in the form of a MTA bus ride.* Keep in mind, I don't talk to strangers . . . well, maybe I do on Swiss Air but not on the MTA. But when he says *hello*, I respond in kind. I ask him where he's from, and he says *guess*. He asks me my name, and I ask him his. I guess that he's Swedish. He is so blond, chiseled and has the bluest eyes. He's also a grown man with a masculinity combined with sensitivity. I am intrigued. My guess is that he's around my age (turns out he is seven years younger). He looks like many Swedish people I've met in Stockholm and in Gothenburg. He says his name begins with a K. I say, "Okay, you're German, if you were Swedish it would begin with a C."

He laughs and says, "You're good. Half right. Guess the other half." I start naming countries, and I'm getting it wrong each time. We're both laughing. Then he says Croatia. I literally squeal with delight. A few people look over at us on the bus. They probably think I'm nuts.

"You know," I say, "I just got back from Croatia. I loved it. It was so beautiful."

He's blown over that I just returned from the Elaphiti Islands, Lopud to be precise. He says, "I really can't believe it," he says, "only Germans and Croatians go there."

"Yes," I say, laughing. "That's what it seemed like to me. Germans, Croatians and now one American."

"Oh, Park Avenue," I say, looking up. "This is my stop. Nice talking to you."

He pauses. "Wait, do you have a card?"

I hand him my card and don't think anything of it. I'm in NYC but my heart is in Berlin. And I'm not looking for anything. I'm just trying to ground myself. I know I'm fragile. I know I need to heal and settle into my new life. But most of all in that precise moment, I know I need to focus on my next client meeting. It's with a COO, and I need to be fully present and engaged in strategy.

"Take care," I say, smiling and stepping out of the bus as he sinks from my consciousness into the choppy waves of seven million faces in Manhattan.

A few hours later, I receive an email from the man on the bus with some photos from Croatia. Attached is a sweet and slightly funny note, "Sorry to disappoint you that I'm not Swedish. But I loved seeing you so happy when I mentioned Croatia. Can I take you for a coffee sometime?"

That gets my attention for a millisecond. I think that's sweet and then I don't think about it anymore. In fact, he will reach out to me many times over the next two months consistently. Each time it will register for a millisecond and then pass through and out of my consciousness into millions of other milliseconds. My heart is still in Berlin.

Then one Sunday morning I wake up after having a very vivid dream about him. It's one of my prophesy dreams, and this one wakes me up. *Holy Shit,* I think… *something is happening here.* And the same morning there is a text from him. At that moment I get it, and I feel myself attracted to him for more than a millisecond.

We meet for a glass of wine and he brings his daughter. She is an angel. In his pursuit of me and his consistency, including daily texts and emails, he has shared his situation. He's legally separated and in the middle of a nasty custody battle. But he's not divorced. They're separated and are living in different residences on opposite sides of town, but still not divorced.

He tells me how drawn he is to me. And I say, *easy breezy beautiful.* I'm cautious, and not in any hurry, which seems to create some sort of safety for him. I'm not asking anything of him. I'm just present to each moment without any attachment to outcome.

He's a Capricorn with lots of Mars and Sun in his chart. He is steady like a goat climbing up a hill — perhaps a goat with a phone, steadily texting and calling. But I don't see him very often. He listens well and picks up on my passion for Misty Copeland and ballet. It turns out that he photographs and films her. He sends me photos of her dancing to Ave Maria that make me burst into tears, because they're so beautiful. Pictures arrive with him and his daughter wishing me a good day. There's a sweetness and a realness about him. But it bothers me that I don't see him very often. I start to feel like I'm an amusement and a distraction from his troubles. It strikes me that he wants me but for some reason can't really engage fully. Emotionally available when I'm with him … but then not. Maybe I'm the same way, as part of my heart is still back in Berlin.

It all comes to a head before Christmas. I call him around sunset, looking South through my apartment window. "I can't do this," I tell him. "Look, you're a special person. I adore your daughter. I'll always have a deep affection for you. But I don't do the cyber friendship thing. I'm a Cancer and Venusian Moon woman. I'm used to more constancy from my relationships. He says, "I understand," and then the phone clicks off. He doesn't call back. We haven't been fully intimate, you know, which makes it easier for me to walk away." So I do. I intend not to look back. I pull the bandaid off quickly. It stings less that way.

It's now a week into the New Year, Friday, January 9th. Friday is ruled by Venus. I'm walking through Madison Park soaking up the Venusian energy. I come across three amazing sculptures of the feminine form. As I stand there admiring them on this chilly day with fresh snowfall, I consider the synchronicity of having just launched a blog called TripleGoddesses. I'm awestruck by this city. I feel blissed out, and I feel an energy. I've always been good at picking up on subtle energy. I feel my way through life, and I know things before I see them. But I can also act and move on those feelings in an intuitive fashion that puts me places. In that moment, standing before the triple Goddesses in Madison Park, I feel him.

I look up and he's there. He looks half scared and half excited to see me. His daughter is with him, and she's smiling from ear to ear. She's a Cancer too. She has the same birthday as the love of my life so many years ago. There's a ripple of energy between all three of us, and I feel pure joy at seeing both of them. I throw my arms around him. He starts apologizing and saying he wants to see me. He's holding me close and whispering this in my ear.

Then we step back and look at each other, as we stand there in a vortex talking. He tells me he's going to Sundance. I tell him I'll be in Paris while he's in Park City, Utah. We're both leaving town at the same time, but we're headed in opposite directions. Many months later this will seem like a bitter metaphor. We'll both be crying as we split up. This is what happens sometimes: different energetic contracts pulling people in different directions. It can happen when two people are living in different chapters of their lives. But at this moment it's all synchronized, moving along the same magnetic pull of our hearts. His daughter looks at him, "Can Kelley *please* take me to the museum?" Then she looks at me.

"Okay," I say, "I would love to sweetheart, as long as it's okay with your dad."

We can't stand there in front of the snowy Goddesses forever. Now we're all getting cold. He says, "I'll reach out." I say, "It was so lovely to see you two beautiful people." I smile. I walk away and realize, *Oh my God, today is his birthday.* His birthday, Friday, Venus (6 = love). I'm struck by the feeling that this is some sort of second chance. It's a big city and we live on the opposite ends of town. The East Side and the West Side. *All the way east* and *all the way west.* The likelihood of this meeting was a total long shot. But the Universe works in mysterious ways, and I know my life, *all of our lives,* are synchronized. No one crosses my path by accident. Life has taught me this with each seemingly coincidental revolution. Something more is coming. I just don't know what.

Three weeks later my phone starts ringing. But I can't answer it right away. I'm on a conference call to Tokyo, as I see his name popping up over and over. When I call him back he picks up on the first ring. We both start laughing. We've developed this tendency to laugh when we both hear each other's voices. We chat for a bit, and then he asks me, "What do you want?"

The question takes me by surprise, and I say, "I feel connected to you and I think we should be friends."

"Good, me too," he says.

We decide that we'll see each other when he's back from Sundance and I'm back from Europe. We follow each other on Facebook while we're away.

When we get back to town and just agree to easy-breezy-beautiful, we don't define easy-breezy-beautiful. We don't put parameters around it, or even name it easy-breezy-beautiful. We don't name *it* anything. But it feels like a big *IT.* Our motto-without-name is *easy breezy beautiful.* It's easy, almost too easy. It's beautiful. It's passionate. It is healing. I feel like I'm home when I'm with this man I met on a bus. I feel awakened by his touch, by the way he looks at me like he wants to devour me, by the way we lie around talking for hours and giggling, watching music videos, and eating marzipan. We pray before dinner with his daughter. We eat lamb and more lamb. We're comfortable around each other in the bathroom. It is *surreally-real*. I feel safe and connected to both him and his daughter.

He opens my creativity. I can write again, really write. I get a book deal without an agent and without pitching anything. Likewise, he gets more and more work. This connection between us feels good for us both. We're both expanding our hearts. We're opening more fully to life. *It* is healing. And it also just *is*.

He tells me he is working on a film project with a famous environmental artist and leading force for filmmaking. I can see how this so fits his frequency. And I tell him so -- that he'll get everything he's lost back and more. I tell him that he will be successful beyond anything he can imagine. He says, "I believe you," and kisses me. "When I see you, I see truth," he tells me. Perhaps he is mine in some unexpected way. I am falling for him. I realize I want to give my whole self to him -- all of me. I'm not holding anything back. This has only happened one other time in my life, and that was 26 years ago, when I first came to New York.

His biggest gift to me is that I feel whole again. I feel like a woman, not some neutered disembodied divorcee. He holds an energetic space when we make love that is so deeply connected, that through him I've reopened fully to life.

Then spring arrives. It's April, and I have another one of my prophesy dreams. I wake up gasping. I know I'm going to lose a good man. I see it in my dream. I gasp and I brace myself for the end. I know that every time a door closes, another portal opens and something even more powerful comes to me. I know this to be my truth but still I brace myself. This one is going to hurt — most of all, because it's been all so good, and he is good.

So when the conversation comes, the one I've been dreading, I try to let it break me open. I try to stay present to myself and to him. I tell him I'm not mad, I'm confused and I don't want to be confused. I say to him, "Did I imagine all of this?" He gets upset with me and says, "Are you crazy? How can you even think I haven't felt everything you have? But I can't do the boyfriend and girlfriend thing. It freaks me out. I have a lot of wounds. And, seriously, I have to do my work on them. I can be friends but I can't be serious."

And this is how life goes. It surprises us. We met on a bus, and we never intended to be serious. We never even defined it. We just went with it. Then somehow our hearts and souls connected and it felt serious. And I realized I was in love.

This I now know though. Making love with him healed, awakened and opened me in a way that I hadn't felt in so long. Being in a shitty marriage had shut all of that down. What I do know is that our connection was a profound spiritual, physical, and emotional connection to goodness — to a profound goodness that we both carry.

It's funny how energy works. If both people are sensitive and open to each other nothing needs to be said because you know it. The energy between us wasn't casual. Kind of never was. And maybe we should have talked about it, defined it. But instead we let the Universe carry us to a point where we had to accept the gift of the sacred exchange between us and that the chapter was closing.

I try to stay open through the grief of losing him. He has been such a precious gift to me — from what he has said to me, and I to him. Now it's time to fulfill the sacred contracts that at this moment have pulled us apart.

Synchronicities are everywhere. They're gateways, really. Receive them. Feel them. Your feelings are the keys to the gates. Your internal dialogue is the gatekeeper. Pass through the gates placed before you. Step aside from your rational mind. Synchronicities have taught me how to wake up to my own self — to my own vulnerability and power as a woman. They expand me into the energy of my destiny. They point the way to the great mystery of our own existence and our path back to the *temple*. And they have given me the most beautiful gifts of my life – gifts for my awakening to the central questions. Who are you? Why are you here?

Yesterday, I got flooded with all my feelings circling back around this. Without naming names, I spoke to the class of how raw I felt. How vulnerable I felt. How much I missed his vibration of sincerity, truth and his profound sensitivity. How acute and painful the loss is for me. His leaving me had left me dumbfounded. What could be more important than the temple?

But I also realized the extent to which we were in different chapters with different priorities. Part of loving someone is to let go and honor free will. So, under that powerful full moon I summoned my courage. This time I summoned the courage to grieve, to fully feel my heart and allow the experience of all of it -- to honor the give-and-take of unconditional love. Loving him unconditionally and generously was, I believe, as much a gift to myself as it was to him. At least this is what I told myself. This is what I hoped.

I was allowing myself to be open to someone who had found me on a bus eight months before. I would never have thought it. Like most New Yorkers, I sit with my sunglasses on and my earphones tucked into my ears.

So I had to recognize that *She* had sent us to each other when we were both fragile. For a time it was a poetic dance, freely expressed without expectation.

I told my students all this. My voice shook and I almost burst into tears. *Keep the Goddess on my side*, I kept telling myself. One of the things I've discovered is that I cannot be false even when I feel the most vulnerable. I cannot dishonor myself by armoring myself.

All this leads me to a deep abiding belief that the Divine Feminine is furthering the complete expression of our whole hearts, connecting us to the highest expression of our hearts.

For me, the Divine Feminine Goddess energy means accessing the Temple that flows within us. It's an energy of acceptance. To arrive within the gates is to surrender to Light; align with Light. Placing our awareness on our feelings, all of our feelings, is the key to the temple. The internal dialogue is the gate keeper.

It's a conscious choice to not turn our back on the temple of our heart. There's a sobriety that comes with that deep knowing, that turning away from the temple of our heart will lead to our slipping further and further away.

Walk back to the temple of your heart. And once you have, don't turn away. Feel all of it. Don't hedge your bets. Love with your whole heart, even if it freaks you out. And if it does, feel that too. Rest with it. Bear witness. Let it breathe. It freaks all of us out sometimes. Risk. Remain open. Live. Don't worry, you'll be better than okay.

Sometimes people walk away from the temple because it is so beautiful that it terrifies them. Sometimes they leave because the connection shines a bright light on their dark places; and they simply can't accept what they see in themselves by virtue of seeing it in another. Sometimes they walk away because remaining in the temple looks foolish.

Even of people I have held close to heart, I have sometimes had to ask, *Why does anyone turn from the temple?*

May we *love*, even in the apparent absence of *love*.

Keep the Goddess on your side.

Chapter 29

Disruptions

How many cares one loses when one decides not to be something but to be someone.

~ Coco Chanel

It can take a long time to get 25 blocks in Manhattan, particularly if you have somewhere to go.

This reality has taught me patience over the years. There is no use getting frustrated with trying to speed the journey. It's 2015 but flying cars haven't arrived yet in New York.

My dear friend and I sit and chat patiently in the back of the cab about fashion, as we make our way uptown. It's Fashion Week in NYC. Thanks to my other dear friend, H, we've been invited to a private showing of the fall/winter collection for Chanel, and it's where we're headed now.

Upon arrival, we see H on the ground floor waiting for us. He keeps us focused as we make our way up three flights of stairs. I find focusing at Chanel insanely difficult. There are so many beautiful pieces of clothing and accessories. I'm easily distracted as much by the beautiful clothes as by the brand itself, what has endured for more than 100 years.

I don't always love the collections, in which, for example, there was recently a very itchy sweater for over 2K and I thought, "Karl, come on… you have got to be kidding me." But I have always been inspired by its founder, a woman who came from less than nothing and made her own destiny. Chanel was one of the true liberators of women. She freed women from the corset. Her clothing designs were centered around freedom and ease of movement. Her designs effected the way we moved, the way we thought, and the way we perceive ourselves today. She was her own creation despite formidable obstacles. This legacy carries into the brand today, the reason why I love it so much.

H says, "Let's go in. They are waiting." It's not every day that Chanel waits for an arrival. What I don't know, but discover soon enough, is that there are ten women sitting in the atelier waiting for us. We're a half-hour late. As we walk in, I can see them impeccably dressed and waiting expectantly for the private showing to begin. A waiter serves Perrier and champagne. There are petit fours. It feels like we are on Rue Cambon, where it all started.

The presentation begins within moments. We sit and watch as we slide into a vortex. We are all clocked into a spell of sorts. Emmanuelle from Paris announces each look and weaves a kind of spellbinding preview of the Chanel collection through the historical lens of the woman who founded the epic brand. I'm feeling a bit elevated and slightly giddy in the rarefied world that is Chanel. Giddy enough to speak to Emmanuelle in French, to which she replies, "Excuse me?" I chuckle and switch back to English. Yes, my French is that bad, but I am happy that I overcame my self-consciousness and tried. We're seated on 57th Street in the atelier with floor-to-ceiling windows, facing the huge Tourneau clock.

It's such a joy, to be in the midst of something so elevated and simultaneously what I consider so down to earth. Chanel herself was this paradox. I love this combination of energy, when something or someone is so authentically grounded in what and who they are. For me, that is the essential power of authenticity. It reinforces a certain liberation of just being. This is what I feel at Chanel. Contrary to what you might think, the staff at Chanel is incredibly friendly and down to earth.

And it's fun! So much fun that my friend and I forget about our reservation for lunch. An hour past time, I say to her, "God, I'm starving. I need to grab one of those little quiches." And she says, "Oh my God, we are an hour late for lunch." We both laugh and acknowledge that we have been floating in another world. We continue to float on air down the three flights of stairs to the ground level.

We also need to eat. The energy of the street hits us hard, and I realize I'm dizzy from being in the Chanel vortex, and dizzy from low blood sugar. I also have a 2 o'clock meeting that doesn't leave time for a proper lunch. My friend suggests that we go to the Plaza for tea, and we end up grabbing take-out salads from the food court and sitting in the little park in front of the famed hotel.

There is something so wonderful about girl time. Both of us love fashion. We love being women. We love just being, and discussing art, fashion, our relationships, and what it means to be a woman. Our time together is special. We get to just be when we are together. We laugh a lot and just support each other. To just appreciate someone who also values friendship and authentic sharing is such a gift.

Then it's time to get to my meeting. She calls Uber. It's going to be 10 minutes. 10 minutes is too long, and I see a cab. I tell her, "Love. Talk to you later. I'm going to grab that cab." It's sitting in front of the Paris Cinema. I hop in.

I say, "31st and 5th." Then I hear a crazy honking behind the cab. I look back to see a truck behind us. Behind the wheel is a construction worker flailing one arm out his window and laying on the horn with the other. Honking never helps in NYC. But it does foreshadow escalation. It also makes my stomach feel flippy floppy. Sound is powerful, and I associate this sound with aggression and escalating emotion. I chuckle to myself and think, *God, just breathe. We'll be moving soon.*

In a split second, I realize I'm wrong. The construction worker is now pounding with two fists on the cab driver's window and screaming, "Fucking move your fucking cab." I say to myself, as if I can actually speak to the mind of the cabbie, "Just drive away. Do not react. Best response is to drive away." The cabbie kicks open his door and jumps out.

Next thing I know they are in each other's face. In the space of seconds, *fuck, fucker, fucking asshole, fuck off, you fucking fat fuck mother fucker fuck!* They are pushing each other and spraying spit in each other's faces. On the other side of the cab, traffic continues passing by. The street has a narrow two lanes. I'm boxed in. There is no way to get out of the cab. I'm going to be late for my appointment if this continues but more than that it's the unfettered rage that is most worrying.

The mate of the construction worker gets out of the truck and tries to pull him away from the cab driver. Now the construction driver tells *him* to fuck off. The royal *we* has descended from our luxurious Parisian style bubble with champagne and petit fours to street level in NYC. I am now far away from the glass walled and rarified atelier that I've only just now floated down from. I've arrived in another energetic field.

Then I roll down my window and say, "Excuse me, gentlemen." I pause. They both stop in mid-fuck to turn to me. In unison, they say, "What?" This is my opening, and I take it. "Well, you're both scaring me," I say. "I hate fighting and my stomach is flippy floppy. I can't get out of the cab because there is traffic on the other side. So what I'm asking you both is to please stop it, or I'll have to open this car door into both of you so I can get out."

Then the construction worker who started the whole thing says, "I'm sorry, ma'am."

I think, W*ow, I am 50 and now I'm being called 'ma'am.' Okay, would rather be called 'Madame,' but whatever.* I just want the fighting to stop.

The cab driver gets back in and shuts his door. The street noise is suddenly hushed, and we pull away.

"Would you please take a deep breath," I say, as we pull out. "You're kind of rattled, and I really would like you focused so we can arrive safely." Without saying anything, he takes a deep breath and then slowly exhales.

"Why didn't you just drive away? I hate fighting," I say to him.

"He started it," he says.

"Who cares? Why didn't you just drive away?"

"If you lived here, you'd know. It happens all the time."

"*I do live here* . . . since 1989, and perhaps it does. That's the problem. What you guys just did is a microcosm of the macrocosm of people being ruled by their emotions and reacting without thinking." I take a breath, and in a more solemn tone tell him, "You know, that's how wars big and small start." Then we're both quiet. He's African and who knows? Maybe he's been closer to war in his life than I have.

"But you stopped it," he says, lifting his eyebrows and glancing at me through the rearview mirror.

"Well," I say. "A man tried to stop it before I rolled down my window and look at him. He got pushed."

"Yes, but you're a woman."

"That is true," I say, laughing.

"Women," he says, chuckling with a big smile on his face.

In that 20 block ride downtown the energy has shifted. As I exit the cab I say, "Thank you for getting me here safely."

"Thank you... for the chat," he says.

I grab my Chanel bag and step out.

Acknowledgements

I thank God, Hashem, Divine Intelligence from the depths of my heart and soul. It is you that makes all blessings possible. You have blessed me beyond words with This Luscious Life. Thank you God.

It is with deep gratitude to my spiritual teachers, Dr. Joseph Michael Levry and Mary Grace O'Hearn who helped me process and understand the deeper meaning of all the experiences of my life and turn them into gold. Your wisdom and unconditional love give me the courage to be my true self. Your presence in my life is beyond words.

I am deeply grateful to my editor and publisher Scott Stanley who believed in me from the start, understood my often nonlinear musings about life and the unseen world and told me to carry around my little Moleskine and make notes. These notes gave birth to this book and to a deep healing in my soul. You are the "doula" of this book and you make me laugh my ass off. Thank you.

Richard Ives my Consigliere. Thank you for protecting me, always telling me the truth and for making sure that I never take a misstep. Our amazing friendship began when I was very fragile and asked you to help me prep for South Africa. And from that point on your support has made all the difference. Thank you for always telling me the truth and looking out for me. You always "see" me and point me to what is in my best interest. Your presence in my life is beyond any label other than you are my Guardian Angel on earth. I love you. Thank you.

Thank you to my sister, Taunya Black who has a unique

understanding of me and having survived an equally brutal childhood, validate this experience. Like me, you survived and thrived. You who kept me from going crazy over the years by your compassionate acknowledgement that certain things did happen. I will always stand in awe of your strength and grace in the face of seemingly insurmountable challenges. Thank you for always cheering for me, seeing the truth and wanting only my greatest happiness. I love you. Thank you.

My niece Ameena Grace who embodies the Divine Shakti and inspires me everyday to be a better woman. Ameena please know always despite the distance of time and space how much your Aunt loves and cherishes you. You are a gift to the world and perfect just the way you are. You are LUSCIOUS

Lisa and Richard Moody At 23 I was a curious, wounded girl looking for her place in the world when I met you. Words cannot express the influence you have had on my life. You embraced me unconditionally and made me part of your family. Your example inspired me to know that what I dreamed could be reality. An authentic life with filled with joy, passion, love, service and adventure. You are two of the most remarkable people I have ever met. As our enduring friendship continues 27 years and counting, my heart continues to feel a deep, love and appreciation for the blessing of you in my life. I love you. Thank you.

Per and Katarina Carlsson How I love the magic of life. Like meeting you in a mutual friends' apartment in Paris 20 years ago and ending up in Stockholm a few short months later. Who knew that this would lead to an enduring friendship that continues to be filled with love, laughter and champagne. We have kept our promise to see each other every year. That is love and love is magic.

Karen Pancholi and Solveig Haupt who rescued me and made

me laugh during the darkest moments. Thank you both for creating the platform for me to escape New York when I most needed a break. You both stood by me with unconditional love and no judgements. You are the best friends a girl could have. Cheers to the Estrogen club. May the Heavenly Light bless you both always. The odyssey of this Luscious Life is so much better with both of you in it!

Artur Tarnowski There will always be a place in my heart for you as you have profoundly influenced me on so many levels. I am grateful and will always hold an enduring, deep love and respect for you.

Aybars Asci When I was a child I used to pray and beg God for a brother. Who knew my "brother" would come to me via Turkey. Hashem delivered big time when he sent you to me. You and your family are so dear to me. Thank you too for holding me up when everything was falling apart and for always being my rock. You have always been there for me without asking for anything in return, for showing me unconditional love. I love you. Thank you.

Karsten Staiger Funny how a chance meeting on a bus and then again in a park months later – seemingly random events but somehow not . . . create magical openings in life. Meeting you helped restore my faith and hope in life; my ability to love and stretch beyond my wounds to do it unconditionally. How could I have known that a four block bus ride would open the portal that thawed the ice and ultimately made this book possible. Having you in my life helped me lower my defenses and just be… be love, be magic, be Shakti, be real, be totally, authentically me   I love you. Thank you.

To each and every one of the following people I give thanks for their generosity, empathy and support in my life: My

Grandmother, Alan Cresto, Tracy Brennan Conte, Elena Polshakov, Julia Marchikova, Sivan Einav, Giuliana Torre, Bibi Khan, Gail Forkosh, Barbara Cohen, Catherine Mountain, Kein Cross, Hermione and David Bushong, Celine Angelici, Carmit Archibald, MD, Zina Kroner, DO, Ana Paula Cota, Karen Pancholi, Gage Coleman, Everyone Associated with Naam Yoga New York, Chris Meyer, Mike Mitchell, Regina Estela and all my amazing clients and Naam Yoga students.

It is connection to that which awakens the heart and soul that makes life luscious. To all those named and unnamed, seen and unseen who have crossed my path, thank you.

ABOUT THE AUTHOR

Based in Manhattan, Kelley Black is a strategic trusted advisor, change management consultant, and executive coach, supporting executives and leadership teams. She is known for empowering men and women to be intuitive leaders, who lead from the heart, create high performing cultures, and make a difference.

She is also known for her Naam Life Coaching practice which provides a spiritual platform for authentic, inspired, heart-centered living. In addition to being certified as a Master Coach, Kelley is a level 1 - 3 Naam Yoga teacher and Harmonyum Healing practitioner.

Kelley lives in New York City and also spends as much time as she can in Paris. She is regularly asked to teach and speak in cities across the globe. She can be reached for speaking or consultation services through her website at: www.KelleyBlack.NYC